THE
ANALYTICAL
PUZZLE

Profitable Data Warehousing, Business Intelligence and Analytics

first edition

DAVID HAERTZEN

Published by:
Technics Publications, LLC
966 Woodmere Drive
Westfield, NJ 07090 U.S.A.
www.technicspub.com

Edited by Carol Lehn
Cover design by Mark Brye

ISBN, print ed.   978-1-9355042-0-7

First Printing 2012
Library of Congress Control Number: 2012940043

ATTENTION SCHOOLS AND BUSINESSES: Technics Publications books are available at quantity discounts with bulk purchase for educational, business, or sales promotional use. For information, please email Steve Hoberman, President of Technics Publications, at me@stevehoberman.com.

Contents at a Glance

Table of Contents

Contents **vii**

My supportive wife, Mary, who had faith that I would complete this book, and provided support through proof reading and feedback.

My computer savvy daughter, Molly, who gives me confidence that my passion for using data to make a better world will continue. Molly has an eye for both clear writing and practical use of data.

My friend, Stephan Hodges, who provided great feedback and ideas. Stephan's experience as a writer and computer expert made for a better book.

My friend, Tony Fike, who gave me great support and inspiration. Tony is passionate about data and using it to make a positive impact on the world.

Allen Messerli, the lead visionary behind the successful 3M Global Enterprise Data Warehouse, who helped me to understand the business case and benefits of the Enterprise Data Warehouse.

My friends and advisors: Judy Hauritz, Jeff Jung, Daniel Smith and Joel Wittenmyer. They gave me insights into specialized aspects of project management and data warehousing.

Allianz Life, Synchrono, 3M, IBM, Mayo Clinic and other organizations that have given me opportunities to learn through experience.

My publisher, Steve Hoberman, who is inspiring with both his knowledge and passion for using data to make the world a better place, and for his support in producing this book.

Times are changing in the field of data warehousing and business intelligence, so I wrote a book to provide a fresh perspective on the field. Some of my favorite books on the subject tell about the benefits of analytics, but fail to explain how it is done. Other books are dated and dwell exclusively on the classic star schema model. Today we need to be concerned with big data, data warehouse appliances, cloud computing, data mining, predictive analytics, visual presentation of data, and mobility.

Upon finishing this book, you will understand what data warehousing, business intelligence, and analytics are. You will be familiar with the goals of and components that make up data warehousing, business intelligence, and analytics. In addition, approaches used by data warehousing professionals will become clear. Examples in the book will enable you to be ready to work and manage others in the field of data warehousing. You will learn:

- How to plan and organize a successful data warehouse project
- How to get the right people involved in the project
- How to determine data warehouse business requirements
- How to choose between a data warehouse and a data mart
- How to load the data warehouse
- How to choose data going into the data warehouse
- How to achieve the benefits of business intelligence
- How to manage the ongoing data warehouse
- How to define a data warehousing architecture
- How to create data models for data warehouses and data marts
- How to avoid traps and pitfalls, so you can avoid problems and succeed
- How to present information to users of the data warehouse and business intelligence system.

Top data warehousing terms are clearly defined in this book, so you will understand data warehousing speak! Knowing these terms will improve your understanding of the benefits of data warehousing. This book will show you how other organizations are benefiting, and also how they conduct their projects in effective ways.

You will be able to create data warehouse and data mart data models. In an extensive section on data modeling, this book shows you how it is done and the kind of data model patterns that apply to each database or data area within a system.

Who Should Read this Book

This book is intended for the following groups of people:

- Data Modeling Team Members (anyone who is involved with data warehousing and data modeling)
- Data Architects
- Data Modelers
- Database Administrators
- Business Experts
- Business Analysts
- Managers.

Prerequisites

To make the most of this book, you need the following background:

- Basic computer background – you understand computers and feel comfortable with them.
- Some data knowledge – you understand a bit about data and are ready to learn more using the tutorials provided in this book. Experience creating or using reports is a plus.

How to Benefit from this Book

This book can be digested straight through, reading all chapters in order, or some readers may prefer to focus on the chapters that provide the most immediate benefit to them. Either way, each chapter is loaded with content and provides substantial benefit. All readers will profit from Chapters 1 and 2, which explain key concepts of data warehousing and business intelligence. The chapters explain both critical technical and business topics.

Chapter Expectations

Chapter	What You Will Gain
CHAPTER 1: Data Warehousing Perspectives	Learn the fundamentals and benefits of this exciting subject. This chapter introduces data warehousing, business intelligence and analytics.
CHAPTER 2: Business Case and Project Management	Learn how to build the business case needed to sell your data warehousing project. Next, learn how to organize a data warehousing and business intelligence project. Make the winning moves and avoid the killer mistakes.
CHAPTER 3: Business Architecture and Requirements	Learn how to elicit and organize business intelligence and data warehousing business requirements. The data warehouse requirements workshop is an effective and rapid way to elicit and document enterprise needs for data warehousing. Learn how to prepare for, conduct, and follow up on effective data warehouse requirements workshops.
CHAPTER 4: Data Warehousing Technical Architecture	Learn to specify the big picture of the data warehousing system, including software components, infrastructure components, technology stack, and non-functional requirements. In addition, gain understanding of cloud based data warehousing and data warehouse appliances.
CHAPTER 5: Data Attributes	Learn about data attributes, the raw material of data warehousing and business intelligence.
CHAPTER 6: Data Modeling	Learn the basics of data modeling, which is data design through pictures. The language and symbols of data modeling are presented, along with step-by-step processes to make your data designs successful. Design patterns for each part of the data warehouse will help you to design the needed databases.
CHAPTER 7: Dimensional Modeling	Learn to model and design databases that directly support business intelligence. Welcome to the world of cubes, stars, and snowflakes, where slicing and dicing, pivoting, drilling down, and rolling up are the things to do.

Chapter	What You Will Gain
CHAPTER 8: Data Governance and Metadata Management	Data governance is the overall management of data, including people, processes, and tools. Learn how to organize a successful data governance program. Learn how to manage metadata for your data warehousing and business intelligence project.
CHAPTER 9: Data Sources and Data Quality Management	Successful data warehousing and business intelligence depends on a supply of clean data. Learn how to identify and understand this important resource.
CHAPTER 10: Database Technology	Learn how to use database technology for your data warehousing project. In addition to relational database technology, you will learn about big data, data warehouse appliances, in memory databases, columnar databases and OnLine Analytical Processing(OLAP).
CHAPTER 11: Data Integration	Learn how to use data integration for your data warehousing project. Topics include: data integration architecture, data mapping, data cleansing, data transformation, and loading data. Selecting the right data movement tool is critical to the success of data warehousing projects. Learn how to determine tool requirements and then acquire the most appropriate tools.
CHAPTER 12: Business Intelligence Operations and Tools	Learn to understand and use business intelligence (BI) operations terms, including slice, dice, drill down, roll up, and pivot. These are the main operations of exploratory BI. Gain an understanding of the types of BI tools that can help with your data warehousing project. Business intelligence tools are used to analyze and present data.
CHAPTER 13: Number Crunching Part 1: Statistics	Learn the basics of descriptive and predictive statistics. You will learn to calculate and understand mean, median, mode, variance and standard deviation.

Chapter	What You Will Gain
CHAPTER 14: Number Crunching Part 2: Data Mining	Gain insights into your enterprise through data mining, which is the application of analytical methods to data. Learn to harness analytical methods such as data mining and statistics to anticipate the future. Learn how enterprises are making more effective decisions by using analytical methods such as: regression analysis, data mining, and statistics.
CHAPTER 15: Number Crunching Part 3: Analytic Application	Learn from an end-to-end example application. This example shows components and design patterns that compose a typical application.
CHAPTER 16: Presenting Data: Scorecards and Dashboards	Gain an understanding of the uses and benefits of scorecards. You will learn how to determine requirements for scorecards, select the best type of scorecard for your needs, and then how to design your scorecard. Gain expertise in the design and use of BI dashboards. Understand important dashboard terms and techniques. Apply methods to mobile technologies such as smart phones and tablets.
CHAPTER 17: Business Intelligence Applications	Gain insight into applications of business intelligence that could of help to your organization. BI finds profitable uses in fields as diverse as risk management, finance, marketing, government, healthcare, science and sports. It is a great tool for fighting crime and detecting fraud as well.
CHAPTER 18: Customer Analytics	Learn how to understand your customers better. Identify the profiles of your most profitable and least profitable customers.
CHAPTER 19: Testing, Rolling Out, and Sustaining the Data Warehouse	Successful business intelligence efforts require that business users must have faith that the system is producing correct answers. Learn how to put together the testing approach that ensures a trusted system. Learn to create and execute a plan for rolling out your data warehouse.

Chapter	What You Will Gain
APPENDIX A: Glossary	Learn to talk the talk. This glossary provides definitions and explanations of the critical data warehousing and business intelligence terms that you must know.
APPENDIX B: Bibliography	Learn to learn. The bibliography points you to further learning opportunities in the field of data warehousing and business intelligence.
APPENDIX C: References	Learn the source of this book's quotes and case studies. The references appendix directs you to supporting information for learning and support of academic papers.

Learn More

You will have an opportunity for follow up learning. At the end of most chapters is a section that points to further learning, including:

- Do it now exercises
- Websites
- Research studies
- Read it now books.

Case Study: 3M a Global Manufacturing Firm

I learned much from Allen Messerli, former 3M Director of Enterprise Information Management, and now principal of Allen Messerli Enterprise Systems, LLC, who was responsible for the business case, design, and delivery of GEDW (Global Enterprise Data Warehouse).

The 3M multi-national manufacturing company headquartered in Saint Paul, Minnesota is an example of the successful use of data warehousing and business intelligence to integrate enterprise data and provide a single version of the truth to management worldwide. The company manufactures over 500,000 products, including tape, sandpaper, adhesive, chemicals, and pharmaceuticals. The diversity and globalization of 3M proved to be a challenge at the beginning of the effort. When the effort started in 1995, the company was organized into over 40 business units, with over 60 subsidiaries, in over 200 countries.

Companion Website and Templates

A companion website that supports this book is available to help you implement your data warehouse and business intelligence solutions. Templates that support the Data Warehousing and Business Intelligence (DWBI) project life cycle are provided: business case, project plans, communication plans, methodologies, etc. The companion website is located at http://www.analyticalpuzzle.com.

About the Author

David Haertzen is an enterprise and data architect with over 40 years of experience. He has provided data services to major organizations like Allianz Life, 3M, Mayo Clinic, IBM, Fluor Daniel Co., Procter and Gamble, and Synchrono. These companies range in size from start up to multinational. As a result, David has extensive experience that he has applied to writing this book.

David is an experienced author, having written several papers and special reports. He is a presenter for organizations such as DAMA. Some of the topics he has talked about are data modeling, data warehousing, data architecture, business intelligence, SQL, and database-related topics. David is also active on the Internet as the editor of the Infogoal Data Management Center and other web sites. His home page is davidhaertzen.com.

David is an instructor for First Place Learning and eLearningCurve. Opportunities to meet his students have enriched his thoughts and enabled him to enhance his course material. He is a graduate of the University of Minnesota and earned an MBA at the University of St. Thomas.

Confessions of the Author

Most books are heavily influenced by the attitudes, values, and beliefs of their authors, and this book is no exception. Here are some of my beliefs and values:

- **Impatience and Sense of Urgency**. Achieving the goals of better customer service and improved business results are a driving passion with me. I lack patience for those who set up bureaucratic or technocratic roadblocks that slow progress toward the goal. Initiative killing statements like "we did that before and it failed" or "people will never agree to that" hold no water with me.
- **Speedy Delivery Does Not Mean Sloppy Delivery**. It is possible to develop something quickly without hurting quality. In fact, products

developed quickly may be of higher quality because there are fewer steps to go wrong, and the original vision and interest is maintained and enforced.

- **Look Inside**. The human resources of an organization are a tremendous asset. It irritates me when a company's management assumes that its own employees lack the ability to make improvements. Data management and related disciplines have been available for many years, so it is likely that existing employees know more than management gives them credit for. Cross functional teams are one way to draw out employee capabilities. For example, a person with a financial analysis background teamed with a person with a data management background can be in a position to build the business case for DWBI. Often, leaps in results are achieved by people who cross from one specialty area into another and "think outside the box" to develop innovative solutions.

Chapter 1
Data Warehousing Perspectives

The secret of success is changing the way you think.

Jack Welch, CEO, General Electric

When you have completed this chapter, you will be able to:

- Understand Data Warehousing and Business Intelligence (DWBI) terms
- Talk about DWBI benefits
- Assess the maturity of DWBI efforts for your organization.

In this chapter of *The Analytical Puzzle*, the following topics are explained:

- Definition of Business Intelligence and Analytics
- Definition of Data Warehousing
- Benefits of Data Warehousing
- The Business Case for Business Intelligence, Analytics, and Data Warehousing
- Operational Data Versus Warehouse Data
- Data Timeliness, Consistency and Comparability
- Decision Support Goals
- What Data Warehouse Is and Is Not
- Data Warehousing Trends and Hot Topics.

What are Business Intelligence (BI) and Analytics?

Business Intelligence (BI) is the set of practices and tools for displaying and exploring data for decision-making. Techniques and tools associated with BI include dashboards, scorecards, drilldown, and slicing and dicing data. Analytics practices take BI to a higher level.

Analytics is the practice of supporting decision-making through number crunching. Analytics supports processes such as customer segmentation, product mix analysis, budgeting, and operations improvements. Some analytic solutions focus on a single domain, rather than the broader domain of the data warehouse. Techniques and tools associated with analytics include data mining, statistical analysis, and regression modeling. Table 01.01 provides examples of BI and analytics.

Table 01-01: Data Warehousing Business Intelligence Scope

Business Intelligence	Analytics
• The system displays average historical temperature. • Customer data is listed in a report or provided on a dashboard. • The number of customers who responded to a sales offer is reported. • A report showing inventory turnover by product is produced.	• The system predicts the weather for next week. • Customers are organized into segments based on multiple factors. • The system recommends a sales campaign offer to make to a customer. • The system recommends actions to optimize inventory levels.

Chapters 12 through 18 of this book provide detailed information about BI and analytics. Data is the raw material needed for BI and analytics, which is where data warehousing comes into play.

Decisions Impact the Bottom Line

Decisions based on BI and Analytics can impact the bottom line by reducing cost and increasing revenues. Costs may be reduced by:

- **Avoiding problems such as poor insurance risks** – Progressive Insurance learned through analytics that credit score is an indicator of insurance risk, which gave the company a competitive advantage. (Davenport 2007)
- **Negotiating improvements in supply** – Prices paid to suppliers can be compared to industry benchmarks, which can identify potential savings.
- **Dropping unprofitable products** – Companies can improve profits by dropping products that cost more to produce and support than they bring in through sales. Analytics identifies those products through a correlation of costs and benefits.
- **Identifying and removing the root causes of waste** – Waste incidents such as scrap and rework are correlated with business process steps and machine settings to determine preventable root causes.

Revenues may be increased by:

- **Understanding and better serving customers** – Behavior and preferences of customers are captured and then analyzed on both group and individual levels. This information may be used to improve the design of websites, as well as to provide service tailored to individual preferences.

- **Focusing on the most profitable products** – High profit products are identified by relating cost and benefit streams. Companies can zero in on the products that provide the best long term profit.
- **Cross selling to customers** – Market basket analytics enables web-based stores like Amazon to recommend additional products. Knowledge of products already purchased helps to avoid making duplicate offers to customers.
- **Capitalizing on trends and events** – Walmart mobilizes its suppliers to provide goods needed in the event of forecasted events such as hurricanes. (Davenport 2007)
- **Growing marketing opportunities** – For example, the United States Census provides statistics and projected trends in the demographic composition of the United States. This data might point to opportunities to provide financial products such as annuities.

Examples of Business Intelligence Results

Improved decision-making can improve organizational results, as shown in Table 01-02. Organizations like Olive Garden, Royal Shakespeare Company, and 3M are great examples of this:

Table 01-02: Decision-Making Examples

Olive Garden	Olive Garden, the Italian restaurant chain, has reduced unplanned staff hours by 40% and wasted food by 10%. (Davenport 2010)
Nike Shoes	Nike uses sensors in running shoes to learn about the habits of its customers. (Davenport 2010)
Royal Shakespeare Company	The Royal Shakespeare Company increased the number of regulars by 70% through customer analytics. (Davenport 2010)
Best Buy	Best Buy found that 7% of their customers account for 43% of their business. (Davenport 2010)
3M	3M is saving $10 million in maintenance and has boosted sales force productivity by 10%. (Gray 2005)
Royal Bank of Scotland (RBS)	The Royal Bank of Scotland has integrated its customer information, creating a single customer view that enables it to better serve and cross sell to its customers. (Friedlos 2007)

See Chapter 17, BI Applications, for numerous examples of the benefits and applications of using data in decision-making.

What is Enterprise Data Warehousing (EDW)?

Enterprise Data Warehousing (EDW) is a process for collecting, storing, and delivering decision support data for an entire enterprise or business unit. Data warehousing is a broad area that is described point by point in this book. A data warehouse is one of the artifacts created by the data warehousing process.

William (Bill) H. Inmon has provided an alternate and useful definition of the data warehouse, which he defines as "a subject-oriented, integrated, time-variant, and nonvolatile collection of data in support of management's decision-making process."

As a total architecture, EDW includes people, processes, and technologies to achieve the goal of providing decision support data that is:

- **Consistent across the enterprise** – Each person accessing the system sees the same values. The customer service department sees the same numbers as the sales department.
- **Integrated** – Data is consolidated from many systems. Customer data may be gathered from customer service, sales, and subscription systems, for example.
- **Standardized** – Data is described using common names and definitions. The definition of a customer is the same in each department.
- **Easy to access from multiple viewpoints** – The direction of data viewing can be shifted from customer to product to geographic area through a point and click portal.
- **Easy to understand** – Information is presented using recognizable approaches such as lists, gauges, and charts with clear labels and descriptions.

What a Data Warehouse Is and Is Not

A data warehouse is a database that contains a *copy* of operational and other data, rather than being a source of original data. This data is often obtained from multiple data sources and is useful for strategic decision-making.

A data warehouse is not another name for a database. Some people incorrectly use the term "data warehouse" as a generic name for a database. Its purpose is not just to maintain historical data. A data warehouse contains specific data that has been gathered for analytics and reporting. It also does not record transactional data as transactions take place. This is managed in application data stores. (A data warehouse may, however, house transactional data after the fact, for reporting purposes.)

Beyond Data Warehousing

Data warehousing is not the solution for all data analytic problems. Data that supports analytics can be obtained and managed through means other than data warehousing. Challenges with data warehousing include:

- **High development cost** – Building a data warehouse can be time consuming and costly.
- **Timeliness of data** – day old data is not good enough for tactical decision-making such as assigning people to incoming work or controlling machines in a factory. Data may be streaming in so fast that it cannot be stored in time to make needed decisions.
- **High volume data** – The petabytes and exabytes of Big Data overwhelm data warehouses.
- **Specialized application** – A specialized application may be better for specific analysis such as risk analysis, actuarial analysis, or investment analysis (Chapter 18).
- **Small and one time data** – The data warehouse may be "overkill" for projects that must be completed quickly and economically.

A data mart may be thought of as a smaller scale data warehouse. A data mart is a database that is part of a data warehouse system where data stored for presentation and user access. Early data mart definitions specified that data marts were targeted to specific subjects and business processes. In practice, the data mart is a database that is organized into facts and dimensions that can cross subjects. Some organizations start with a smaller scale data mart effort and then progress toward the Enterprise Data Warehouse.

Data analysis can provide worthwhile results whether done using data in a spreadsheet, a data mart, a data warehouse or Big Data across many servers!

Assessing Data Warehouse BI Maturity

"How Mature is our DWBI Effort?", you may be asking. You can develop your own answers to this question by completing the DWBI Maturity Profile; Table 01-03 provides an example. The Maturity Profile helps you determine where your DWBI efforts need improvement.

DWBI Maturity Profile:

- **Organization Background** – provide a profile of the organization, including topics such as:
    - o Organization name
    - o Legal organization
    - o Industry
    - o Geographic area
    - o Revenue
    - o Employees.
- **History** – Describe the history of DWBI at the organization, including prior projects.
- **Executive Support** – Identify the support provided by executive sponsors such as the CEO and CFO.
- **Competencies** – Describe the skills and capabilities that are in place, such as:
    - o BI Competency Center
    - o Data Integration Competency Center
    - o Data Governance.
- **Usage** – Describe the current state of DWBI users and analysts:
    - o How many users are there?
    - o What percent of employees are using the DWBI?
    - o Do users see DWBI as mission critical?
    - o Do users trust the data and analysis from DWBI?
    - o How is DWBI usage divided by management level?
    - o How is DWBI usage divided by functional area?
    - o What is the level of analytical capability?
- **Data Sources** – Describe and enumerate the data sources that feed the DW. How dispersed is the data?
- **Data Integration Tools** – Identify the data integration tools available and in use.
- **Data Warehouse Platform** – Describe components of the data warehouse platform (hardware/software/DBMS).
- **Data Warehouse Size** – Quantify the amount of data storage consumed by the data warehouse. Include frequency of update and growth rate.
- **BI Tools** – Identify the BI tools and applications that are in place and in use.
- **Results** – Describe the benefits obtained from the use of DWBI, both quantitative and qualitative.

Table 01-03: Data Maturity Profile Example

DW BI Maturity Profile	
Organization Background	First Place Toys Corporation (FPTC) is a fictional corporation headquartered in the state of Minnesota. This 200-person company achieved $24 million in revenue last year by distributing niche lines of toys worldwide.
History	The company developed its first successful data warehouse in 2008 with a focus on sales analysis. The data warehouse has been extended several times, adding support for customer service, manufacturing, and financial analytics.
Executive Support	The senior executives of FPTC are very supportive of the data warehouse. Gary Benedict, the company CEO, is the chief sponsor and has become a believer.
Competency Centers	The company has developed competencies in the areas of business intelligence, data management, and data integration. The company has 2 specialists who focus on business intelligence and 1 specialist who designs databases and develops data integration. In addition, the company has developed relationships with consulting firms who extend these capabilities.
Usage	The data warehouse is widely used at FPTC. Over 25 percent of the company's employees regularly access the system, guiding their activities and decisions using portals, dashboards, and scorecards populated with data warehouse data.
Data Sources	The data warehouse is populated from multiple sources. Accounting data is sourced from a PC-based software package, sales information is sourced from web-based shopping cart software, and manufacturing data is obtained from an open source system.
Data Integration Tools	The company uses Microsoft SQL Server 2008 Integration Services (SSIS) to integrate data.
Data Warehouse Platform	The data warehouse related databases are hosted on SQL Server 2008. Some of the data is stored as cubes using SQL Server Analysis Services (SSAS).
Data Warehouse Size	The data warehouse contains approximately 550 Gigabytes (GB) of information. It is growing at a rate of 15 percent yearly.
BI Tools	The company uses Microsoft SQL Server 2008 Reporting Services (SSRS) to generate reports. It also uses Microsoft Excel 2010 for additional analysis and computation.
Results	The company has achieved a return on investment (ROI) of 215 percent. The investment in data analytics has resulted in lowered costs of inventory and improved customer service.

DW and BI are Management Disciplines

Proven management disciplines, such as Corporate Performance Management, are enhanced and supported by data warehousing and business intelligence. For example, scorecards for motivating and evaluating employees require data that is often gathered through a data warehousing effort and made available through BI tools, as illustrated in Figure 01-01.

In my experience, people outside of the IT and BI departments are often power users of data and related tools. They may build elaborate systems using desktop tools such as spreadsheets to build models and integrate data. Great benefits can be gained by bringing together the users who are the most knowledgeable about data (the "power users") and the data warehousing/BI team.

Unfortunately, power users often find themselves spending a large portion of their time gathering and manually manipulating data, rather than analyzing the data and producing value. In addition, numbers produced by independent spreadsheets often produce inconsistent answers, which undermine the credibility of the results. Data warehousing addresses the manual effort by automating the gathering and storage of data. In addition, data warehousing addresses the problem of inconsistent data by providing a source of consistent and cleansed data.

Figure 01-01: Data Warehousing and BI are Management Tools

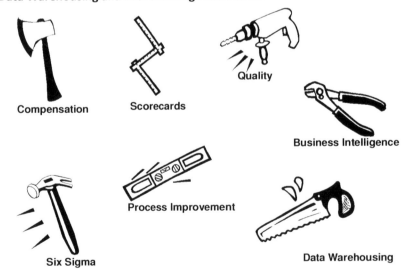

Compensation

Scorecards

Quality

Business Intelligence

Six Sigma

Process Improvement

Data Warehousing

Operational Data vs. Data Warehouse Data

Operational data is data that many people are familiar with, such as the current checking account balances, customer service call statuses, and today's sales amounts. Operational data emphasizes current values. The databases that store this kind of data are optimized for transaction processing, meaning the design of the database is normalized to avoid duplication of data. Each fact is represented in one place to support fast and frequent updating.

Operational data is different from data warehouse data. Data warehouse data is focused on historic and trend value – what was the data in the past and how is it changing. Examples of historic data include checking account balances as of the first day of the month for the last five years; average customer service call time by month; and total sales amounts by month. Instead of a normalized database design, a multi-dimensional design organized into facts and dimensions is used for part of the data warehouse. Chapter 7 explains how that works and shows you how to create a multidimensional data model.

Data warehouse data is optimized for analytical processing, rather than transactional processing. The analytic data stored in the data warehouse is different from operational data. Operational data is:

- Optimized for Transaction Processing
- Frequently Updated
- Designed using Entity Relationship Modeling.

In contrast, data warehouse / analytic data is:

- Optimized for Analytical Processing
- Not Updated (It is loaded instead)
- Designed using multiple patterns including Entity Relationship Modeling and Multidimensional Modeling.

High Quality Data

High quality data is needed for data warehousing and business intelligence in order to produce good answers. Some characteristics of high quality data are:

- **Timeliness** – Data is up to date as of the same point in time.
- **Consistency** – The same answers are produced each time and each place. Reports consistently produce the same answers, which makes reporting more dependable based on consistent data and consistent formulas.
- **Comparability** – Numbers can be added and compared. They can be summed, averaged, analyzed with statistics, etc.

See Chapter 9, Data Sources for Data Warehousing and Business Intelligence, to learn how to assess and improve the quality of your data.

Decision Support Goals

The data warehouse supports the Decision Support function of the organization, which typically has the following goals:

- Make fact based decisions
- Make timely decisions
- Make profitable decisions that reduce costs and increase revenue.

These decisions can support a number of stakeholders

- Customers
- Employees
- Shareholders
- Suppliers
- Community.

Here is another take on decision-support roles. Decision support is the use of business intelligence to make profitable decisions that (1) reduce cost or (2) increase revenue. You want to make sure that business decisions serve your stakeholders, the people affected, such as customers, employees, shareholders, suppliers, and the community, by making fact-based, timely decisions based on an analysis of the numbers.

Data Warehousing Enterprise Architecture

Solid enterprise architecture is critical to the success of data warehousing efforts. The ANSI/IEEE Standard 1471-2000 defines the architecture of software-intensive systems as "the fundamental organization of a system, embodied in its components, their relationships to each other and the environment, and the principles governing its design and evolution."

The Enterprise Architect (EA) builds and communicates blueprints that model the enterprise and IT solutions. These models identify the people, processes, and technologies that are needed to enable the enterprise to succeed in its mission. Architecture is organized into a number of domains, each of which provides value to data warehouse architecture. Architecture domains, illustrated in Figure 01-02, include business architecture, information architecture, software architecture, and technology architecture.

Chapters 3 and 4 dive into each architecture domain and show how they support the success of data warehousing and business intelligence. This includes definitions as well as examples of deliverables, such as documents and models. Each domain includes subdomains as listed in Table 01-04. When you have completed Chapters 3 and 4, you will have an overall understanding of enterprise architecture and the specifics of data warehouse architecture.

Figure 01-02: Enterprise Architecture Pyramid

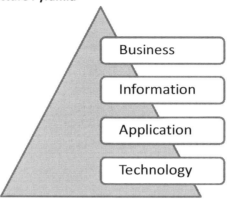

Table 01-04: Enterprise Architecture Sub-Domains

Business	Information
• Business Requirements • Business Rules • Organization Structure • Critical Success Factors • Business Process Design and Modeling • Mission / Vision	• Data Governance • Data Integration • Data Architecture • Master Data Management • Data Delivery Architecture • Data Modeling • Data Quality • Content Management • Dashboards and Analytics • Business Intelligence • Data Mining and Analytics • Enterprise Reporting • Corporate Performance Management
Application	**Technology**
• Enterprise Application Integration • Custom Application Development • Services Definition • Process Alignment • Services / Event Architectures	• Servers • Networks • Telecom • Operating Systems • Desktop • Middleware • Database Infrastructure • Security • Storage • Other Hardware

Data Warehousing Trends and Hot Topics

The fields of data warehousing, business intelligence and analytics are continually growing and changing. The industry is buzzing with new developments. In addition, innovations in technology impact data warehousing. It is imperative to know about them in order to solve the Analytical Puzzle. Hot topics are identified here and more fully explained in this book.

- **Agile Data Warehousing and Business Intelligence** – agile approaches reduce time to value by delivering results at regular intervals
- **Big Data** – multi-terabytes of typically unstructured data is critical to modern analytics and contributes to the success of companies such Google, Facebook and Amazon
- **Data Warehousing in the Cloud** – a method to rapidly ramp up and manage data warehousing capacity without investing in fixed infrastructure
- **Data Warehouse Appliances** – vendor provided solutions that include both hardware and software greatly increase performance through Massive Parallel Processing (MPP)
- **Columnar Databases** – new database software that stores and retrieves data by columns rather than by rows is dramatically improving data warehouse performance
- **In Memory Databases** – this software boosts performance by storing data in memory rather than on hard disk
- **Federated and Virtual Databases** – data distributed in multiple data stores can be made to look like a single data store, avoiding the cost and time of copying data
- **R** – this open source analytics language with supporting software is gaining wide acceptance in both the business and academic community
- **Predictive and Prescriptive Analytics** – predicting who will be a profitable customer and prescribing the best offer to make, provides competitive advantage
- **Data Mining** – analyzing data to find patterns and gain new knowledge using statistical methods is rapidly advancing
- **Data Visualization** – improved tools are enabling data to be better understood through graphical displays
- **Mobile Computing** – the growing use of smart phones and tablet computers is making business intelligence available to new audiences and requires new ways of thinking.

Key Points

- Business Intelligence (BI) is the practice of supporting decision-making through the presentation and analysis of data.

- Analytics takes BI to a higher level by applying number crunching to support processes such as customer segmentation, product mix analysis, budgeting, and operations improvements.

- Data Warehousing is a total architecture for collecting, storing, and delivering decision support data for an entire enterprise.

- BI improves decision-making, which can impact the bottom line by reducing costs and increasing revenues.

- BI requires high quality data that is timely, accurate and comparable.

Learn More

Deepen your knowledge of data warehousing and BI through these resources:

Do It Now!	Assess you organization's Data Warehousing and BI Maturity. Download and complete the assessment available at the support website for this book: http://www.analyticalpuzzle.com
Visit a Website!	Visit The Data Warehousing Institute – a premier organization that provides information about data warehousing and business intelligence: http://www.tdwi.org/ Wikipedia provides a great overview of data warehousing, including a history starting in the 1960s: http://en.wikipedia.org/wiki/Data_Warehouse The BeyeNETWORK is a web portal that brings together knowledge from numerous BI experts. Allen Messerli has written an excellent article series titled "Reinventing Business: Enterprise Data Warehouse Business Opportunities for Manufacturing" that help you to develop a business case: http://www.b-eye-network.com

Read about it!   These books provide excellent overviews of the economics of analytics and EDW:

Ayres, Ian.   *Super Crunchers: Why Thinking-By-Numbers is the New Way to be Smart.* New York NY: Bantam Books, 2007.

Davenport, Thomas H., and Jeanne G. Harris. *Competing on Analytics: The New Science of Winning.* Boston, MA: Harvard Business School, 2007.

Leadership is attending to conditions that would keep growth from happening.

Peter Senge

Project management skills are essential to successful data warehousing and business intelligence efforts. Putting together the right people, process and technology is critical.

In Chapter 1, you were introduced to Data Warehousing and Business Intelligence. You saw that great benefits can be gained through use of data warehousing and business intelligence. Organizations such as 3M, Nike Shoes and The Olive Garden are great examples to aspire to.

In this chapter, you will learn about the management of successful data warehousing / business intelligence projects. The chapter is organized in two sections:

- Developing the Business Case
- Data Warehouse Project Management.

Data warehouse and business intelligence projects are not just about creating a new data warehouse or data mart from scratch. Increasingly, organizations have an existing data warehouse in place and need to improve or extend it. The following are the types of projects that may be undertaken:

- Conducting a pilot or proof of concept
- Creating a new data warehouse or data mart
- Adding new data to an existing data warehouse or data mart
- Creating new outputs from an existing data mart – dashboards, scorecards, reports, data mining analysis, etc.
- Consolidating or partitioning data marts
- Providing reporting and/or BI as part of a larger project
- Improving performance of existing data warehouses or data marts
- Correcting data problems in existing data warehouses or data marts.

Six Steps to Developing the Business Case

Data Warehousing Business Intelligence (DWBI) requires an investment before benefits are returned. To start or improve a DWBI program, it is essential that the business case being presented to executive management, show that the DWBI program will provide benefits that exceed costs. In this chapter, you will learn how to develop a Business Case (BC) document and presentation that shows that the program is worth investing in.

A Business Case, also known as Cost Benefit Analysis (CBA), is built using the steps described in Figure 02-01, Business Case Steps. By following these steps and using the templates downloadable from the book's website, you will be on your way to preparing and presenting the case for implementing or improving DWBI.

Figure 02-01: Business Case Steps

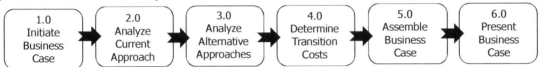

BC STEP 1.0 – INITIATE BUSINESS CASE

Initiating the Business Case includes forming a cross functional team, setting objectives for the business case, and determining the scope of the business case. These deliverables are produced:

- BC Objectives
- BC Scope Statement.

Scope identifies the boundaries of an effort: which subjects are inside and outside the boundaries of the DWBI initiative. Certainly, data that does not support decision-making will be excluded. For example, see Table 02-01, Data Warehousing Business Intelligence Scope.

Table 02-01: Data Warehousing Business Intelligence Scope Example

In Scope	Out of Scope
1. Shared Data	1. Operational details
2. Account	2. Regulatory Data
3. Asset	3. Supplier
4. Codes	4. Product Details
5. Customer	
6. Employee	
7. Pricing	
8. Product Identifiers	

Controlling scope is a way to reduce the risk that the effort will spiral out of control and become a "runaway project." The executives to whom you present the business case are likely to ask penetrating questions to ensure that the effort is a success. Scope items can include:

- **Analysis Subjects** – what topics are included: product shipments, customer complaints, hotel reservations?
- **Organization Scope** – is this a department, business unit, or enterprise effort?
- **Level of Effort** – is a new data warehouse being created or is this a specific extension to an existing system?

After the Business Case is accepted the scope will be further refined. The section of this chapter titled "Defining Scope and Objectives" provides details.

BC STEP 2.0 – ANALYZE CURRENT APPROACH

After initiating the business case, the next step is to examine the Current Approach to the analytics that support decision-making. Quantification is important, so this includes an analysis of the financial impact of the current approach and a projection of that impact into the future.

A template that will help you to develop the business case is available on the companion website for this book. It includes a section for specifying the costs and benefits of the Current Approach.

The Current Approach is a description of the way the 'world' is now and is likely to be if changes to the Current Approach are not made. This includes: costs and benefits, people and organizations, as well as data and systems. The Current Approach can be described through multiple means including:

- Narratives
- Cost / Benefit Spreadsheets
- Context Diagrams that show the inputs and outputs of the Current Approach
- Business Process Diagrams that show the steps used to acquire and analyze data.

Outputs include current costs and benefits such those as described in Table 02-02. The costs and benefits of the current state are then projected into the future.

Table 02-02: Current Costs and Benefits

Current Costs	• Analyst time to acquire and manipulate data • Rework cost due to poor quality data • Fines and penalties due to late or unavailable data • Cost of lost business due to dissatisfied customers • Problem counts (returns, cancellations, warranty claims, drop outs, repeat crimes, medical errors, law suits, etc.) • Hardware costs • Software costs • IT people support costs
Current Benefits	• Revenue by product, market, channel, etc. • Rate of output (cases analyzed, products created, sales campaigns planned, etc.)
Current Outcomes	• Customer satisfaction level measured by Net Promoter Score (NPS)

Dig into the numbers and gain a thorough understanding of the metrics that describe how your organization achieves results. This includes financial and metrics such as:

- Number of workers performing an activity
- Number of units processed
- Cycle time per unit of work
- Compensation rates
- Software license costs.

BC STEP 3.0 – ANALYZE ALTERNATIVE APPROACHES

The third step is to generate ideas for alternate approaches and next examine those approaches, including a financial impact analysis. This analysis includes a projection of cost scenarios with both direct and indirect costs and benefits. The output of this step is compared to the output of BC Step 2:

- Future cost scenario component of BC
- Future benefit view of each alternative approach.

The Future Approach is a description of the way one wants the world to be. In the current state, this includes costs and benefits, people and organizations, as well as data and systems. In the future world, it is likely that benefits will be higher than in the current state and that those benefits will exceed the costs.

DWBI provides many benefits that can be included in the Business Case. Evaluate which DWBI benefits are applicable to your organization, such as:

1. Avoiding the costs and risks of not using DWBI
2. Improved communication inside and outside the organization based on shared information and definitions
3. Improved risk management by understanding risk root causes
4. Accelerated time to market by rapidly identifying opportunities
5. Increased sales by improving product offerings
6. Increased sales by improving campaign effectiveness
7. Decision-making supported by providing a consistent basis of comparison
8. Improved customer relationships by identifying customer needs
9. Improved customer retention through 'stickiness'. The customer sees a unified view of accounts and services, making it less likely that the customer will leave.
10. "Single Version of the Truth" – consistent information
11. Improved up sell and cross sell results by responding to customer buying habits
12. Reduced costs of publishing product and catalog data by avoiding duplication
13. Reduced costs of errors and rework by identifying and correct the root causes of errors.

On the other side of the equation are the costs of DWBI, which include:

1. Time and attention of management to oversee development and implementation
2. Software and hardware
3. DWBI programs and projects
4. Custom development
5. Transition costs
6. Ongoing costs such as maintenance and support.

Benefits can be both direct and indirect. Table 02-03 shows examples of both kinds of benefits.

Table 02-03: Direct and Indirect Benefits

Direct Benefits	Indirect Benefits
• Revenue increases • Output rate increases – goods produced, crimes solved, students graduated, etc.	• Productivity increases • Risk reductions

The business case could be presented with a range of improvement estimates based on scenarios such as:

- Pessimistic (worst case) 20% improvement, i.e., $20M benefit
- Target (typical case) 30% improvement, i.e., $30M benefit
- Optimistic (best case) 40% improvement, i.e., $40M benefit.

Inability to identify the root cause of problems can be a challenge in business case development for business intelligence. Use of BI methods may reveal root causes and patterns that require follow up efforts to address the root causes. The business case may speculate on root causes and potential findings of BI efforts.

The Benefit Impact Matrix (see Table 02-04) is a tool that can help you to associate root causes with their financial impacts.

Table 02-04: Benefit Impact Matrix

Root Cause	Effect	Enterprise Impact	Metric	Annual Impact
Non-integrated customer data	More customer service calls	Higher customer service expense	Customer service staff cost	$12 Million
Non-integrated customer data	Dissatisfied customers	Lost customers	Customer turnover cost	$210 Million
Product design flaw	Product replacement requests	Increased service cost	Product replacement cost	$5 Million

BC STEP 4.0 – DETERMINE TRANSITION COSTS

The fourth step is to determine the cost of moving from the current approach to the future approach. To move from the current approach to the future approach requires an investment known as transition cost or project cost. The resulting deliverable is:

- Transition cost component of BC

Transition costs are a key part of the business case. It costs money to go from here to there. Transition costs include elements such as:

- Business process redesign
- Business requirements
- Computer hardware
- Computer software
- Software development
- Data integration
- Training.

BC STEP 5.0 – ASSEMBLE BUSINESS CASE

The fifth step is to correlate and refine the business case results. Examples of financial calculations for the business case are provided in Table 02-05. Deliverables are prepared that compare the current approach and proposed future approach, along with the costs required to transition from the current to future approach. The deliverables from this step are:

- BC Detail Document
- BC Presentation.

Table 02-05: Financial Calculations (Examples)

Item	Calculation
Return on Investment (ROI)	(gain – cost) / cost
	Extend over 5 years
Payback Time (number of years until gain exceeds costs)	(yearly payback) / cost
Net Present Value (NPV)	Discounted value of gains over 5 years
	Discounted cost over 5 years
Internal Rate of Return (IRR)	Cost of Capital – Net Present Value

The presentation includes a table of contents that outlines the business case such as the example in Figure 02-02. It is important to create a consistent story that sells the benefits to the enterprise.

Figure 02-02: Business Case Executive Summary Contents

```
┌─────────────────────────────────────────┐
│  Data Warehousing Business Case          │
│                                           │
│   ❑  Overview                             │
│                                           │
│   ❑  Scope                                │
│                                           │
│   ❑  Current Approach                     │
│                                           │
│   ❑  Future Approach Blueprint            │
│                                           │
│   ❑  Roadmap and Transition Costs         │
│                                           │
│   ❑  Bottom Line                          │
└─────────────────────────────────────────┘
```

BC STEP 6.0 – PRESENT BUSINESS CASE

The final step is to present the business case and proposals to the decision makers. Here the decision makers are educated about the key points of the business case and (presumably) give their approval to proceed.

Case Study: 3M, Global EDW Business Case

The 3M business case for its Global Enterprise Data Warehousing (GEDW) included transition costs, ongoing costs, business benefits, and IT benefits. The original $50 million in transition costs invested beginning in 1995 were quickly recouped. Ongoing maintenance costs were $2.6 million per year. The ongoing maintenance costs are more than offset by annual savings of over $10 million per year in maintenance and customer service costs. Projected lifetime benefits of over $1 billion have been realized.

The results and impact are substantial. Applications encompass logistics, inventory analysis, supplier analysis, cross-selling, and customer penetration. The system went live in 1996, and net benefit within the first five years was expected to exceed $100 million. Projected benefits included reduction of indirect procurement cost by $350 million, improvement of sales force productivity by 10%, and reduction of supply chain, marketing communications, finance, and IT costs by more than $500 million. Revenue improvements related to improved customer penetration, faster product commercialization, customer retention, and price management also contributed substantially to the bottom line.

Additional benefits identified by Allen Messerli, former 3M Director of Enterprise Information Management, include:

- Meeting Sarbanes-Oxley Act (SOX) auditing requirements without adding systems or costs
- Increased cross-selling, customer penetration, and customer relationships
- Improved supply chain excellence indices
- Providing global customer and supply chain visibility
- Six sigma implementation.

The well documented and presented business case enabled the GEDW team to gain the needed executive support to carry the program forward.

Data Warehousing Project Management

In this section, you will learn about the management of successful data warehousing / business intelligence projects. Topics include:

- Defining Scope and Objectives
- Finding the Right Sponsor
- Producing the Project Roadmap and Plans
- Organizing the Team
- Executing the Plan
- Finishing the Project
- Avoiding Major Data Warehouse Mistakes.

DEFINING SCOPE AND OBJECTIVES

Scope specifies the boundaries of the project. It tells what is in and what is out. The scope definition started in the business case will be expanded, if needed, when the project is underway. This effort includes:

- Overview of the project (Mission, Scope, Goals, Objectives, Benefits)
- Scope plan
- Scope definition
- Alternative development.

Defining the correct scope and setting realistic objectives are critical to any project's success, and a data warehouse project is no exception. Scope defines project boundaries including:

- Business requirements addressed
- Anticipated/planned users
- Subject Areas such as inventory transactions or customer service interactions
- Project success criteria, including quantified planned benefits.

Defining an overly large project scope and letting scope grow in an uncontrolled fashion (scope creep) are certain to cause project failure. Remember you cannot please everyone:

> *I cannot give you a formula for success,*
> *but I can give you a formula for failure: try to please everybody.*
>
> Herbert Bayard Swope

Enterprise vs. Departmental Focus

The choice of Enterprise Data Warehouse vs. Departmental Data Mart is critical to the success of data warehousing projects. This choice is a major component of project scope. Examples of factors that arise with each focus, based on my experience, are shown in Table 02-06.

Table 02-06: Enterprise vs. Departmental Focus

Factor	Enterprise Focus	Department / Functional Focus
Organizational Scope	Enterprise Wide	Business Unit or Business Process Focused
Time to Build	Multi-year phased effort	Single Year effort
Sponsorship Required	Executive Sponsor	Management Sponsor
Complexity	High	Medium
Typical Cost	Often a multimillion dollar effort	Often less than $1 million effort

The project may require both an Enterprise Data Warehouse and one or more Data Marts. The Technical Architecture chapter explains more about this choice.

FINDING THE RIGHT SPONSOR

The role of the project sponsor is critical to the success of the data warehousing project. This individual is a senior management person who takes overall responsibility for a project. Seek out a project sponsor who has both a large stake in the project outcome as well as authority over the resources needed for the project.

The project sponsor fills a number of roles including:

- Owner of the business case

- Harvester of benefits
- Overseer of the project
- Link to upper management.

Data warehousing champions complement the work of the project sponsor. Look for people who will promote data warehousing efforts across the organization. They make sure that the project is aligned with enterprise goals and help to sell the project to the rest of the organization.

The scope of a DWBI effort is also highly dependent on the level of authority of the project sponsor. If the sponsor is the CEO or CFO, then the scope can be enterprise wide. If the sponsor is a business unit head, then the scope is likely the business unit. If the sponsor is a department head, then the scope is likely limited to a single department.

Conversely, an Enterprise Data Warehouse project requires a higher level executive sponsor with more authority and resources than is required for a Departmental Data Mart project.

PRODUCING THE PROJECT ROADMAP AND PLANS

A roadmap is a high-level plan that coordinates multiple project plans. The project roadmap is larger in scope than a single project plan. It encompasses a series of projects that carry the organization forward to longer range objectives. It is often best to build the data warehouse through a series of smaller projects that are coordinated using a project roadmap.

A project plan is a document, or set of documents, that describes a project in terms of its objectives, scope, schedule, budget, and resources. The project plan supports the execution and control of a project to ensure its success by:

- Acting as a communication tool between decision makers and team members
- Guiding the project phases and activities.

Project planning includes these activities:

- Developing the Work Package Plan which includes an Activity List and Work Breakdown Structure
- Developing Project Schedule which includes a Project Timeline and Critical Path
- Determining Resource Requirements
- Assembling a Cost Estimate and Project Budget

- Approving the Project Plan.

Key Project Questions

Your project plan should ensure that these key questions are answered.

- What are the expected outcomes of this project?
- What are the inputs and outputs?
- Why is this project being done?
- When will the project begin and end?
- How will the outcomes be accomplished?
- Where will the project take place?
- Who is involved with this project?
- Who is the customer?
- Who is the sponsor?
- Who will contribute to the project?
- What methodology will be used (waterfall vs. agile)?

Developing The Work Package Plan

The Work Package Plan is a detailed plan that breaks a project down to the activity level. The first part of developing the plan includes building an activities list using techniques such as brainstorming, templates, and checklists. This is followed by these further efforts.

- Identifying activities
- Selecting activities
- Reconciling activities
- Organizing activities.

This book describes many of the activities and corresponding deliverables that are needed to carry out successful data warehousing and business intelligence projects. Use the activities listed in Table 02-07 as an idea starter when planning your project. Each of these activities is described in later chapters of this book.

Not all activities identified in the first pass should be included in the project plan. Review each activity and select only activities that are within the project scope and contribute to desired outcomes.

The list of activities may contain activities that are duplicates or very similar. Reduce the number of activities by combining duplicate activities. Create manageable tasks that require between 8 and 40 hours to complete. Shorter tasks lead to micromanagement while longer tasks lose visibility. The result is a reconciled list of activities that is easier to manage.

Table 02-07: Data Warehousing and Business Intelligence Activities

• Determine enterprise mission, vision and strategies	• Model and design fine grained facts
• Conduct proof of concept	• Model and design aggregated facts
• Build capability maturity model	• Model and design atomic data warehouse
• Elicit functional requirements	• Obtain data source documentation
• Elicit non-functional requirements	• Conduct data profiling of data sources
• Specify data architecture direction	• Obtain XYZ source system data
• Create data architecture context diagram	• Design and develop BI metadata
• Specify technical architecture direction	• Design and develop reports
• Determine data warehouse technology stack	• Design and develop scorecards
• Acquire infrastructure	• Design and develop dashboards
• Determine databases required	• Design and develop portals
• Determine data sources	• Design and develop analytic models
• Establish Data Governance	• Tune databases
• Establish Metadata Management	• Secure the data
• Establish Information Lifecycle Management (ILM)	• Document processes and procedures
• Identify candidate metrics and KPIs	• Train end users
• Define metrics and KPIs	• Create test plan
• Determine dimensional tables needed	• Implement test plan
• Create Dimension Fact Matrix	• Rollout solution to end users
• Model and design dimensions	• Conduct post-project evaluation

Organizing activities into a Work Breakdown Structure (WBS) is the next step. A WBS is a hierarchical organization of project activities that facilitates management of the current effort. Figure 02-03 depicts this hierarchical organization of project tasks.

Figure 02-03: Work Breakdown Structure Hierarchy

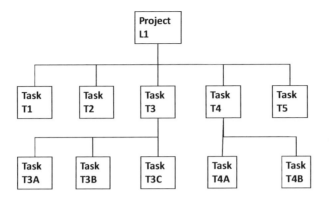

The WBS should support project goals and objectives. For example, the project goal may be to create a framework that supports Enterprise Performance Management (EPM) and objectives include:

- Establish a foundation for EPM
- Establish EPM for Customer Experience
- Establish EPM for Financial Excellence
- Establish EPM Operational Excellence
- Establish EPM for Employee Growth and Retention.

In this case, the WBS would be organized to support these objectives. The objective "Establish a foundation for EPM" would include activities such as:

- Conduct proof of concept
- Build capability maturity model
- Elicit non-functional requirements
- Create data architecture context diagram
- Specify technical architecture direction
- Determine data warehouse technology stack
- Acquire infrastructure
- Establish Data Governance.

The more specific objectives like "Establish EPM for Customer Experience" and "Establish EPM for Financial Excellence" address specific business requirements and are aligned with specific activities needed to deliver on those requirements. Focusing on objectives supports early delivery of value.

Each high level objective can be organized into activity groups based on major data warehousing work efforts:

- **Vision** – Document the future state and supporting business case
- **Requirements** – determine the needs and features of the data warehouse
- **Architect** – Specify the business and technical architecture of the data warehouse
- **Design** – Specify system details including: data models, data mapping and dashboard layouts
- **Build** – Create deliverables including: databases, data integration jobs and dashboards and acquire supporting technology
- **Quality Assurance** – Test the data warehouse to make sure that it meets requirements
- **Roll out** – Deliver value that meets the objective in a sustainable manner.

Developing the Project Schedule

After activities are defined and organized into a WBS it is time to develop the overall project schedule. This requires estimating the duration of each activity and arranging activities in sequence.

Estimates for activities are best prepared by the people responsible for that activity. This takes advantage of expertise and leads to commitment by the estimators. Steps include:

- Determining project roles – reference Table 2-10 for project roles
- Obtaining an estimator for each project role
- Estimating duration and elapsed time for each activity
- Correlating the estimates.

Next, arrange activities into sequence. To do this, consider dependencies between activities, risk reduction and delivery of value. There will be dependencies at a high level. Design activities must come before build activities. There will also be dependencies at a detail level; for example, database tables must be created before they can be loaded with data.

Data warehousing and business intelligence projects have specific risks that can be mitigated, in part, through intelligent project scheduling using methods such as those identified in Table 02-08.

Table 02-08: Risk Mitigation through Project Scheduling

Risk	Mitigation
Data sources have data quality problems	• Schedule data profiling activities early. • Include data source reviews with business experts in the project schedule.
High data volume causes slow load of data warehouse	• Schedule data volume estimation early in the project. • Include performance testing with data volumes that exceed estimates early in the project as part of technical architecture activities.
Root cause analysis finds unanticipated problems	• Include points in the schedules where the project schedule can re-evaluated based on project findings.

Schedule the project so that value is delivered early. Avoid schedules that stack all value delivery at the very end. This mitigates the risk that opportunities are lost due to late project completion.

Determining Resource Requirements

Staffing resource requirements are determined by adding the duration time for each person role and time period. The number of people in each role required depends on the hours needed and the overall schedule length. A shorter delivery period may require more people.

Assembling the Project Budget

The budget is an itemized projection of the resources needed for the project, including the amount of money needed for each item. Here are some of the major items that should be included in the budget:

- People (Employees, Consultants)
- Hardware
- Software (Development, Infrastructure)
- Data acquired from external sources.

The people budget can be determined by multiplying the hours estimated in the Resource Requirements Plan by the rates. The projections for hardware, software and external data depend upon the Technical Architecture selected. Be sure to add some contingency time in case the project does not go as planned due to factors such as:

- Discovery of additional requirements
- Data quality problems
- Loss of critical personnel
- Competing priorities.

Waterfall vs Agile approaches

There are two high level approaches to project management, the waterfall approach and the agile approach. Specifically these apply to data warehousing projects. The waterfall approach organizes the project into activities that are planned in detail and then executed as planned. The waterfall method is proven to produce results, however, it is vulnerable to risk that require adaptation to changed circumstances.

The agile approach recognizes that adaptation to change is a critical success factor in projects and builds in flexibility for change. Agile methodologies have worked very well for me in practice. The agile approach produces rapid results and enables team learning. Critical components of the two approaches are described in Table 02-09.

Table 02-09: Waterfall to Agile Approach Comparison

Strategy Area	Waterfall	Agile / Iterative
Time to Value	• At the end of a lengthy process	• Multiple deliveries at regular intervals
Time Periods	• Time is divided into sequential phases	• Work is divided into iterative time periods called "Sprints".
Documentation	• Focus is on thorough specifications	• Focus is on delivering "code" / functionality not documentation • Documentation is generated from the code • Code can consist of metadata / declarations rather than procedural code
Team Location	• Team may be distributed	• Team is often co-located in a "war room" (except in Distributed Agile).

ORGANIZING THE TEAM

The right team is critical to any successful project and data warehousing projects are no different. Table 02-10 describes the roles that are needed for an effective data warehousing project team. The project manager should seek extended team members who can help if the project is blocked for some reason.

Table 02-10: DWBI Project Roles

Role	Description
Data Warehousing Champions	The data warehousing champions complement the role of the data warehousing sponsor. They provide executive support for the project. They make sure that the project is aligned with enterprise goals and help to sell the project to the rest of the organization.
Project Manager (PM)	The Project Manager provides project leadership. This includes preparing project plans and then following up on those plans to keep the project on schedule. The PM manages risks, issues and project communications.
Business Subject Matter Experts (SMEs)	The SMEs understand the business and provide detailed business requirements.
Business Analyst	The business analyst elicits and documents business requirements.
Enterprise Architect	The enterprise architect makes sure that the project is aligned with enterprise directions in the areas of business architecture, data architecture, technical architecture, and infrastructure architecture.
Technical Trainer	The technical trainer provides training in data warehouse tools and techniques. We recommend training team members before they start using new tools or techniques to develop the project.
Data Architect	The data architect provides a broad perspective on data.
Data Modeler	The data modeler builds and communicates data models, which are visual representations of the data. The data modeler works with business and subject matter experts to elicit and define data requirements.
Database Administrator	The database administer configures and manages databases. This is an important role that makes sure that data is efficiently managed and protected.
Technical Architect	The technical architect determines the technical solution at the project level. These individuals work with enterprise architects and others to make sure that the details support the overall architecture.
Data Integration Designer/Developers	The Extract Transform Load (ETL) designers and developers move data to where it is needed to support the data warehouse system. In many cases, this is about 70 percent of the project effort (Kimball 2004), so it is important to do this efficiently.

TRAINING THE TEAM

Make sure the data warehousing team is trained in the skills needed for success. Review each role and team member for needed skills and train as needed. Team members may require skills in areas such as:

- Project Management
- Data Warehouse Architecture
- Data Warehouse Modeling
- Requirements Analysis
- Specific Tools.

EXECUTING THE PLAN

When the data warehousing project is under way, execution becomes paramount. In the best projects, the participants are inspired and are focused on positive outcomes for the organization. The project manager must keep the project under control while insuring that stakeholders are informed of progress.

A focus on positive outcomes is a critical ingredient in project success as the data warehousing project plan is being executed. For example, if improved decision making and productivity of actuarial data analysts are goals, make sure that project team members are aware of that. You might have team members do a "otcp in" with actuarial analysts to show them what the life of the actuarial analyst life is like and how it will be improved by the project. Team members then know that skimping on quality delivery will have negative results for fellow workers.

Status reports and meetings coupled with proactive follow up are important tools in the effort to keep a project under control. Each week team members should report their status toward assigned tasks.

The Workflow Chart is a way to gain control and visibility to tasks that require repetitive steps. Figure 02-04 shows a Workflow Chart for data discovery and mapping which shows each data source to be discovered and mapped along with assigned analyst, subject matter experts (SMEs) and Status. For each task there is a planned date identified by a letter P and when complete, an Actual date identified by an A. The workflow steps include:

- **Obtain Documents** – Locate data source documentation.
- **Define Inputs** – Obtain definitions for data source attributes.
- **Profile Inputs** – Query data source to gain understanding.
- **Map Data** – Map data source to data target.

- **Data Quality** – Assess data quality.
- **Publish Results** – Produce a report documenting findings.

Figure 02-04: Data Discovery and Mapping Workflow Chart

Data Source Name	Obtain Doc Date	Define Input Date	Profile Input Date	Map Date	Data Quality Date	Publish Results Date	Analyst Name	SME Name(s)	Status
CRM	P 7/12 A 7/09	P 8/1 A 7/28	P 8/15	P 9/1	P 9/15	P 10/1	J Smith	B Rose M Heart	In Progress
PIM	P 7/12 A 7/13	P 8/1 A 8/2	P 8/15	P 9/1	P 9/15	P 10/1	A Nelson	W Neuton	In Progress
Sales Order	P 7/12	P 8/1	P 8/15	P 9/1	P 9/15	P 10/1	J Smith	B Rose M Heart	Planned

The project manager must take aggressive action to keep the project on track. Two tracking tools are the Issue Log and the Risk Log. The Issue Log is a document that tracks problems which must be solved. It includes a description of the problem, person assigned to solve the problem, date discovered, date corrected and status. If the assigned person cannot solve an issue in a timely or satisfactory way, the project manager should determine the root cause of the problem and push for resolution.

The Risk Log identifies problems that have a possibility of occurring. It includes a description of the risk, potential impact to the project, likelihood of occurrence and a mitigation approach to deal with the risk should it occur. Gaining visibility of risks and taking steps to handle them is critical to project success.

It is also critical to make data content visible to team members and project stakeholders. For example, if data is being obtained from a data source, display the data to make sure that it is what is expected. Also, data that is being placed in the data warehouse should be shared to avoid surprises later. Walkthroughs of data warehousing deliverables also serve to keep project stakeholders interested and committed. Make sure that the project complies with earlier specified goals and architectures by comparing the actual project with plans and recommendations.

FINISHING THE PROJECT

When finishing the data warehousing project it is important to set the data warehouse on a sustainable course and to learn from experience. Read Chapter 19 of this book learn about setting the data warehouse on a sustainable course.

A "Lessons Learned" session is a good way to learn from the data warehousing experience. Request that project stakeholders identify aspects of the project that went well and those that need improvement by completing a survey. Then correlate the information and host a meeting to review the results. The Lessons Learned meeting is an opportunity for project stakeholders to express themselves as well as learn from the viewpoints of others.

Case Study: 3M, Enterprise Data Warehouse Continued

The 3M Global Enterprise Data Warehouse (GEDW) is an effort that goes well beyond a single project. It is an ongoing effort guided by critical principles and a roadmap. Gaining executive support and buy in was an early step and a critical success factor.

Executives supporting the GEDW program were top level executives who provided multiple perspectives. Allen Messerli indicated, "It was important that the GEDW not be dominated by a single business area. If the Chief Financial Officer (CFO) were the sponsor, then the solution would be a financial data mart, not the desired Enterprise Data Warehouse (EDW)."

The initial GEDW was developed over a five-year period. Allen Messerli recommends that an EDW be built in phases, not in one big bang. Each phase should deliver value within six months or less. Then each successful delivery paves the way for approval and support for the next phases.

Project Management Tips

In order to succeed in data warehouse projects, it is wise to be aware of best practices and common pitfalls. Use these tips to improve your projects.

- Before starting, diagnose the readiness of your organization for data warehousing and business intelligence.
- Make sure that your data warehouse project is aligned with the strategies of your organization.
- Use SMART goals including metrics. SMART – specific, measurable, assignable, realistic, and time-based goals.
- Work with key users – people in the business who are actually going to use the system for decision-making.
- Work with executive management who can sponsor and promote the data warehouse.
- Make sure to educate your organization so that it understands data warehousing and business intelligence.

- Start the project with an experienced project manager and data warehouse architect.

AVOIDING MAJOR DATA WAREHOUSE MISSTEPS

You can avoid or reduce common data warehousing missteps by being prepared. Follow the suggestions described in Table 02-11 to prevent or recover from problems.

Table 02-11: Data Warehouse Missteps

Misstep	How to Prevent
Focusing on technology instead of people and process	Put people and process ahead of technology. Make sure that people's needs and business requirements are at the center of the effort.
Lack of sponsorship and management support	Remember to find and involve executives from both business and IT who support and sponsor the data warehousing and business intelligence effort. The sponsor must have a stake in the outcome along with authority to push through the program.
Overly ambitious or undefined scope	Insist that the effort proceed step by step so it can build on a record of success. The scope must be clear and documented to prevent confusion and set focus.
Undefined requirements	Use the requirements elicitation and documentation process described in Chapter 3 of this book. Remember if what is needed is unclear, the project, will likely fail.
Failure to consider future requirements	The way to prepare for future requirements is to be aware of the organization's long-term vision and to design flexible systems that can be adapted to support that vision.
Unrealistic expectations	Emphasize to sponsors and other stakeholders that the data warehouse will be built step by step and, therefore, will not satisfy every desire immediately. Keep communicating to avoid unrealistic expectations. The recommendation to "Under promise and over deliver" is a good one.

Misstep	How to Prevent
Failure to architect a long-term solution	In order to avoid tactical solutions that do not last, create a flexible architecture using the approaches explained in Chapters 4 through 11 of this book.
Failure to obtain high quality data	Establish a data quality effort based on the Six Steps to Data Quality Management, as described in Chapter 9, Data Sources and Data Quality Management.
Trying to turn the prototype into the final solution	The prototype is designed to show the potential of the data warehouse, not to be the actual data warehouse. Prototypes often lack data quality management and other important features needed for the final solution. Communicate the prototype approach from the beginning to avoid this trap.
Designing around one tool/vendor	Domination of the project by a single vendor or promoter of a single tool can lead to an inflexible solution that cannot grow to support the needs of the organization. Instead, take charge of the effort and build to a strong architecture.
Failure to scale up	Some data warehouse systems work well for small volumes of data, but cannot be expanded when volume expands. Avoid this problem by building on database and other technology that can expand, rather than desktop databases that limit expansion.
Failure to store data at the right level of detail / grain	It may be tempting to store data at a summarized grain of detail rather than at a finer grain of detail. This can cause problems when it is desirable to drill down to detailed information to better understand root causes. Be sure to analyze the level of detail, including the need to drill down.

Key Points

- Avoid common data warehousing mistakes such as focusing on technology instead of people and processes.

- Build an effective Business Case to sell the DWBI effort.

- Obtain executive sponsorship and management support.

- Clearly define scope to a challenging but achievable level.

- Answer basic project questions (what, why, when, how, where and who) which are critical to project success.

- Successful execution is critical to the winning project. Keep in control of the project through monitoring and strong follow up.

Learn More

Expand your knowledge of how to organize a data warehousing and business intelligence project. These resources can help.

Visit a Website! See the Gantthead Data Warehouse Process for steps needed to manage a data warehouse project.

http://www.gantthead.com

The Project Management Institute (PMI) is a leading association of project management professionals.

http://www.pmi.org

Read about it! This book shows how to manage data warehousing and BI Projects:

Hughes, Ralph. *Agile Data Warehousing: Delivering World-Class Business Intelligence Systems Using Scrum and XP.* iUniverse, 2008.

A factor present in every successful project and absent in every unsuccessful project is sufficient attention to requirements.

Suzanne & James Robertson (Robertson 2004)

When you have completed this chapter you will be able to:

- Understand and use business architecture and business requirements terms.
- Describe business capabilities and create a business capability heat map.
- Elicit and organize data warehousing and business intelligence business requirements.
- Conduct a successful business requirements workshop.

In this chapter of *The Analytical Puzzle*, the following topics are explained:

- Business architecture
- Business goals, capabilities, and strategies
- Business requirements
- Functional and non-functional requirements
- Conducting the business requirements workshop.

Business architecture and business requirements are critical to the success of data warehousing and business intelligence projects because they provide linkage and alignment with enterprise goals.

Business Architecture

Business architecture is a strategic blueprint of an enterprise, or unit of an enterprise, including analytic capabilities. The business architect builds a picture of how multiple views of the future combine to support the organization's stated vision and mission. The multiple views include functional decomposition of the business value chain into business functions and capabilities. The first order of discussion is the enterprise mission, vision, and strategies.

Peter Drucker (Drucker 1974) has recommended these critical questions and their corresponding decisions:

- What is our business? (Mission)

- What will our business be? (Vision)
- What should our business be? (Strategies)

The layers of enterprise mission, vision, and strategies are described in Table 03-01.

Table 03-01: Enterprise Mission, Vision, and Strategies

Mission	The mission statement is a short description of the fundamental purpose and approach of an enterprise. It answers fundamental questions including: - Who are we? - Why do we exist? - How do we do business? The answers to these questions serve to keep all parts of an enterprise "on the same page", as well as to inform external stakeholders such as customers and investors. The focus is on the present. A mission statement might say "First Place Toys is an agile company that develops toys in order to help children develop small motor skills. We accomplish this goal by extensive quality and safety testing."
Vision	The vision statement is an inspirational picture of the future of an enterprise which provides guidance for strategic planning. The vision describes where an enterprise will be in a successful future. For example, a vision statement may indicate the enterprise will be the "Leading Provider in the field of Manufacturing Automation".
Strategy	A strategy is a long-range plan for managing resources to implement a vision. A strategy could be a long-range plan for improving the effectiveness of a capability, such as innovative product development or excellent service. In general, the enterprise architect contributes to enterprise strategies by proposing them, and by developing business architectures that support the strategies.

The enterprise mission, vision, and strategies provide guidance and direction to the business architect who models the business needs in the form of the business value proposition. It is the primary benefit that an organization offers its customers. This model may be broken down into lines of business architecture. Figure 03-01 shows a typical business value chain that is widely applicable to many enterprises. The value chain framework is an aid to understanding the business functions and capabilities that an enterprise needs to fulfill its mission.

Figure 03-01: Business Value Chain

The value chain is part of the enterprise picture. Figure 03-02 shows that the value chain translates to core business capabilities that impact stakeholders, including employees, customers, suppliers, investors, regulators, distribution channels, and business partners.

Figure 03-02: Model of the Enterprise

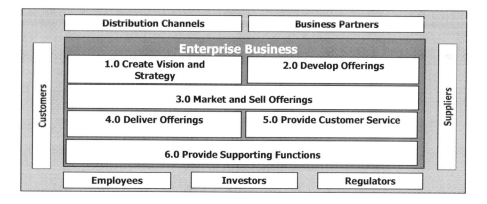

Business functions can be decomposed into lower level capabilities. Then each of the capabilities can be assessed for current and desired maturity. For example, the "Develop Offerings" business function could be decomposed into the following capabilities (among others):

- Evaluate existing offerings to market opportunities
- Research needs of customers and markets
- Evaluate customer feedback.

The maturity level of these capabilities is evaluated using a scale divided into multiple levels, such as aware, trailing, par, leading, and excelling. Table 03-02 describes these maturity levels.

Table 03-02: Capability Maturity Levels

#	Maturity Level	Description
5	Excels	The enterprise has established a capability that is a competitive advantage over peer enterprises, as determined through benchmarking and competitive intelligence.
4	Leads	The enterprise has a level of capability that is ahead of peer enterprises.
3	Par	The enterprise has a level of capability that is similar to peer enterprises.
2	Trails	The enterprise has some level of capability that is behind the level of peer enterprises.
1	Aware	The enterprise realizes that a capability exists and wants to pursue it.

Objective metrics and targets will aid in the evaluation of maturity. A metric is a direct, quantified measure of performance including revenue, cost, unit sales, and complaint count. Targets are quantified goal levels for specified time periods. Targets can take into consideration benchmarks of peer enterprises and strategic choices. Key Performance Indicators (KPIs) are metrics that support strategic goals and are defined in terms of targets.

The Heat Map is a comparison of the current (as-is) maturity level to the desired (to-be) maturity level. Figure 03-03 shows an example of a Heat Map. In this case, three business capabilities are evaluated.

In each case, the as-is maturity level is less than the desired to-be maturity level. For the business capability "evaluate existing products to market opportunities", the as-is is a level 2 (trailing) and the to-be is at a level 4 (leads). The difference between the as-is and to-be is the gap. When there is a gap of one level or less, moderate improvements could close the gap. However, when the gap is two or more levels, more extreme, transformational change is required.

Figure 03-03: Business Capability Heat Map Example

Business Capability	Level 1 Aware	Level 2 Trails	Level 3 Par	Level 4 Leads	Level 5 Excels
Evaluate existing offerings to market opportunities		As-Is		To-Be	
Research needs of customers and markets	As-Is		To-Be		
Evaluate customer feedback		As-Is	To-Be		

You might ask, "Why not excel at all business capabilities and have a goal of level 5 for each capability?" Each organization can only do so much and must focus on strategic competencies. The industry low cost leader may pursue customer service at a par level, while excelling at offering low prices. Another firm might provide premium products and services for a premium price.

The business architect will work with the enterprise to determine the gaps that are highest priority to close. This typically requires a prioritization of capabilities and linking those capabilities to enterprise goals and strategies.

Often, many root causes for the low maturity of capabilities are due to a lack of data and analytical tools for decision-making. In fact, the same information can have many uses.

Putting together a complete business architecture is a multiyear effort.

Data Warehousing Business Requirements

Business requirements describe the needed data warehousing solution in business terms. Eliciting and managing business requirements include these activities, which will be described in more detail shortly:

- Homework (Research of Documents)
- Enterprise Goals and Objectives
- Identify User Groups
- Requirement Interviews

- Requirement Workshops
- Sizing
- Data Exploration.

Business requirements are sometimes known as functional requirements and are the focus of this tutorial section. Technical requirements, sometimes known as non-functional requirements, will be explained in Chapter 4, Data Warehousing Technical Architecture.

HOMEWORK FOR DATA WAREHOUSE REQUIREMENTS ELICITATION

Be sure to do your homework before eliciting requirements from others for the data warehouse and business intelligence effort. By doing your homework, you acknowledge the prior data warehousing efforts that have been made, avoid looking uninformed, and save others time by not asking questions that have been previously addressed.

First, you must understand previous data warehousing efforts:

- Who was involved?
- What were the results?

Researching documentation can help you get a handle on your organization's current and prior state of data warehousing. You can examine documents such as:

- Enterprise mission, vision, and strategy statements
- Business plans
- Annual reports
- Business unit plans
- Data strategy and roadmaps
- Data warehousing project plans
- Requirements specifications.

In addition, computer-based information can provide insight into the requirements of existing systems:

- Database layouts
- Data models
- Metadata repositories
- ETL jobs
- Programs.

IDENTIFY BUSINESS INTELLIGENCE USER GROUPS

Identifying and engaging the right people to participate in data warehousing and business intelligence efforts is key. Focus on decision makers such as:

- Executives
- Managers.

The people who analyze data are subject matter experts (SMEs) who will provide valuable input. Examples are:

- Financial Analysts
- Marketing Analysts
- Information Consumers.

The people who create reports usually have great insights because they are asked by the business to create business intelligence reports. They often have a backlog of requests and "wish lists" that can be translated into data warehousing requirements.

DATA EXPLORATION

Analytics users may have difficulty knowing or expressing their data requirements. Consider challenging potential users to discuss their problems, pain points, and wish lists to find out what they need.

Business users of data are often saying "I'll know it when I see it." Create situations where analytics users can experience possible data. This can be done by creating demonstration outputs such as mocked up reports, dashboards, and scorecards. Demonstration outputs can be created by using a quick Proof Of Concept (POC) data mart. Be sure to display in bold letters that the samples are mock ups only and are not ready for use, or some users will have the false expectation that the information will be immediately available.

INTERVIEW BUSINESS INTELLIGENCE USERS

There are a number of good reasons to interview individual business intelligence users for data warehousing requirements. The reasons include:

- Obtaining facts beyond research
- Verifying research facts
- Answering open issues and questions
- Encouraging buy in by participation.

Here are some suggestions to make the interview process productive:

- Start on a positive note – a friendly smile, good eye contact, and firm hand shake help to establish rapport
- Prepare an agenda and questionnaire
- Be friendly and flexible, within limits
- Talk business, not computer buzzwords
- Use the Kipling Questions as a means of generating ideas for questions that elicit requirements:

> *I keep six honest serving men, They taught me all I knew; Their names are what and why and when and how and where and who.*
>
> Rudyard Kipling

Here some sample questions for the interview:

- What are the expected goals of your area?
- How do you measure results? (Metrics)
- What are the critical success factors of your job?
- How do you identify opportunities and problems?
- What business dimensions are important to your analysis and decision-making? (Products, Customers, Vendors, Time)
- What are your current sources of information?
- What is your vision for the future of your area?
- What questions would you like the new system to answer?

GROUP METHODS

A facilitated group session is often a great way to elicit requirements. Requirements are produced in group sessions faster than using individual interview methods. In a facilitated group session, the meeting participants have the opportunity to bounce ideas off of each other and reach a consensus on the requirements.

See the BI Requirements Workshop section of this chapter for a practical approach to conducting group data warehouse requirement sessions.

DOCUMENTING REQUIREMENTS

There are a number of documents that can be used to specify requirements at various levels. Table 03-03 describes many of these documents.

Table 03-03: Requirements Document Types

Document	Description
Needs and Features	A document that describes high-level requirements (needs) and then provides details about the characteristics (features) that are required to fulfill the need. For example – • Need 7: System will provide a scorecard display that includes multiple perspectives. • Feature 7-1: System will display scores relating to the Financial Perspective. • Features 702: System will display scores relating to the Product Perspective.
Requirements Specification	A document that provides a detailed description of the essential and desired functions of the system. It provides more details than the Needs and Features document. See Table 03-04.
User Story	A document, often the size of a 3 by 5 card, which describes a feature of the system from the user point of view. The User Story is an artifact that supports Agile projects. For example – *The Production Manager will be able to view the production for an entire region, and be able to drill all the way down to individual production lines to find and correct the root causes of production problems.*
Use Case	A document that describes system requirements in terms of interactions between the system and its users. It supports object-oriented analysis and design and is a recognized Unified Modeling Language (UML) artifact. It includes scenarios for both the most common (the "happy path") and exception cases. Each use case includes: • Name and identifier, such as UC-1099 • Description of the use case goal • Identification of the actors – people who participate in the use case • Assumptions about conditions that must be satisfied for the use case to complete • Steps that must be taken to perform use case tasks, including sequence, conditions and exceptions • Variations in the overall use case flow • Non-functional requirements - describe the manner in which a system must carry out the functional requirements.

Document	Description
SIPOC	SIPOC is a high-level description of a process that is organized into the following subjects: • **Process** – the name of the process stated as a verb followed by a noun, such as "Receive Inventory" • **Suppliers** – the sources of inputs to the process, such as persons or software systems • **Inputs** – the things that trigger and are used in the process, including data • **Process steps** – the series of activities that compose the process • **Outputs** – the results produced by the process • **Customers** – the people who receive the outputs.
User Interface Specification	A document that defines and describes how a person will interact with the system. This often includes display and report layouts, such as scorecard and dashboard layouts. A rough layout of a graphical user interface is often referred to as a "wireframe" or "mockup"; it helps people to visualize solutions. See Chapter 16 to learn more about this.
Data Model	A graphic representation of the data and information needed to support the functionality of the system. It is used to understand the data and design the database(s). Data modeling is described in Chapters 6 through 8 of this book.
Data Dictionary	An artifact that contains definitions of the data, along with descriptions of its characteristics, such as data type. A Data Dictionary is a kind of Metadata Repository. See Chapter 5 for a description of the data characteristics captured in a typical Data Dictionary.
Metric and KPI Specification	A component of the data dictionary that defines and describes metrics and KPIs. A metric is a direct, quantified measure of performance, and KPIs (Key Performance Indicators) are metrics that support strategic goals and are defined in terms of targets. This specification is also described in Chapter 5.

FUNCTIONAL REQUIREMENTS

Functional requirements are the features and functions of a system; that is, what the system does for those who use it. Each requirement is assigned a requirements number, which is used to track the requirement and to ensure that the requirement is satisfied, as illustrated in Table 03-04.

Table 03-04: Functional Requirements Example

#	Description	Priority
307	The system will provide users with KPIs that support sales campaign management including: • Campaign returns per 1000 items mailed	High
308	The system will enable categorization of sales by Region, Territory, District, Manager, and individual.	High
301	The system will enable summary and drill down of general ledger transactions by year, quarter, day, and individual transaction.	Medium

NON-FUNCTIONAL REQUIREMENTS

Non-functional requirements describe the manner in which a system must carry out the functional requirements. Table 03-05 shows a non-functional requirement example. These requirements are often detailed in architecture documents. The need to provide a specified level of performance while utilizing specified technology is a non-functional requirement.

Table 03-05: Non-Functional Requirements Example

#	Description	Priority
951	Non-Public Private Information (NPPI) will be encrypted, both while being moved and when stored (at rest).	High
952	A Disaster Recovery (DR) hot site must be provided to ensure that service will be restored within two seconds without loss of data, should the main site experience a service interruption.	High
953	Naming of tables and columns will conform to the XYZ Corporation data modeling standard.	Medium

Case Study: 3M, a Global Manufacturing Firm

Alignment with corporate business goals, as well as executive vision, strategy, and investment, were important factors in the 3M Global Enterprise Data Warehouse (GEDW) success story. The GEDW team demonstrated to the CEO and other senior executives, through both one-on-one communications and executive committee review, that GEDW contributes to the achievement of 3M business goals. The executive committee provided support to the project both through funding and through management commitment.

In addition to working with the executive committee, the GEDW team elicited requirements by interviewing 250 mid-level managers. (Watson 2004) In addition, the GEDW team streamlined its requirements gathering approach by deciding on and implementing high-level principles. A critical principle explained by Allen Messerli is "Touch It, Take It Data Sourcing." Using this principle, the team extracted all data from touched source systems when the source systems were first accessed. "This best-practice approach is faster and less costly" than continually going back to the source system to extract more data, according to Messerli.

A second critical principle is that the GEDW must support action by the business, which requires detail about business events and transactions. Allen Messerli explained that establishing a "role-based, event-driven culture" was essential to success. Events and transactions captured in GEDW include customer touch points such as customer calls, as well as system activities such as order processing steps. It is a high-level requirement that business users be able to drill down to actionable date to make a difference.

A third critical principle is the "one face, one voice" philosophy, which declares that information made available to stakeholders must be consistent. This means that customers, suppliers, distributors, and employees have tailored yet consistent views of company information.

Data Warehousing Requirements Workshop

> *Large projects' requirements change many times before they're completed. Important requirements usually remain important as the business changes, while others change or even evaporate. Prioritization lets you deliver the most important requirements first.*
>
> Dave Quick

When you have completed this topic you will be able to:

- Conduct a successful Data Warehousing Requirements Workshop
- Prepare the Inputs for the Session
- Define Objectives of Requirements Sessions
- Develop the Agenda
- Produce Results
- Follow up the Session.

Would you like to learn a productive way to elicit requirements while building support for your data warehousing project? The Business Intelligence Requirements Workshop is a great way to get that done. Read further to learn:

- Benefits of Data Warehousing Requirements Sessions
- Who does what?
- Room Layout and Equipment
- Building and Maintaining Momentum.

Obtaining requirements rapidly using the requirements workshop has numerous benefits:

- Increased Productivity
- Improved Solution Quality
- Rapid Results
- Longer Lasting Results
- Enhanced Teamwork and Cooperation
- Lower Development Costs.

ROLES AND RESPONSIBILITIES

The successful BI Requirements Workshop requires a team effort with assigned roles and responsibilities:

- Session Leader Facilitator
- Data Warehouse Modeler
- Scribe
- Executive Sponsor
- User Manager
- Business User.

The Facilitator leads the BI Requirements Workshop and has responsibilities including:

- Setting goals and preparing the agenda
- Keeping the session on task and within scope
- Encouraging participation
- Gaining and articulating consensus
- Leading exercises such as brainstorming or consensus building
- Identifying follow up tasks and gaining commitment for next steps.

The Data Warehouse Modeler asks questions to identify the data required to support business intelligence. This may include diagramming facts and dimensions or asking related questions, such as: "What is being measured here?" or "How would you slice and dice that information?"

The Scribe records the minutes of the session including:

- Participants
- Decisions
- Requirements.

PREPARING FOR THE SESSION

Again, Rudyard Kipling and his questions will come to our aid. Prepare for the session by answering these and similar questions:

Why   Why are we holding this meeting? (Identify problem, opportunity, or challenge.)

Who   Who will attend the meeting, and who will play each role?

What   What are the inputs and outputs of the meeting?

How   How should the meeting be conducted?

When   When should the meeting be scheduled, and how long should it last?

Where   Where should the meeting be held, and with which facilities?

EXECUTIVE SPONSOR AND USER MANAGER ROLES

The Executive Sponsor provides a high-level picture of the goals of the Business Intelligence program. The sponsor also shows that executive management is committed to the program. The User Manager provides expert input and encourages team member participation. Business Users provide subject matter expertise.

ROOM LAYOUT

Focus on the goals of the workshop. Arrange the room using Figure 03-04 as example, to be effective for workshop activities. Encourage interaction between participants, while focusing on the business intelligence requirements.

Figure 03-04: Room Layout

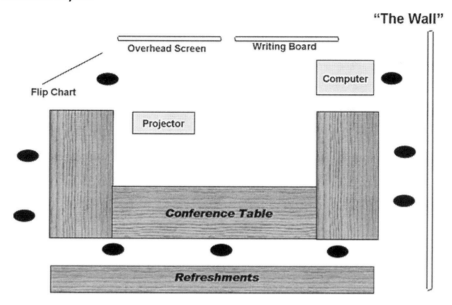

GROUP METHODS AND TECHNIQUES

The Session Facilitator will use group methods, techniques, and ground rules (Figure 03-05) to ensure a successful BI Requirements session:

- **Asking Questions and Probing for Answers** – The facilitator will provoke thinking using the Kipling Questions. Open ended questions such as "How would you measure success?" are good for clarifying problems. The lean admonition to "ask why seven times" to drill down to root causes is a great way to probe for answers.
- **Generating Ideas** – Brainstorming, brain writing, and the Nominal Group Technique are ways to encourage idea generation.
  - o Brainstorming involves a rapid listing of ideas without the inhibition of evaluation.
  - o Brainwriting is a structured technique to generate many ideas in a limited period of time. Participants bring 3 ideas. The team is broken into small teams who generate ideas and record them on sticky notes in 5 minute rounds. Ideas are clustered and shared with the larger group.
  - o Nominal Group Technique is a decision making technique that encourages participation. After an introduction, participants individually record their ideas on paper. Next, participants share their ideas. This is followed by a group discussion. Finally, the ideas are voted on and ranked.

- **Evaluating Ideas** – Determining which ideas are best is a multi-step process. First, criteria must be identified and weighted. The criteria form one side of a matrix. Second, the degree that each idea satisfies the criteria is evaluated using a consistent scale, such as a 1 to 5 scale. Finally, the weighted score of each idea is determined by multiplying the score by the criteria weight. The sum of the weighted scores will provide an overall rank for each idea. This scoring process can be done by individuals or a group. These scores are used to select which ideas are implemented.

- **Consensus Building** – Consensus is reached when a group decision has been made wherein a majority of the participants agree with the decision, participants feel heard, and participants support the decision. The facilitator builds consensus by stating ideas and asking for agreement or disagreement as well as the reasoning behind agreement or disagreement.

- **Using Presentation Materials and Equipment** – The successful facilitator is skilled with both presentation materials and electronic equipment.
  - **Facilitator Tool Kit** – Be ready with supplies: markers, flip charts, sticky notes, and easels.
  - **Equipment** – The facilitator requires computer with presentation software, diagramming software, and a projector.

- **Dealing with Difficult Group Members** – Difficult members may derail facilitated group sessions. Be ready to address these challenges:
  - **Non-participator** – This person says little and does not participate in discussions. Periodically ask this person questions about topics where the person can contribute. Also, structure methods so that each person contributes, for example using brainwriting.
  - **Monopolizer** – This person dominates discussions to the point where others do not have a chance to participate. First, set ground rules such as the five minute rule, which limits discussion of each topic. Second, ask the person to focus on the identified topic. Third, summarize the person's points and then move on by inviting others to provide their perspective.

- **Encouraging Participation** – The facilitator can encourage participation by asking questions of non-participative members; dividing the group into smaller teams, which gives each participant more "air time"; and by asking participants to individually write and then share ideas.

Figure 03-05: Ground Rules

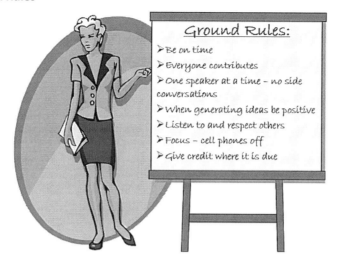

OUTCOMES OF EFFECTIVE BI REQUIREMENTS SESSIONS

The BI Requirements Workshop can have a number of positive outcomes:

- Requirements are documented
- Benefits are identified
- Costs of not having BI are identified
- Business processes, including analytical business processes, are identified
- Business roles are identified and related to the business processes
- Participants better understand BI and the BI program
- Preliminary measures and KPIs are identified and related to business processes
- Potential analytic data is explored
- A list of business questions that the business wants to see answered are specified
- Preliminary facts and dimensions are identified
- Preliminary models are created
- Risks and mitigations are identified
- Follow up tasks are identified and assigned
- Forward momentum is increased.

The benefits and costs elicited are great supporting material for the business intelligence business case, which in turn is critical to the success of the program.

REQUIREMENTS SESSION FOLLOW UP

Realizing the outcomes of the BI Requirements Session requires follow up. In this case, you will:

- Document and distribute the results of the session
- Update requirements documents
- Follow up on "Action Items" identified during the session
- Schedule a second session to validate the requirements.

Key Points

- Elicit DW business requirements using a sound methodology.

- Get the right people involved in the requirements gathering process.

- Group sessions are an effective way to elicit requirements. This approach is faster than a series of individual interviews and has the advantage of building consensus and resolving differences.

- Group sessions have drawbacks that should be compensated for. For example, not everyone may participate and the group may engage in groupthink. Be sure to include individual sessions to obtain a balanced view.

- Lack of documented and agreed upon requirements is a leading cause of project failure.

- Exploring data can help users to visualize their requirements.

- Interactive group sessions are an excellent way to elicit and document data warehousing and business intelligence requirements.

- A successful requirements session requires thorough preparation.

- A productive requirements session is a team effort that includes the roles of facilitator, executive sponsor, scribe, data modeler, and business experts.

- Group methods, such as setting ground rules and idea generating techniques, boost output of requirements sessions.

- Follow up is required to implement the requirements identified through requirements sessions.

Learn More

Build your know-how in the areas of business architecture and business requirements using these resources.

Visit a Website!

APQC is an industry organization that has built an excellent library of business capabilities and business processes.

http://www.aqpc.org

The International Institute of Business Analysis (IIBA) has developed outstanding guidance for eliciting and documenting business requirements. Check out their Business Analysis Body of Knowledge® (BABOK® Guide).

http://www.iiba.org

Read about it!

This book shows how to define business architectures and elicit requirements:

Laursen, Gert H. N., and Jesper Thorlund.
  *Business Analytics for Managers: Taking
  Business Intelligence Beyond Reporting.*
  Hoboken, NJ: Wiley, 2010.

Chapter 4
Data Warehousing Technical Architecture

From an architects' point of view, the hard part is to find the natural places to locate boundaries and define the appropriate interfaces needed to build a working system.

Einar Landre

In this chapter, you will learn about technical architecture, data architecture and data warehouse architecture and how to define them. You will learn to do many things.

- Understand technical architecture terms and concepts.
- Identify data architecture components needed for data warehousing and business intelligence.
- Understand and present the big picture of data warehouse architecture.
- Present the data warehouse technology stack which is the set of technologies selected for a data warehouse implementation.
- Recognize databases needed to produce your data warehouse.
- Compare data warehouses to data marts. This book explains the functions of each and shows where they are the same and where they are different.
- Identify data sources – the places where you are going to get data to populate your data marts and data warehouses are explained.
- Manage the business intelligence application architecture portfolio.
- Put together the technologies needed to support data warehousing and business intelligence.

Solid architecture is critical to data warehousing. The ANSI/IEEE Standard 1471-2000 defines the architecture of software-intensive systems as "the fundamental organization of a system, embodied in its components, their relationships to each other and the environment, and the principles governing its design and evolution." This chapter presents Technical Architecture, Data Architecture and Data Warehouse Technical Architecture. Data warehousing architecture is an application of technical architecture and data architecture targeted to the data warehouse.

Technical Architecture

Technical Architecture presented in this book is a combination of Application Architecture and Infrastructure Architecture. Major topics of technical architecture are described in the next section of this book:

- Functional and non-functional architecture requirements
- Technical architecture principles
- Buy, build, or re-use approach
- Architecture roadmaps.

FUNCTIONAL AND NON-FUNCTIONAL REQUIREMENTS

The recommendation "Begin with the end in mind" is very true for data warehousing and business intelligence. The end that we have in mind is a system that satisfies both functional and non-functional requirements. The data warehouse is a system that does what it is supposed to do.

Functional requirements (business requirements) are needs identified by the business relating to data and business processes. For example, you may be looking for a system that provides information about customers, territories and products that supports the business processes of selling and customer support. See Chapter 3, Requirements for Data Warehousing and Business Intelligence, for guidance on how to elicit and organize business requirements.

Non-functional requirements are needs about performance and IT chosen practices. Performance includes issues such as required system availability and recoverability. It depends on the volume of data and number of users expected for the data warehouse. IT chosen practices include selected technologies (the "technology stack") and standards.

TECHNICAL ARCHITECTURE PRINCIPLES

Technical architecture principles are critical to the success of data warehousing efforts. In my experience, these principles are often expressed in terms of "ilities", such as those described in Table 04-01.

Table 04-01: Technical Architecture Principles

Principle	Description
Adaptability	The ability to be effective in changing circumstances.
Affordability	The ability to achieve goals at costs that are within the financial means of an enterprise.
Auditability	The ability to record the circumstances and history of a process for later review.
Extensibility	The ability of a solution to accept new functionality.
Interoperability	The ability to exchange and use functionality across organizations and systems.
Maintainability	The ability to make changes to a system to keep it operating correctly.
Manageability	The ability to obtain information about a system and to control it.
Recoverability	The ability to restore a system to operational status without loss of data and within a required time period.
Reliability	The ability to consistently perform according to specified standards.
Scalability	The ability of a system to increase throughput and maintain responsiveness under conditions of increased load.
Supportability	The ability of a system to be serviced such as through the use of a help desk.
Understandability	The ability for a system to be comprehended or interpreted by people who use or support it.

BUY, BUILD, OR RE-USE APPROACH

A critical question for data warehousing efforts is how to obtain the software resources that make up the data warehousing system. There are three options:

1. Re-use existing resources
2. Buy a new resource
3. Build a resource.

Re-using existing resources can often save money and deliver a superior and more maintainable solution. If an organization buys or builds new components every time there is a new project, then the portfolio of resources will soon become bloated and expensive to maintain. Re-use can also have drawbacks. Existing resources may not meet current functional or non-functional requirements.

Buying a new data warehousing resource can save time and money over building a resource. Buying is a good choice when products are available for a price less than building a new resource, and meet a large percentage of your requirements. Purchased software may have more features and fewer problems than homegrown software, for example. In addition to software, pre-built industry data models are available which can also save time and money.

Complete turn-key solutions, known as data warehouse appliances, are available for some applications. The data warehouse appliance integrates multiple components: hardware, software, and data models. This can result in money savings, risk reduction, and faster implementation.

Building a resource can be a good answer when there are no existing resources to re-use and when purchased resources that meet requirements are not available for a reasonable price. Building a solution, or part of a solution, can result in a competitive advantage for your organization when it has a capability that is not readily duplicated by competitors. Cost is also a factor. Purchased software often has per user or per computer charges, while in-house developed software can be made available to internal users without additional licensing fees. On the other hand, building a solution can take a lot more time than adapting existing resources or purchasing a new data warehouse resource.

In general, I recommend "re-use before buy, and buy before build." Re-use means using an existing asset. For example, if your organization owns an ETL tool that meets requirements, it may cost less to re-use that tool than acquiring a new tool. Buying is acquiring an asset by purchasing or licensing it. The alternative is to build an asset. Table 04-02 illustrates considerations for this decision. Some combination is likely. When requirements and technology stack are known, create a list of needed resources and specify possible sources of supply for each item. This organized approach leads to effective sourcing with minimal duplication and waste.

Table 04-02: Comparing Re-use, Buy, and Build of Software Tools

	Pro	Con
Re-use	• Avoids new license fees • Current staff is capable of using tool • Does not add complexity to technology portfolio	• Existing tools may not be best of breed • Existing tools may be built on obsolete technology • Existing tools may no longer be supported by vendors
Buy	• Newer tool use may result in more productivity • Newer tool may support newer environments	• Additional purchase or licensing cost • Additional training costs • Complexity added to technology portfolio
Build	• Avoids licensing fees • May result in competitive advantage • Standard languages such as Java will be supported for years	• Pulls focus away from business goals • Depends on a limited number of internal developers

TECHNICAL ARCHITECTURE ROADMAPS

Data warehousing architecture helps to answer critical questions:

- What is the current state of data warehousing and business intelligence?
- What is the desired future state of data warehousing and business intelligence?
- What are the high-level steps that must be taken to move from the current state to the future state?

Roadmaps identify actions that must be taken to achieve the desired future state. In addition, roadmaps specify intermediate future states that must be passed through to achieve the ultimate future state.

Data Architecture

Data Architecture or Information Architecture is a blueprint for the management of data in an enterprise. The data architect builds a picture of how multiple sub-domains of data combine to support the organization's stated vision and mission. The multiple sub-domains include data governance, data quality, ILM (Information

Lifecycle Management), data framework, metadata and semantics, master data, and finally business intelligence. Figure 04-01 visually depicts these sub-domains.

Figure 04-01: Data Architecture Sub-domains

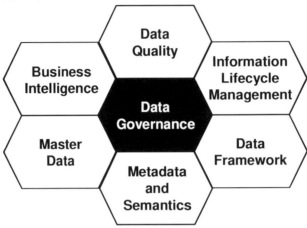

Each of the data architecture sub-domains has a role in the successful data warehousing and business intelligence project. Table 04-03 identifies and describes each of the sub-domains and identifies places in this book that provide further information.

Table 04-03: Data Architecture Sub-domain Descriptions

Data Governance (DG)	The overall management of data and information, including the people, processes, and technology that improve the value obtained from data and information by treating data as an asset. It is the cornerstone of the data architecture. See Chapter 8, Data Governance and Metadata Management, for more information.
Data Quality Management (DQM)	The discipline of ensuring that data is fit for use by the enterprise. It includes obtaining requirements and rules that specify the dimensions of quality required such as: accuracy, completeness, timeliness, and allowed values. Chapter 9, Data Sources, describes the use of DQM to improve the data utilized in DWBI.
Information Lifecycle Management (ILM)	The discipline of specifying and managing information through its life from its inception to disposal. Information activities that make up ILM include classification, creation, distribution, use, maintenance, and disposal. ILM is described in Chapter 8, Data Governance and Metadata Management.

Data Framework	A description of data-related systems in terms of a set of fundamental parts and the recommended methods for assembling those parts using patterns. The data framework can include database management, data storage, and data integration. This chapter shows the organization of the data framework and additional chapters provide supporting information: • Chapters 5, 6, and 7 – Data Attributes and Data Modeling • Chapter 8 – Data Governance and Metadata • Chapter 9 – Data Sources • Chapter 10 – Database Technology • Chapter 11 – Data Integration
Metadata and Semantics	Information that describes and specifies data-related objects. This description can include: structure and storage of data, business use of data, and processes that act on the data. Semantics refers to the meaning of data. Metadata is described in Chapter 8, Data Governance and Metadata Management.
Master Data Management (MDM)	An activity focused on producing and making available a single authoritative source of master data, the essential business entities such as customers, products, and financial accounts. Master data is data describing major subjects of interest that are shared by multiple applications. Consistent master data is a critical ingredient in the data warehouse. See Chapter 9, Data Sources, for more information.
Business Intelligence	The people, tools, and processes that support planning and decision-making, both strategic and operational, for an organization. Business intelligence is a focus of this book and its many aspects are described in: • Chapter 12 – BI Operations and Tools • Chapter 13 – Statistics • Chapter 14 – Data Mining and Analytics • Chapter 15 – Analytic Pattern • Chapter 16 – Presenting Data • Chapter 17 – BI Applications • Chapter 18 – Customer Analytics

Given the frameworks of Technical Architecture and Data Architecture, it is now time to focus on Data Warehousing Technical Architecture.

Data Warehousing Technical Architecture

Data warehousing technical architecture builds on the classic system pattern: input, process, and output. Figure 04-02 shows a simplified picture view of the data warehouse system. This is the type of diagram included in earlier generation books and presentations about data warehousing. We will start with this view and then dive deeper.

Figure 04-02: Simplified Picture – The Data Warehouse System

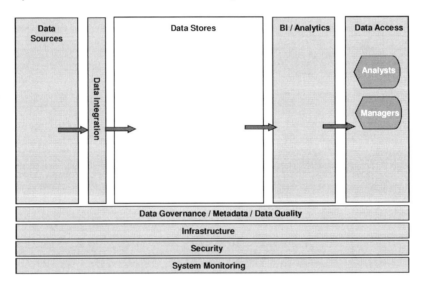

Each part of the data warehousing technical architecture is addressed in this chapter and expanded in later chapters.

- Data Sources
- Data Integration
- Data Stores
- BI / Analytics
- Data Access
- Data Governance
- Metadata
- Data Quality
- Infrastructure
- Security
- Systems Monitoring

The data warehousing system flow starts with a data extract process, which pulls data out of data sources and loads the extracted data into an intermediate data store such as staging areas for the atomic data warehouse. Data may be transformed at the same time as the extract or after the load. Figure 04-03 shows the next level of detail.

Figure 04-03: Next Level – The Data Warehouse System

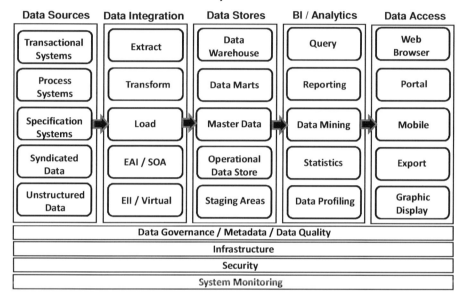

Next, data from data stores may be manipulated and moved between and within internal data stores. For example, data might be moved from an atomic data warehouse to a dimensional data mart. Query, reporting, data mining, statistics and data profiling tools each access data in their own particular format. This book describes how to design each of these areas so that analysts can access that data.

The data warehousing architecture includes a metadata layer and a system monitoring layer.

As you will recall from previous discussions, data warehousing and business intelligence are complementary and supplement each other. Data warehousing is about the data – it integrates and stores the data needed for the analytics required by the business. It includes databases, data movement, data integration, and data cleansing.

Business intelligence is the result of analyzing the data that was brought together through data warehousing. It includes producing reports, dashboards, scorecards, and analysis.

DATA SOURCES

Starting from the beginning, data sources (Inputs) are the places where data is obtained. There are typically multiple places to store data. This architecture chapter introduces data sources and Chapter 9, Data Sources, provides greater depth about this topic.

Data sources are the origination points of data. These founts of data include:

- **Transactional Systems**, which contain business activity such as receipts and purchase orders
- **Process Oriented Systems**, which contain workflow information
- **Specification Systems**, which contain plans, settings, and rules
- **Syndicated Data**, which is obtained outside the organization, and is used to enrich internal data, such as customer profiles
- **Big Data** is typically unstructured and consists of text, images, video, and audio. The advent of social media data has increased the importance of Big Data.

DATA INTEGRATION

Data is obtained from data sources through data integration approaches such as:

- **Extract, Transform and Load (ETL)** – a process where data is obtained from a data source, modified, and placed in a data target through batch means. This is the primary method for obtaining data for most data warehouses. A related method is "Extract, Load and Transform (ELT)" where data is transformed after it is loaded.
- **Enterprise Application Integration (EAI)** – a method of integration between software applications that utilizes application program interfaces (APIs). This approach provides immediate data and useful for near real-time data warehousing.
- **Enterprise Information Integration (EII)** – a method of data integration that provides access to multiple data sources without the need to move the data to a common database such as a data warehouse. This method supports a federated schema, which makes multiple data sources act like a single data source. This method can save the cost of developing new physical data warehouses and copying data.

Data integration tools move data into a data integration and storage area, which is another part of the architecture.

So, what factors should be considered when integrating data? There could be a customer who is defined in the Enterprise Resource Planning (ERP) system with their orders, shipping information, and so forth. The same customer is then identified in the Customer Relationship Management (CRM) system or database where there is information recorded about potential sales activities, customer service, and so forth. The data warehouse is a place where this data can be put together, providing a 360 degree view of the customer and our relationship with them.

After data has been extracted and the physical storage areas created, it is time to pump the data through the data warehousing system. It is moved from the data sources to a staging database, then to the data warehouse and to the data mart, where it is then available for BI queries by the business user.

These key activities are needed to support this process:

- **Mapping** – Data sources are aligned with their data targets. You will decide what data goes where.
- **Transforming** – Data is modified to meet requirements and formatting for where it lands.
- **Enriching** – Additional data may be added, such as geocoding.
- **Loading** – Data is inserted into the databases.

Data Integration Tools are a category of software that moves/copies data from one location to another, as well as scrubbing and cleansing the data. ETL (extract, transformation, and load) tools, as well as more real time integration tools like ESB (enterprise service bus) fall into this category. As you look at the overall effort and work that goes into a data warehousing project, the bulk of the work actually falls to the data integration tool. This tool is *critical* to the success of the project.

Chapter 11, Data Integration, provides further information on this subject.

Once data is integrated and stored, it is moved to an exposed data area where it is available to analysts and managers. Those who are going to make use of that data will access it using business intelligence and analytic tools.

Case Study: 3M, a Global Manufacturing Firm

Scalability was a primary driver when establishing the technical architecture for the successful 3M Global Enterprise Data Warehouse (GEDW). The system must support a global enterprise with over 100,000 employees and 50,000 trading partners that require data returned in seconds. The system would start with 500 users and grow to 30,000 users. The GEDW team evaluated a number of platforms and then decided on the Teradata® database engine to manage the databases associated with GEDW, and Information Advantage® MyEureka!® to support analytic applications. The technical architecture started with two database server complexes and one application server complex.

The database servers were built on Teradata Massively Parallel Processing (MPP) technology, with server complexes consisting of 48 to 80 CPUs organized into multiple nodes. Storage started at fifteen terabytes stored in a disk configuration that supports failover (RAID5). High availability is supported by failover control between processing nodes and use of a RAID5 disk.

The data includes structured data such as customer orders and shipment records, as well unstructured data like documents and product images. Also, GEDW provides data critical to data warehouses, such as master data, reference data, digital asset data, and metadata. (Messerli 1999)

Allen Messerli recalls the achievement, "We just did it and made it work! 3M had independent transaction systems in 62 countries, all feeding into the GEDW." This resulted in a streamlined system. Messerli explained, "We got rid of all our separate physical data marts and other data stores." (Hackathorn 2002)

Data Storage

Now, let's look at the data stores required to support the data warehouse system.

The data warehouse system is not going to be composed of just one database. Multiple databases or areas of databases will be required, with each database having a particular role in the data warehousing architecture. Sometimes it may be efficient and effective to combine multiple roles into a single database like the Enterprise Data Warehouse (EDW) or the Operational Data Store (ODS).

Data Warehouse: This database is organized into subjects, such as customer, product, sales transaction and so forth. The EDW contains a full set of data with an enterprise scope. The Atomic Data Warehouse area contains normalized data, meaning one fact or piece of information in one place. The data warehouse is larger in scope than the data mart and may provide data to one or more data marts.

Data Mart: This database is organized by business process, rather than data subject, so there may be receipts, issues, insurance policy, transactions, and so forth. It is a sub-set of data needed to analyze particular events or facts, so it is smaller in scope than the data warehouse.

- Focused on presentation and querying, to enable business people to quickly understand and use data. In this case, fast data output is critical, as is analysis for pulling data out, understanding it, and using it.
- Integrated using conformed dimensions, which are database tables that contain properties that consistently identify and categorize data, using agreed upon labels. These are descriptors that help us index and cross reference business processes.
- Denormalized or designed as cubes or a star schema, which provides faster access for reporting and analytics.

Staging Areas: These are databases where data is staged, integrated, and stored, prior to being made available through data warehouses and data marts.

MDM Hub (Master Data Management): Master data includes the core business and reference entities, such as customers, products, and locations.

ODS (Operational Data Store): ODS stores the data resulting from operating a business, such as orders, deliveries, receipts, issues, purchase orders, etc. The ODS can also act as a data integration hub and data warehouse.

PDS (Process Data Store): Data for supporting business process activity to provide near real-time business intelligence. This data is associated with BAM (Business Activity Monitoring). The PDS is a relatively new kind of database that is gaining in importance.

Data Mining Database: This database contains data that is optimized for use by data mining software. For data mining, it is best to store the data in flat structures, which is different from the data mart, described above.

Big Data: Data that is so voluminous (over 2TB) that it cannot be managed using traditional databases such as relational databases. This data is typically unstructured, and consists of text, images, video, and audio. This data is spread across many servers.

Data Warehouse vs. Data Mart

So what is the difference between a data warehouse and a data mart? Sometimes these terms are used interchangeably, but technically they are not the same thing. For the purposes of our architecture, we are going to discuss the distinctions between the two of them.

The data warehouse is:

- Focused on integration and storage.
- Loaded quickly to provide users with the most current data.
- Organized by subjects, such as customer, product, and so forth.
- May contain both normalized data, called an atomic schema, meaning one fact or piece of information in one place, as well as denormalized, which allows planned data redundancy.

Data Warehouse Architecture Patterns

The choice of where and how to store the data for the data warehousing system is a critical architectural question. Part of the issue is the data warehousing architecture pattern, which is explained in Table 04-04. Data warehousing patterns include:

- Independent Data Marts
- Coordinated Data Marts
- Centralized Data Warehouse
- Hub and Spoke
- Federated.

Table 04-04: DW Architecture Patterns

Pattern	Description
Independent Data Marts	Multiple databases containing analytic data are created and maintained by different organizational units. The databases tend to be inconsistent with each other, having different dimensions, measures and semantics. There is "no single version of the truth" and it is a challenge to perform cross data mart analysis. These weaknesses make the independent data mart the least desirable of the architecture patterns.
Coordinated Data Marts	Data is harmonized across multiple analytic databases or areas of databases. Each database meets a specific need such as customer segmentation or product analysis. There are shared dimensions and semantics between the databases. For example, customer and product dimensions are consistent across the databases. Consistent dimensions and semantics support a logical enterprise view.
Centralized Data Warehouse	An Enterprise Data Warehouse (EDW) contains atomic data, summarized data and dimensional data. This is provided through a single database. Logical data marts are built from this database to support specific business requirements. Analysis between subject areas is facilitated by data being stored in a single database.

Pattern	Description
Hub and Spoke	The hub and spoke architecture is similar to the centralized data warehouse architecture except that there are physical data marts instead of logical data marts. A cost and complexity element is added due the need to copy data from the central data warehouse to the distributed data marts.
Federated	The federated data warehouse architecture makes data that is distributed across multiple databases look to users like a single data source. Common keys such as customer and product identifiers are used to tie the data together. This approach reduces the expense and time needed for data movement. The approach may have a high overhead and slow response time because queries between data sources in multiple locations can be inefficient.

Data Model Patterns for Data Warehousing

A data model is a graphical view of data created for analysis and design purposes. While architecture does not include designing data warehouse databases in detail, it does include defining principles and patterns for modeling specialized parts of the data warehouse system.

Areas that require specialized patterns are:

- Staging / landing area – looks like source systems
- Atomic Data Warehouse – uses normalized ERD (Entity Relationship Diagram)
- Data mart – uses dimensional modeling – the star schema, the snowflake schema or the cube.

In addition to these specialized patterns, the architecture should include other pattern descriptions for:

- Naming of tables and columns
- Assignment of keys
- Indexing
- Relational Integrity (RI)
- Audit history.

A **Data Modeling Tool** is a software tool that provides a way to analyze database requirements using a graphical representation of the data needed to support the business, and then design the database(s) that will house the data. In other words, pictures are used to describe the data. On the surface, this looks like a drawing tool for creating graphics, but a data modeling tool provides a detailed design capability, which includes the design of tables, columns, relationships, rules, and specifying business definitions. A Data Modeling Tool will enable you to design a better database and also to communicate with team members about the data.

Data modeling is described in greater detail in Chapter 6, Data Modeling, and Chapter 7, Dimensional Modeling.

Operational BI

Look at Figure 04-04, Operational BI, which shows operational business intelligence, which is decision-making about the business for more tactical use. Distinctive features of Operational BI include: Process Data Stores, Business Rule Engines, Business Activity Monitoring, Virtual Data Warehouses, and Complex Event Processing. Operational BI supports the organization that needs to make a decision such as "should we upgrade a customer from coach class to first class", or "to grant credit". Immediate answers may be required, and data stores such as the ODS and the PDS may be consulted. Those data stores will be updated in near real time fashion, which means the data is as up to date as is practical.

Figure 04-04: Operational BI (See oval entries.)

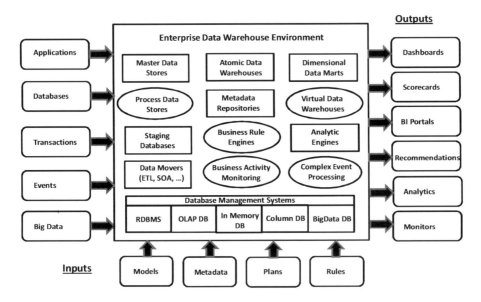

The data that populates transactional systems and the data warehouse is the "tip of the iceberg", compared to multi-terabyte volumes of unstructured data known as "Big Data". Your organization may have upwards of 80 percent of its data allocated to text, images, video, and audio. Technical architecture needs to consider this Big Data factor.

Database Versions

Database categories such as data warehouse, data mart, ODS, and PDS were just described. During the system lifecycle, which includes the development, testing, and ultimate use of these databases, multiple versions of each database should be maintained. Data warehouse architects need to be aware of and plan for multiple databases and versions of databases. Figure 04-05 shows an example of multiple database versions.

Figure 04-05: Database Versions

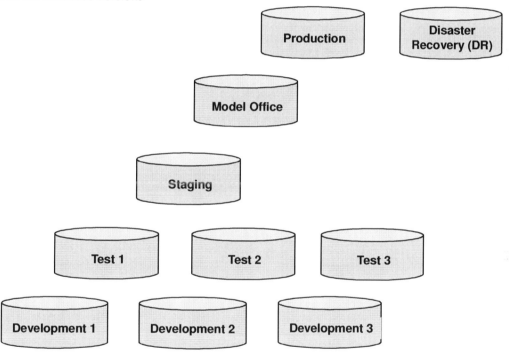

Development is where all sourcing, loading, application, and reporting SQL and program code is coded and prepared. ETL developers, DBAs, and data modelers are also developing the databases. One or more versions of the data warehouse database will be needed to create and try out the proposed designs. In Figure 04-05, a number is appended to the database role name to indicate a version number. In this example, there are three copies of the development database so that multiple people can develop at the same time without interfering with each other.

Once the database has been designed and developed, and coding completed and unit tested, there will be a need to perform testing on the data, so multiple versions of the test database may be needed. Testing may be performed by QA (Quality Assurance) people, often with the participation of business users.

After testing has been completed, a staging version of the database is needed to prepare for the initial data load for production. This is not the same data staging that is part of the daily data movement pipeline.

When the system is ready to "go live" and people are ready to use it for business, then a production version of the system is created. In addition, the architectural plan should cover disaster recovery (DR), in case the production database goes down. This could mean a backup copy of the database.

BI / Analytics

Decision Making which includes Business Intelligence is the part of the data warehousing system where business users make use of the data stored in the data warehouse by analyzing it and preparing presentations. Business people tend to either act like farmers, harvesting a crop of known information, or explorers, who are seeking new patterns. The data warehouse architecture must support both types of access.

Data warehouse architecture includes the selection and use of the following types of BI/Analytics tools:

- **Query Tools** are business intelligence software tools that select data through queries and present it as reports and/or graphical displays. The business or the analyst is able to explore the data and produce reports and outputs that are desired and needed to understand that data.
- **Reporting Tools** are software tools that produce repeatable reports and graphic outputs. Reports are output in predefined formats, often on a schedule unlike query tools, which are more ad hoc in nature.
- **Data Mining Tools** are software tools that find patterns that are useful for predictive analytics and optimization analytics in stores of data or databases. See Chapter 19, Data Mining, for more information about this topic
- **Statistics Tools** are software tools that enable the analysis of data. There is a substantial overlap between statistics tools and data mining tools. Both can be used to describe and understand data as well as to draw conclusions about data and to make predictions. Statistics Tools work with data samples while data mining tools work with larger volumes of data (aka Big Data).
- **Data Profiling Tools** are software tools that support understanding data through exploration and comparison. These tools are used to access existing

data and explore it. The tool looks for patterns such as typical values, outlying values, ranges, and allowed values, so that you can better understand the content and quality of the data. It is very important to not just look at the definition of the data, but to actually look at the content of the data to see what is there. Application developers are notorious for using data columns for unintended purposes, so knowing what should be in a column and knowing what's actually populated in that column is very important for accuracy in reporting.

Chapter 12, Business Intelligence Operations and Tools, supplies additional information about each tool category.

Data Governance, Metadata and Data Quality

The topics of data governance, metadata and data quality were introduced earlier in this chapter under the heading of Data Architecture.

Metadata

Supporting this process is metadata, which is information that describes the whole process and the data. The data included in system monitoring, a function that supports all areas, tracks what is happening as information moves from one place to another. More details are provided in Figure 04-03, Data Warehousing Architecture.

A **Metadata Repository** is a software tool that has both a user interface and a database component to record, maintain, and look up data that describes other data. There are two kinds of metadata: business metadata and technical metadata. A metadata repository should enable you to build a metadata dictionary, which describes important business terms, as well as the technical components of the data warehouse, such as tables, columns, data maps, and indexes. See Chapter 8, Data Governance and Metadata Management, for more information.

Data warehousing Infrastructure

The successful data warehouse system is built on a fundamental framework of hardware and software known as the infrastructure. Data warehouse technical architecture includes a big picture view of the infrastructure as well as recommendations concerning the components that make the infrastructure.

A view of a data warehouse infrastructure from layered perspective is illustrated in Figure 04-06. Components that can influence data warehouse and business intelligence performance are described in this section, including:

- Communication Channels
- Storage Devices
- Database Servers
- Database Appliances
- ETL Servers
- Query and Reporting Servers
- Analytics Servers
- Applications
- Workstations.

The diagram shows that disk drives or disk pools can be shared by multiple database servers. The database servers can in turn be configured as a cluster, enabling high availability and redundancy. Multiple databases can be hosted by a single database server.

Figure 04-06: Data Warehouse Layered Infrastructure Architecture

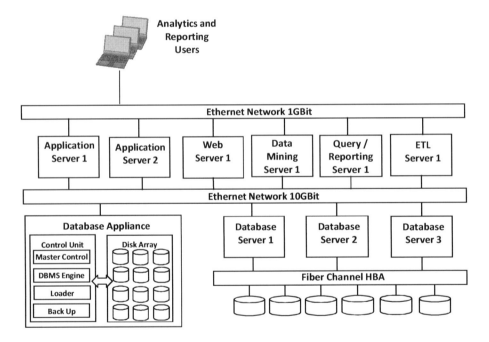

Servers are computers configured to host or run specific applications or services. They may be designed as standalone computers or in a group of load sharing computers known as a cluster. A single physical computer or cluster of computers can support multiple servers by employing virtual machines. Each virtual server has its own operating system (OS) and can be controlled independently. Virtual servers offer flexibility with a potential loss of performance due to shared resources.

In the case of data warehousing, each server tends to be assigned to a specific role. When developing data warehouses it is possible to place multiple functions on a single workstation computer. My main workstation computer is loaded with a variety of database management software and other tools. This will not work well for a production system with more than a few users or with over 200 GB of data.

The base characteristics of a server can be described in a specification such shown in Table 04-05. Each high level component of the server is identified. Together these characteristics describe the server configuration. I recommend that your organization standardize on configurations for each server role: database server, calculation server, ETL server, application server, web server, etc. These standard configurations will be part of the data warehouse reference architecture.

Table 04-05: Database Server Specification Example

Component	Description
Processor	Intel Itanium 3.22 GHz
Virtual	No
Operating System	Microsoft Windows Server 2008
Server Model	Dell PowerEdge 600x
CPU / Core Count	4 CPU with 4 cores – 16 cores total
Internal Memory	48 GB
Internal Storage	4 x 300 GB 15,000 rpm HDD
Fiber Channel HBAs	8 x Dual Port 4 Gbps
LAN Connections	4 x 10/100/1000 Ethernet
Database Software	Microsoft SQL Server 2008 R2 Enterprise

These specifications are heavy in the use of acronyms, abbreviations and technical terms. Table 04-06 contains terms and definitions to help you to interpret server specifications. In addition, this chapter includes further explanations about components of the infrastructure architecture.

Table 04-06: Infrastructure Terms

Term	Description
Cache	Main memory that is reserved to contain data. Performance is improved because main memory data is faster to access than HDD data.
Core	A processor within a CPU chip that can execute instructions. It is an engine within a physical CPU.

Term	Description
CPU	Central Processing Unit – a physical chip that handles the processing for a computer.
Fiber Channel HBAs	A high speed network connection typically used to communicate with HDDs. HBA stands for Host Bus Adapter.
GHz	Gigahertz – a measure of CPU cycle speed. Expect 1.5 to 4 GHz.
Gigabyte (GB)	1 billion (1,000,000,000) characters
Grid	A high speed network of computers that are utilized to solve a single problem in parallel.
HDD	Hard Disk Drive
LAN	Local Area Network
MPP	Massively Parallel Processing – multiple independent processors are coordinated to produce results.
Petabyte (PB)	1,000,000,000,000,000 characters
RAID	Redundant Array of Independent Disks – data is stored across multiple hard with the same data being stored in multiple places.
RPM	Revolutions Per Minute – the rotation speed of Hard Disk Drives. Current top speed is 15,000 RPM.
SAN	Storage Area Network – a pool of disk drives that is accessed through a high speed network connection.
SDD	Solid State Disk Drive
Server	Server – a computer system configured to host or run specific applications or services.
SMP	Symmetric Multi-Processor – a computer system consisting of multiple tightly coupled processors of the same type, running the same operating system and sharing resources.
Terabyte (TB)	1 trillion (1,000,000,000,000) characters
Virtual Server	Virtual Server – a server that runs on a Virtual Machine, which is software that gives the appearance of a physical computer including support for an Operating System.

Communication Channels – sometimes referred to as "the pipe" are the means of carrying data between devices. Types of communication channel include:

- Ethernet Network – A family of networking protocols that enable Local Area Networks (LANs). There are multiple transmission rates available ranging from one Gigabit per second to 100 Gigabit with 10 Gigabit being considered high performance.
- Fiber Channel HBA – a high speed network optimized for use in connecting to disk drives.
- InfiniBand – a high speed (up to 120 Gigabit) that is used to connect processors such as within a data warehouse appliance.

Storage Devices – devices that store data include Hard Disk Drives (HDD) and Solid State Disk (SSD) devices. Hard disk drives utilize a physical spinning disk, which can be the factor that slows down the data warehouse. Make sure to use 15,000 RPM disks or faster rather than the roughly 5,000 RPM disks found on work stations and home computers. SDDs have no moving parts and so are much faster than HDDs and are equivalent to 50,000 RPM. Unfortunately, SDDs may have longevity issues, supporting a limited number of data rewrites.

The size of the storage device is a critical consideration. In general, it is faster to store data on four 250 GB devices than on a single one TB device because the four devices can be searching data in parallel.

Storage devices can be organized into a Storage Area Network (SAN) such as the example network described in Table 04-06. SANs commonly have 50 to 100 individual HDDs to improve performance and reliability. The SAN can provide data to multiple database and application servers through a high speed Fiber Channel HBA network. This approach is an economical way to organize and share data.

Table 04-07: Storage Area Network (SAN) Specification Example

Component	Description
Fiber Channel HBAs	8 x Dual Port 4 Gigabytes per second (Gbps)
SAN Switch	16 port SAN Fiber Channel Switch
External Storage	1 x IBM DS4800 with 10 x EXP810 Expansion Units – 80 x 300GB 15K rpm HDD
RAID Type	RAID-5 (striping with parity)
Raw / Usable Storage Space	8 TB / 24 TB

Database Servers – a system that runs database management software such as IBM DB2, Microsoft SQL Server or Oracle DBMS. It may also run specialized columnar database software such as SybaseIQ or Vertica. Database servers are typically based on general purpose SMP architecture, which can be used for other purposes such as running application software.

Database software manufacturers provide reference architecture documents, which show example configurations which support specified performance levels. For example, Microsoft has developed a "Fast Track" architecture which shows the sizes of database servers needed to support SQL Server 2008 for data warehouse workloads. The specification includes amount of storage supported specified in terabytes, processor specification (number of CPUs and cores), main memory, operating system, DBMS version, fiber channel HBA and disk storage.

Data Warehouse Appliances – a specialized system that is optimized to provide database services using MPP architecture. The Data Warehouse Appliance includes multiple tightly coupled computers with specialized functions plus one or more arrays of storage devices which are accessed in parallel. Specialized functions include system controller, database access, data load and data backup.

Data Warehouse Appliances provide high performance. They can be up to 100 times faster than the typical Database Server. Consider the Data Warehouse Appliance when more than 2TB of data must be stored.

See Chapter 10, Database Technology, to learn more about database technology including data warehouse appliances and columnar databases.

ETL Servers – servers that run Extract Transform and Load (ETL) software such as Informatica PowerCenter or Microsoft SQL Server Integration Services (SSIS). The ETL software should be placed on its own server.

Query and Reporting Servers – servers that support query and reporting software such as IBM Cognos or SAP Business Objects. The query and reporting software should be placed on its own server.

Analytics Servers – servers that support data mining and statistical software. This software should be placed on its own server. Some analytic software places a heavy load on hardware. For example, software that projects insurance capital requirements may generate a large number of scenarios and require hundreds of CPUs and/or cores in order to complete calculations in a timely manner. This may require high performance computing approaches such as grid computing, supercomputing or cloud computing.

Applications – systems that are the data sources for the data warehouse systems. See the discussion of Data Sources in Chapter 9, Data Sources and Data Quality Management.

Workstations – computers used directly by data warehouse end users. Workstations may include large multiple display screens to support data visualization.

Data Warehousing Technology Stack

Now we will catalog the technologies selected to support our warehousing architecture. The data warehouse technology stack is the set of technologies selected for a data warehouse implementation. Table 04-08 is an example of the data warehousing technology stack for First Place Toys, Inc.

Table 04-08: Data Warehousing Technology Stack Example

Technology Role	Technology Selected
DBMS for Data Warehouse	Microsoft SQL Server 2008 R2
DBMS for Data Marts	Microsoft SQL Server 2008 R2
Data Integration Tool	Microsoft SSIS 2008
Query and Report Software	Microsoft SSRS 2008
Statistics Software	System R (Open Source)
Data Mining Software	RapidMiner from Rapid I
Data Modeling Tool	Computer Associates ERwin 8.2
Scenario Generator	Internally developed

Data Warehouse in the Cloud

Cloud computing can be an effective way of managing data warehouse infrastructure and the technology stack. Using cloud computing, a data warehouse environment can be rapidly established by purchasing services from either internal or external sources. This means less money and time to productivity, however, security and performance issues must be considered.

What is cloud computing? The National Institute of Standards (NIST) has created a practical and often quoted definition.

> *Cloud computing is a model for enabling ubiquitous, convenient, on-demand network access to a shared pool of configurable computing resources (e.g., networks, servers, storage, applications, and services) that can be rapidly provisioned and released with minimal management effort or service provider interaction. This cloud model is composed of five essential characteristics, three service models, and four deployment models. (NIST 2012)*

A cloud computing environment includes the following essential characteristics (NIST 2012):

- **On-demand self-service** – the cloud environment enables consumers to provision system resources (e.g. data storage, server time) through system requests without need to interact with provider personnel
- **Broad network access** – a variety of customer devices such as workstations, laptops and smart phones can access cloud resources over the network.
- **Resource pooling** – resources such as server time and data storage are shared and then allocated based on multi tenancy consumer demand
- **Rapid elasticity** – virtually unlimited cloud resources can be acquired and released
- **Measured service** – use of cloud resources via services is monitored and consumers are charged on a pay-per-use basis.

Cloud computing is deployed "as a Service" (aaS) and includes a number of service models:

- **Data as a Service (DaaS)** – data and/or database services (e.g. Microsoft SQL Azure) are provided
- **Software as a Service (SaaS)** – consumers are provided complete applications (e.g. Netsuite®, Oracle On Demand®, salesforce.com®) through thin client interfaces such as web browsers or mobile applications
- **Platform as a Service (PaaS)** – providers (e.g. Amazon Web Services®, force.com®, Microsoft Windows Azure®) supply consumers with a platform including computer languages, libraries, services and utilities which can be used to support consumer provided applications
- **Infrastructure as a Service (IaaS)** – providers (e.g. Amazon Web Services®, Rackspace®, Verizon®) supply consumers with basic computer resources such as CPU, networks and data storage enabling the customer to deploy supporting software and applications.

Clouds can be deployed through a number of delivery modes (NIST 2012):

- **Public cloud** – the cloud provider makes its service available to the general public so consumer resources are pooled with those of the resources of other consumers in the general public
- **Private cloud** – the cloud provider makes its service available for the exclusive use of a single organization with infrastructure being on-premises or off-premises
- **Community cloud** – the cloud provider makes its service available to a group of organizations or consumers who share common interests such as an industry association
- **Hybrid cloud** – a cloud that has characteristics in common with multiple other modes (e.g. public, private, community clouds).

Data warehouse in the Cloud can provide a number of benefits. Advantages of cloud based data warehousing include:

- **Rapid start up** – a lengthy process acquire and build infrastructure is avoided
- **Avoid over buying** – a data warehouse can start small and grow dynamically, avoiding the need to buy excess capacity to support future growth
- **Support peak periods** – capacity can be increased to support processing for month end and year end peak periods for example
- **Scalability and elasticity** – resources and their costs can be easily scaled up and cut back as needed
- **Reduced costs** – the economies of scale drive down the cost of infrastructure
- **Load balancing** – additional computer resources can be utilized to maintain high availability and performance
- **Environment Support** – multiple environments such as development, test, staging and disaster recovery are supported.

Data warehousing in the Cloud does present challenges. The Cloud is not the best approach for every situation. Challenges associated with the Cloud include:

- **Importing data** – mechanisms must be developed to provide enterprise data to the cloud
- **Communication channels** – data movement over the network can be a bottleneck
- **High costs for data transfer** – cloud vendors often charge by the volume of data moved to the cloud

- **Data latency** – the data in the cloud may not be current
- **Query speed and computation speed** – cloud solutions are often slower than on premise platforms such as data warehouse appliances
- **Control of security** – requirements for security must be considered such as authentication, authorization, vulnerability and security event monitoring, and data access logging
- **Legal protection** – data could be lost or unavailable in cases where the cloud provider runs into legal problems.

Use of best practices can help to overcome many data warehousing in the cloud challenges.

- **Standards** – use standard APIs and languages to provide flexibility in case it is necessary to change cloud vendors
- **Reference architecture** – develop architectural patterns that can be consistently applied to the cloud including data warehousing
- **Plan for required workload** – determine the patterns and volumes of likely workload
- **Network bandwidth** – make sure that there is enough network bandwidth – get a big pipe
- **Upload changes only** – send only changed data to the cloud rather than complete data refreshes to reduce bandwidth costs and improve performance
- **Determine best delivery model** – private clouds or hybrid clouds may address weaknesses public clouds
- **Security** – require the cloud provider to provide security features such strong authentication, data encryption and audit logs of data access
- **Monitor performance** – detect and avoid problems such as "killer queries" that slow performance
- **High performance guarantees** – negotiate high performance SLA guarantees to supply calculation intense activities and timely data warehouse queries
- **High availability** – negotiate high availability SLA guarantees
- **Contingency** – have a backup plan in case of service outages or other problems, which includes a backup copy of the data.

Data warehousing in the cloud provides many opportunities to improve results, increase flexibility and reduce costs. This is a technology that should be considered as part of data warehouse technical architecture.

Managing, Operating, and Securing the Data Warehouse

To achieve benefits from business intelligence, it is important to manage the data warehouse to make sure that it continues to provide value and risk of loss is avoided. This includes activities such as:

- Obtaining feedback from BI users
- Assuring the quality of the data
- Monitoring the performance of the data warehouse
- Securing the data warehouse from threats
- Enabling governance of the overall system.

The management of data warehousing is further described in the Chapter 19, Testing, Rolling Out, and Sustaining the Data Warehouse.

Data Warehouse Security

It is essential that data warehouse data be secured both when it is in motion and when it is at rest. Data that is being copied as part of data integration is in motion while data stored in a database such as the data warehouse is at rest.

All data should be assigned a security classification based on its sensitivity, such as:

- **Public** – data can be freely shared.
- **Confidential** – data must be protected, such as credit card numbers, social security numbers, or account balances.
- **Highly Confidential** – data is of strategic importance such as plans to acquire a company.

Data must be secured appropriately. Those who access data must have appropriate security clearances, depending on their roles and need to access data. This includes login authentication and determination of access permissions. Network, database and application security controls should regulate who can access data. Sensitive data should be encrypted both when stored in databases and when on the move through ETL.

Data masking techniques should be used to hide sensitive data from view. This can be used for test data as well as for data displays.

Data Warehouse Architecture Tips

This section explains things that you can and should do to make your data warehouse architecture more sound and flexible.

First, begin to work with real data early. That means looking at your data sources and understanding what is there, rather than just theorizing about the data and not understanding what it really is.

Second, I recommend using a consistent technology stack. You should decide on technology stack items such as the data integration tool, metadata repository, and so forth. Deciding on a technology stack and sticking to a consistent tool for each task makes data warehouse tasks easier. You will build up skills and capabilities in each area and be able to reuse work between areas.

Third, work with data source experts. Data source experts are people who understand the data sources, including people in the business who are working with the systems – business experts. People in information technology who work with that data and make changes for maintaining programs and so forth can also be included.

Fourth, develop architecture for the real world, which has multiple data sources and multiple data marts, using a federated approach. Generally, you will find that it is unrealistic to assume there is just going to be a single data source, single data warehouse, or single data mart, because multiples may be required. New systems often include something called a data mart, which might be reused or included in our overall federated approach.

Fifth, I advise including external data such as syndicated data, which can really improve the value delivered by the data warehouse system. Include unstructured data such as text, images, audio, and video in your plans. This is important to the modern data warehouse.

Finally, I recommend designing for scalability. Work with infrastructure architects who can design for growth. A scalable system can grow by expanding the hardware and software, enabling the data warehouse to support more data and more work.

Data Warehouse Architecture Traps

On the other hand, there are traps – things that you should avoid. Become aware of the following traps of data warehouse architecture.

First, do not attempt to do the "do-all" data warehouse on your first project. In other words, avoid building a big data warehouse to cover everything. It will take too long, get complicated, and probably not deliver the value that everyone is expecting. Begin with smaller steps and successes.

Second, do not build a rigid system. Make sure that you create a flexible system that can be enhanced and expanded as the need grows.

Third, avoid using a variety of tools, which is just the opposite of a consistent technical stack. If each person picks only the tools they are comfortable with, it is going to be more complicated and expensive to build and maintain. Flexibility and consistency will be lost and people will be unable to move between projects. Instead, use a consistent technical stack.

Fourth, do not start without preparation. Obtain training on how to use new tools and learn what the best practices are. Attend classes, and if your budget permits, bring in consultants who can demonstrate how to use the tools for a given project to reduce the learning curve.

Fifth, do not save the most difficult work for last. This is important, because you may get to the end of the project, discover problems, and be unable to get the most difficult parts of the project to work. Instead, tackle the most difficult parts of the project early and the rest of the project is more likely to be straightforward.

Sixth, do not report on staged data. As illustrated in the warehouse diagram, the staged data area contains data that comes directly from its data sources; it has not been cleansed and integrated for use by the analytics tool. Ralph Kimball explicitly warns against using staged data for reporting and analytics. (Kimball 2008)

Finally, avoid fighting a religious war. You may encounter people who subscribe to the Ralph Kimball, William Inmon, or Agile philosophies of data warehouse architecture. Each has its strengths and weaknesses which can be adapted for your project. A religious war would mean spending your time debating the differing views and deciding between them, rather than producing results.

Learn More

Build your knowhow in the areas of data warehousing technical architecture using these resources.

Visit a Website!	The Wikipedia provides a great overview of data warehousing, including a history beginning in the 1960s: http://en.wikipedia.org/wiki/Data_Warehouse http://en.wikipedia.org/wiki/Data_warehouse_appliance
Get Research!	Search the web for research reports (filetype=pdf): • Forrester Wave Data Warehouse

- Gartner Magic Quadrant Data Warehouse

Read about it! This book shows how to architect data warehouses using Microsoft SQL Server technology.

Rainardi, Vincent. *Building a Data Warehouse: With Examples in SQL Server.* Apress 2008

Inmon, W. H. and Krish Krishnan. *Building the Unstructured Data Warehouse.* Technics Publications, LLC; First edition, (January 1, 2011).

Include unstructured data to take your data warehouse to the next level.

Key Points

- Technical Architecture Principles provide non-functional requirements such as adaptability, extensibility, scalability, and understandability.

- The Data Warehousing Architecture Picture includes data sources, data movers (ETL), data integration and storage, and data that are exposed for analysis.

- Metadata, often defined as "data about data", provides critical documentation about the DWBI system.

- The Data Warehouse Architectural Pattern is a critical choice. The top patterns include independent data marts, coordinated data marts, centralized data warehouse, federated as well as hub and spoke.

- The Data Warehouse Technical Stack is the selection of tools used to analyze, design, build, operate, and maintain the data warehouse. Tool categories in the technical stack include metadata repository, data modeling tool, data movement tools, databases, and reporting/BI tools.

- The Data Warehouse Infrastructure Architecture is the combination of hardware and software that enables the operation of the data warehouse. Infrastructure elements include servers, storage devices, communication channels and operating systems.

In God we trust, all others bring data.

W. Edwards Deming

When you have completed this chapter, you will be able to:

- Define data, information, knowledge, and wisdom
- Categorize quantitative and qualitative data attributes
- Write effective definitions for data attributes
- Name data attributes
- Specify metrics and KPIs.

In Chapter 4, you became aware of the technical architecture of data warehousing and business intelligence. You gained perspective on the big picture of data warehousing and business intelligence.

In this chapter, you will add to your perspective by understanding the essential ingredient of data warehousing and business intelligence, the data itself. Data is the raw material through which we gain understanding. It is a critical element in data modeling, statistics, and data mining. Figure 05-01 shows data as the foundation of the pyramid that leads to wisdom and informed action.

Figure 05-01: Data in Perspective

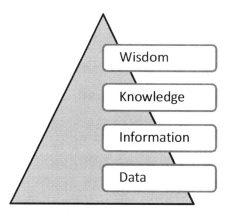

Later in this book, you will learn more about gaining wisdom for making effective decisions. For now, keep in mind the definitions in Table 05-01 quoted from the DAMA Dictionary of Data Management (DAMA 2008).

Table 05-01: Data, Information, Knowledge, and Wisdom Defined (DAMA 2008)

Term	Definition
Data	Facts represented as text, numbers, graphics, images, sound or video. Data is the raw material used to create information.
Information	Data in context. The interpretation of data based on its context, including the 1) the business meaning of data elements and related terms, 2) the format in which the data is presented, 3) the timeframe represented by the data, and 4) the relevance of the data to a given usage.
Knowledge	1. Understanding; cognizance; awareness of a situation. 2. Expertise; familiarity gained through experience and association. 3. Understanding the significance of information; information in perspective, integrated into a viewpoint based on the recognition of patterns (such as trends and causes) based on other information and experience.
Wisdom	1. Accumulated knowledge; deep understanding, keen discernment and a capacity for sound judgment. 2. Knowledge in context; knowledge applied in the course of actions.

Raw Data

Raw data is a set of data points without the additional context that would result in information. For example, a set of raw data of weights in pounds for five year old children might look like this:

(40, 52, 41, 43, 38, 42, 46, 39)

A set of raw data can be used as input to analysis, which can be put to good use. See Chapter 15 for insights into the use of statistics applied to analyzing raw data. Analysis and understanding are typically obtained by bringing together multiple data points and putting them in context. For example, you may want to understand the roles of weight influencing factors such as the school district, child height, gender, parental education level, and birthdate. An expanded set of data points, Table 05-02, shows an example.

Table 05-02: Data Points in Context

#	School District	Birth Date	Gender	Weight	Height	Parent Education Level
1	196	1/2/2006	F	40	44	16
2	196	4/3/2006	M	52	54	12
3	196	10/12/2005	F	41	41	20
4	201	12/31/2005	M	43	42	8
5	202	3/17/2006	F	38	40	12
6	196	5/12/2006	M	42	43	18
7	201	11/21/2005	M	46	51	12
8	202	5/3/2006	F	39	40	18

Attributes

There are a number of words with the same or similar meaning, which apply to individual pieces of data. Some of the more frequently used words are listed here:

- Attribute
- Property
- Data Element
- Field
- Column
- Cell
- Data Point.

For now, this book uses the word "attribute" when describing an individual piece of data. An attribute is a characteristic of an entity (person, place, thing, or idea) or a relationship between entities. Attributes characterize entities and relationships by containing data values. Some examples of attributes are:

- Customer Order Number
- Account Balance Amount
- Marital Status Code
- Product Description
- Skill Level Code.

Attributes can be further described by drilling into their definition and usage. Attributes can have names, data types, domains, initial values, rules, and definitions. Each of these characteristics of an attribute is described in Table 05-03. Key

Performance Indicators (KPIs) are attributes of special interest and will be described in more depth later in this chapter.

Table 05-03: Data Characteristics

Characteristic	Description
Name	Each attribute has a name, such as Account Balance Amount. An attribute name is a string that identifies and describes the attribute.
Datatype	The datatype is the format of the data stored in the attribute. It specifies whether the value must be a string, a number, or a date (for example). In addition, it specifies the size of the attribute. Datatype is also known as the data format. Examples of datatype are decimal(12,4), character(50), and date.
Domain	A domain such as Currency Amounts is a categorization of attributes by the range of values that can be stored in the attribute.
Initial Value	An initial value, such as 0.0000, is the default value that an attribute is assigned when it is first created.
Rules	Rules are constraints that limit the values that an attribute can contain. For example, "the attribute must be greater than or equal to 0.0000". The use of rules helps to improve the quality of our data.
Definition	An attribute definition is a narrative that conveys or describes the meaning of the attribute. For example, "Account balance amount is a measure of the monetary value of a financial account such as a bank account or an investment account."

Qualitative and Quantitative Attributes

Qualitative attributes are descriptive or categorical, rather than numeric. Mathematical operations like addition and multiplication do not apply to qualitative attributes. Examples are:

- Gender
- City name
- Nationality
- Brand preference.

Qualitative attributes can be further classified as nominal and ordinal. Nominal attributes are descriptors whose values imply no order, while ordinal attributes have order. Examples of nominal attributes are credit card number, brand preference, and state code. In contrast, a good example of ordinal attributes is the Likert scale that is often used in surveys: 1=Strongly disagree; 2=Disagree; 3=Neutral; 4=Agree; 5=Strongly agree.

Quantitative attributes are numeric. Mathematical operations like subtraction and numeric comparison may be applied to quantitative attributes. Examples are:

- Inventory Count
- Unit Price
- Temperature
- Failure Rate.

Quantitative attributes can also be further classified into categories. For example:

- **Interval** – The interval category has no "true" zero, so division and multiplication do not apply. Examples of interval attributes include: time of day, credit scores, and temperatures measured in Celsius or Fahrenheit.
- **Ratio** – For the ratio category, there is a "true" zero, so division and multiplication do apply. Examples of ratio attributes include: time durations, counts, weights, and temperatures measured in Kelvin.

Attributes in each category have different properties and operations that can be performed with them. *Distinctiveness* specifies attributes which can be compared as equal or not equal. *Order* implies attributes are put in sequence – compared for less than or greater than. *Additiveness* specifies that attributes can be added and subtracted. And finally, *multiplicativeness* asserts attributes can be multiplied and divided. Table 05-04 shows how these properties and operations apply to nominal, ordinal, interval, and ratio type attributes.

Table 05-04: Qualitative and Quantitative Attribute Properties

Property	Operation	Nominal	Ordinal	Interval	Ratio
Distinctiveness	= ≠	X	X	X	X
Order	LT GT		X	X	X
Additiveness	+ -			X	X
Multiplicativeness	* /				X

Naming Attributes

Attributes with descriptive, unique names greatly improve communication and make data models and associated databases much easier to understand and use. The goals are to:

- Make names understandable
- Make names consistent – the same name for the same thing (avoid synonyms)
- Make names distinct – different names for different things (avoid homonyms).

A proven method of creating meaningful and distinctive names is creating qualified names from modifier words, prime words, and class words, in that order. This pattern has proven very effective.

- **Prime Word** – The major noun that is the subject of a data attribute, such as customer, employee, asset, or product.
- **Modifier Word** – An optional adjective that modifies the subject of a data attribute, such as current, prior, or preferred.
- **Class Word** – A categorization of a data attribute such as: code, amount, or date.

The examples shown in Table 05-05 should help you to better understand the benefits of using qualified names with prime, modifier, and class word components.

Table 05-05: Attribute Naming Examples

Qualified Name (Do this)	Unqualified Name (Avoid this)
Last Received Amount	Amount
Order Issued Indicator	Issued
Open Order Count	Open Orders
Purchase Order Number	Order Number

There tends to be a small, fixed number of class words for each enterprise. A typical list of class words, based on my own experience, is provided in Table 05-06. Using a standard abbreviation for each class word will make attribute names more consistent.

Table 05-06: Class Words

Class Word	Abbreviation	Description
address	addr	A descriptor of the location of an entity, such as a street address or email address.
amount	amt	A monetary measure of something, such as a premium amount.
code	code	A word or abbreviation that classifies and/or describes a set of specific values.
count	cnt	The number of something obtained by adding one for each occurrence of an item such as inventory count.
date	date	A day identified in a calendar, typically including year, month, and day of month, such as 2007/02/14 (yyyy/mm/dd).
description	desc	A narrative that provides an explanation about or definition of something.
identifier	id	A reference that identifies a specific instance of an entity. It is often a logical or natural key.
indicator	ind	A two valued descriptor such as: true/false and yes/no.
name	nme	One or more words that describe what an entity is called, such as first name, product name, or city name.
number	nbr	A string that identifies or describes an entity. Values are often determined by an external organization such as social security number or driver's license number. It is often but not necessarily numeric. For example, a license plate number could contain letters (DLZ 879).
object identifier	oid	A system assigned identifier for an object. This type of identifier is used internally for efficient access and storage. It is often a physical key. It has meaning only within systems and is not used by/or known to the business.
percent	pct	A number described in terms of parts per hundred; rates are excluded.
quantity	qty	A numeric measure of something other than money, such as item order quantity.
rate	rate	A quantity of something measured in terms of a fixed quantity of something else Employment rate and error rate are examples.
text	text	A block of textual information other than a name or description. Customer comment text and correction procedure text are examples.
time	time	A point in time on a specific day.

Key Performance Indicators (KPIs)

KPIs are a type of data element that is of particular interest in the world of business intelligence and analytics. A KPI helps an organization define and measure their performance by indicating how well they are progressing towards a specific goal. KPIs have characteristics in common with other data elements including:

- Name
- Datatype
- Domain
- Initial Value
- Rules
- Definition.

Additional characteristics of metrics and KPIs are described in Table 05-07.

Table 05-07: KPI and Metric Characteristics

Characteristic	Description
Responsibility Level	Categorize the KPI as one of the following: • **Operational** – detailed information needed by supervisors to monitor operations and support immediate action, such as current customer orders, today's inspection results, and shipment backlogs. The data tends to be atomic and immediately actionable. • **Tactical** – department information needed by managers to improve processes through midterm efforts. It includes data such as weekly worker productivity, process breakdown trends, and unscheduled maintenance costs. • **Strategic** – enterprise information needed by executives to carry out long term plans such as improvement in market share or customer engagement. Strategic KPIs are often expressed as a percentage such as plant uptime percent, on time shipment percent, and asset availability percent.

Characteristic	Description
Responsible Business Roles	Identifies the job roles that are measured by the KPI. This includes identification of drilldown levels of the KPI.
Targets and Priority	Specifies target levels of the metric for each business role, as well as its priority for each role. Rules that specify notifications and alerts for when a KPI deviates from the target should be specified.
Align to Enterprise Scorecard Categories	Relates the KPI to strategic categories such as those proposed in the Balanced Scorecard (BSC): • Customer Satisfaction • Financial Performance • Organizational Learning • Production and Innovation
Frequency of Review	Specifies how often the KPI should be reviewed and analyzed. Operational KPIs should be reviewed multiple times during the day, tactical KPIs should be reviewed daily or weekly, and strategic KPIs monthly or quarterly.
Data Composition and Sources	Specifies the data that makes up the KPI and from where the data should be obtained. Includes sources of drilldown details.
Presentation Type	Specifies the appropriate presentation type for the KPI, such as: • Bar Graphs • Broken Line Graphs • Pie Charts • Histograms • Gauges • Reports • Trees.

Key Points

- Data attributes are isolated facts that are stored in the form of numbers, letters, or images.

- There is a hierarchy where data, information and knowledge build toward wisdom.

- There are many words for pieces of data, including attribute, property, data element, field, column, cell, and data point.

- Data has further characteristics that provide understanding and enable its management – name, data type, domain, initial value, rules, and definition.

- Qualitative attributes are descriptive or categorical, rather than numeric, and are classified as nominal and ordinal.

- Nominal attributes are descriptive without sequence, while ordinal attributes have order.

- Quantitative attributes are numeric, subject to mathematical operations, and are classified as interval and ratio.

- Assigning consistent, meaningful names to attributes makes attributes easier to understand and use. A proven pattern of attribute naming builds the attribute names from a combination of modifier words, prime word, and class word.

Learn More

Build your know-how in the area of data element basics using these resources.

Visit a website!   Data Management International (DAMA) is a global association of professionals who are dedicated to the practice of data management: http://www.dama.org

The KPI Library is a great place to learn about business performance, bench marking, and KPIs.

http://www.kpilibrary.com/

Read about it!   This book addresses data and its use in data mining and other analytics.

Pyle, Dorian. *Data Preparation for Data Mining.* Morgan Kaufmann, 1999.

The cost of a model is more than compensated for by future savings. It not only presents an accurate picture of the product for the executives, but it also gives the tool-makers and production men an opportunity to criticize and to present manufacturing problems.

Henry Dreyfuss, Designing for People

When you have completed this chapter, you will be able to:

- Understand data modeling terms and concepts
- Create conceptual, logical and physical data models
- Structure data models using normalization.

In Chapter 5, you gained some perspective by understanding the essential ingredient of data warehousing and business intelligence. Data is the raw material through which we gain understanding. Now you will learn to take data to the next step, the data model.

Data models, whether used for data warehousing or other purposes, are designed using commonly understood symbols and terminologies. This section will provide you with that grounding.

Data Modeling Tools

Data modeling involves visualizing data using graphical tools. You will want to obtain a data modeling software package or use graphical capabilities in existing software. See the Data Management Center Data Modeling Directory for a list of data modeling tools and other resources.

http://www.infogoal.com/dmc/dmchome.htm

Data Modeling Levels

There are three levels of data models (see Figure 06-01):

- **Conceptual Data Model** – a high-level model that describes an area of interest.
- **Logical Data Model** – a detailed data model that describes a solution using business terms. This model is independent of any specific implementation technology.
- **Physical Data Model** – a detailed data model that defines database objects. This model is needed to implement the models in a database and produce a working solution.

Figure 06-01: Data Modeling Levels

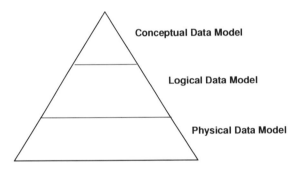

A Conceptual Data Model is a data model that describes an area of interest.

- Produced for areas of interest that consist of subjects (or domains)
- May be expressed in Unified Modeling Language (UML)
- Includes domain models and class models
- Useful at an enterprise level to describe the data domains of an entire enterprise
- Created during early project phases and for determining project scope.

A Logical Data Model is a data model that describes a solution to a problem in business terms.

- Created on a detailed level using entities, relationships, and attributes
- Uses Entity-Relationship Diagramming (ERD)
- Created during requirements and design phases
- Not specific to any particular database.

A Physical Data Model is a data model that describes a database-specific solution to a problem.

- Created on a detailed level using entities, relationships, and attributes
  - o Entities become tables (with some adjustments)

- o   Relationships become foreign keys
- o   Attributes become columns
- Uses Entity-Relationship Diagramming (ERD)
- Performed during design and build phases
- Specific to a particular database, including optimization and constraints.

Industry Data Models

One way to save time and money is to use an Industry Data Model, which is a data model that has been created to serve a particular industry or functional area. These models are available from software vendors and industry organizations. The benefits of using one of these models include:

- Saving time and money
- Improved, more thorough model
- Leveraging many experts.

Starting with an industry model is recommended over creating a new model "from scratch", in many cases. Industry models usually must be modified to match the requirements of individual organizations. In most cases, industry models cannot be used as-is, right out of the box.

Section 6A – Entity Relationship Modeling

Entity Relationship Modeling is a style of data modeling that has proven to be very effective for understanding data at a logical level and implementing relational databases, at a physical level. This book uses the Information Engineering (IE) data modeling notation. Example diagrams have been prepared using ERwin from Computer Associates. Other notations and tools may differ somewhat from the example diagrams provided in this book.

> *The principles of database design are nothing more than formalized common sense.*
>
> C. J. Date

Entities

A core part of the Entity Relationship Model is the entity. An entity is a person, organization, place, thing, activity, event, abstraction, or idea of interest to the enterprise. Think of entities as singular nouns.

As described earlier, an entity can be:

- A person
- An organization
- A place
- A thing
- An activity
- An event
- An abstraction or an idea.

Specific examples of entities include:

- Customer
- Department
- Product
- Job step
- Order receipt.

Entities are represented by rectangles in logical data models.

At the top of the entity is the entity name. In Figure 06-02, the Customer entity attributes include:

- Customer id
- Customer status
- Customer name.

An entity in our model can be thought of as a template that identifies characteristics of a typical real world instance of the entity.

In the Table 06-01, notice how entity instances correspond to the entities which represent real world customers. There are headings for customer id, customer status, and customer name. The values associated each entity instance are listed below:

- Customer id 1001 with customer status of active and customer name of Ace Auto Glass is listed first
- Also, there is customer id 5703 with customer status of active and customer name of Best Paints
- Finally, there is customer id 8207 with customer status of Pending and customer name of Ajax Plumbing.

Listing sample entity instances is a great way to better understand entities and make sure that practical solutions are designed.

Figure 06-02: Entities

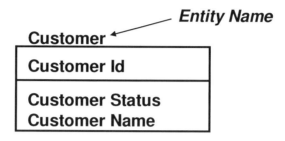

Table 06-01: Entity Instance Example

Customer ID	Customer Status	Customer Name
1001	Active	Ace Auto Glass
5703	Active	Best Paints
8207	Pending	Ajax Plumbing

Attributes

The next concept to understand in the Entity Relationship Model is the Attribute.

An attribute is a characteristic of an entity or a relationship. It describes entities and relationships by containing data values.

Some examples of typical attributes are:

- Customer Status Code
- Customer Name
- Sales Order Number
- Account Balance Amount
- Marital Status Code
- Product Description
- Skill Level Code.

Figure 06-03 is a diagram of an entity. Inside the rectangle are the attributes.

The two attributes above the internal line are designated as the primary key. A primary key is a set of one or more attributes that uniquely identify an instance in an entity or table and have been designated as primary. Each entity has one primary key.

Figure 06-03: Attributes

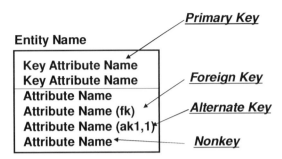

Below the line are additional attributes. Next to one of the attributes, in parentheses, are the letters "fk". This stands for foreign key, which is a set of one or more attributes that are also the primary key of a related entity, thus enabling navigation between the entities. An entity may have multiple foreign keys.

The attribute with the letters "ak" in parentheses is an alternate key. An alternate key is a set of one or more attributes other than the primary key that can be used to identify an instance in an entity or table. An entity may have multiple alternate keys. In addition, an entity can be described by numerous other attributes that are not keys.

An attribute name is a string that identifies and describes an attribute. We've already discussed the three typical parts of attribute names – modifier, prime word, and class word. An example is "Previous Inventory Count" where "Previous" is a modifier word, "Inventory" is a prime word and "Count" is a class word.

Part of building a complete data model, is specifying the metadata for each attribute.

Relationships

The next concept to understand in the Entity Relationship Model is the Relationship. A relationship is an association between two entities that helps build our understanding of the data and often represents a business rule about the relationship between the two entities.

Relationships may be expressed as verbs or verb phrases. Data modeling focuses on binary relationships. For example:

- Customer places order
- Region contains district
- Employee has developed skill
- Sales representative is responsible for territory.

Relationships are diagrammed by drawing a line between the related entities. Figure 06-04 depicts two entities, Customer and Order, that have a relationship specified by the verb phrase, Customer Places Order.

Figure 06-04: Relationships

Next is a deeper dive into the details of relationships.

CARDINALITY

Cardinality specifies the number of instances of an entity that may participate in a given relationship, expressed as one-to-one, one-to-many, or many-to-many. Figure 06-05 provides examples of cardinality.

In a one-to-one relationship, a Person plays the role of one and only one Employee.

In a one-to-many, one Student owns many Books.

In a many-to-many relationship, many Employees have many Skills. Each Employee may have many Skills, and each Skill may be possessed by many Employees.

Figure 06-05: Cardinality

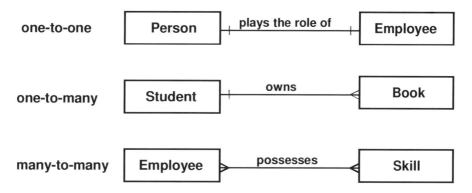

Cardinality is specified by putting symbols on the relationship line near each of the two entities that are part of the relationship. Two symbols are used. One expresses minimum cardinality while the other expresses maximum cardinality. If no symbol is used, then cardinality is unknown.

Minimum cardinality is expressed by the symbol furthest away from the entity. A zero indicates that an entity instance is optional, while a bar indicates an entity instance is mandatory and that at least one is required.

Note that some tools allow you to specifically state the actual minimum and/or maximum number allowed. For example, a minimum of 1 and a maximum of 6.

Figure 06-06 provides examples of cardinality, using entity A and entity B.

In the first case, an instance of entity A *may* have one instance of entity B (represented by what looks like a zero and a one on the right side of the relationship), and entity B *must* have one and only one instance of entity A (represented by what looks like a one on the left side of the relationship).

In the second case, entity A *may* have *one or more* instances of entity B (represented by what looks like a zero and a crow's foot), and entity B *must* have one and only one instance of entity A.

Figure 06-06: Cardinality Introduction

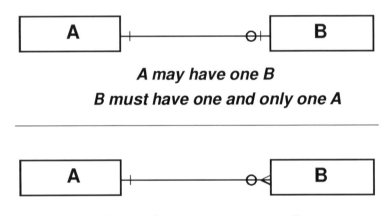

A may have one B
B must have one and only one A

A may have one or more B
B must have one and only one A

Here are some examples.

Employee has a relationship to Position. The cardinality symbols are left off which indicates that cardinality is not known or not yet determined. In practice, data modeling tools require that cardinality be specified, so this case only appears on whiteboard diagrams.

In the second example, it is optional for a Student to own a Book, so an O symbol is used to depict that.

In the example of Employee has Skill, it is thought that an employee must have at least one skill, so a vertical bar is used to show that this is mandatory.

Figure 06-07: Minimum Cardinality

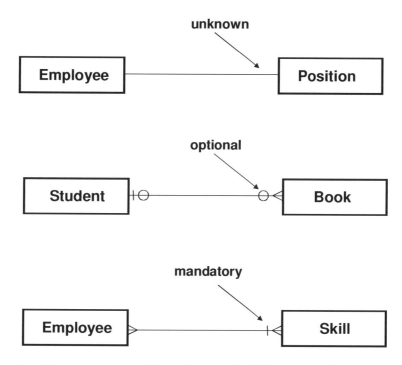

Maximum cardinality is expressed by the symbol closest to the entity. A bar means that a maximum of one entity instance can participate, while a crow's foot, which is a three-prong connector, means that many entity instances may participate in the relationship at the same time. This means a large unspecified number.

If there is a single bar, this means that both minimum and maximum are one. That is there must be one and only occurrence of the entity.

Examples of maximum cardinality are illustrated in Figure 06-08. In the first case, Employee has a role of Music Lover. There are no symbols, so both the minimum and maximum cardinality are unknown. In the second case, there is a single bar near Transcript, which means that a Student must have one and only one Transcript. Finally, in the last example, the crow's foot means that an Employee can have many Skills.

Figure 06-08: Maximum Cardinality

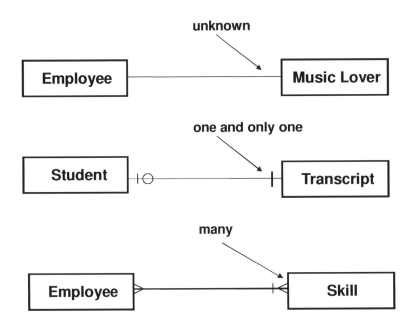

Exclusive Supertype / Subtype

A supertype/subtype relationship exists when two or more entities share common attributes and relationships, but each is also unique in its own way. The supertype entity is a generalization of the subtype entities and has all of the shared attributes and relationships. Each subtype is a specialization of the supertype and has the attributes and relationships that make it unique. With a supertype/subtype relationship, all of the attributes and relationships of the supertype are inherited by the subtypes, meaning the attributes and relationships of the supertype also apply to the subtypes. This relationship is also known as the "is a kind of" relationship, as in 'The subtype is a kind of the supertype.'

The example in Figure 06-09 shows the Party entity, which is the supertype entity. A Party is a generalization of Individual and Organization, which are subtypes of Party. It could be said that an Individual is a kind of Party and an Organization is also a kind of Party. In this book, we will use a half circle to indicate a supertype/subtype relationship. An exclusive relationship means that a Party can be an Individual or a Party can be an Organization, but it cannot be both. To show that it is an exclusive supertype/subtype relationship, use a half circle with a cross.

Figure 06-09: Exclusive Supertype / Subtype

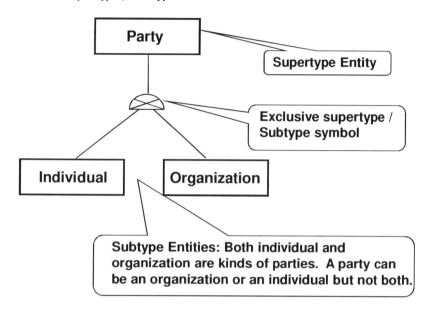

Non-Exclusive Supertype / Subtype

A non-exclusive supertype/subtype relationship is represented by the half circle without the cross. Non-exclusive means the supertype can be more than one of the subtypes at the same time. In Figure 06-10, Buyer is the supertype, while Produce Buyer and Poultry Buyer are subtypes. The inheritance symbol does not have a cross in it, so a Buyer could be both a Produce Buyer and a Poultry Buyer at the same time.

Figure 06-10: Non-exclusive Supertype / Subtype

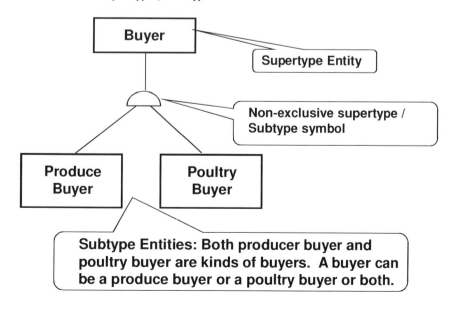

Derived Data

Derived data is another type of data for us to consider. It is data that is calculated or determined from existing data. Examples of this are totals and formulas.

For example, Total Cost Amount can be derived by adding Fixed Cost Amount and Variable Cost Amount. It is not necessary to create an attribute for Total Cost Amount, because it can be easily calculated. This saves storage, plus it simplifies maintenance because there is no need to change Total Cost Amount if the Fixed Cost Amount or Variable Cost Amount is changed.

Normalization

Normalization is a data modeling process that organizes data effectively and without redundancy. Atomic Data Warehouses have normalized designs. There are five levels of normalization:

- **First normal form** – separate repeating attribute groups.
- **Second normal form** – separate attributes that depend on only part of a composite key.
- **Third normal form** – separate non-key attributes that represent facts about other non-key attributes.
- **Fourth normal form** – separate two or more independent, multi-valued facts for an entity.
- **Fifth normal form** – eliminate interdependent attributes.

FIRST NORMAL FORM

First Normal Form occurs when an entity contains no repeating groups or attributes – see Figure 06-11. The student entity on the left has a repeating group consisting of course number and course grade. This is a problem because update anomalies could occur. Plus, there is a limitation of three courses.

To normalize, split the student entity into a student entity with an attribute that relates to student number, the key of student. Then create an entity called student grade, which has keys of student number and course number. Now a student can have course grades for many courses.

Figure 6-11: First Normal Form

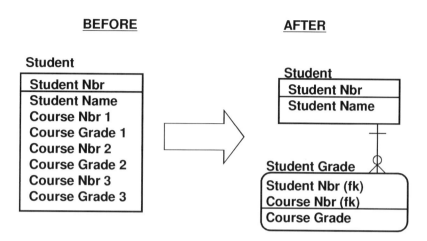

SECOND NORMAL FORM

Second Normal Form occurs when an entity is in First Normal Form and every non-key attribute is completely dependent on the primary key. In Figure 06-12, department is dependent only on department number and not on an employee number or start date. A change to department name requires a change of that attribute numerous times, once for each employee assignment.

This problem can be avoided by creating the Department entity and simplifying the Employee Assign entity. The department entity has a key of department number and a non-key attribute of department name. The new Employee Assign entity no longer contains Department Name. This approach has eliminated redundancy. Now, Department Name exists once for each Department Number.

Figure 06-12: Second Normal Form

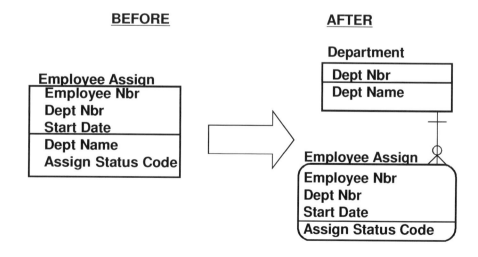

THIRD NORMAL FORM

Third Normal Form occurs when an entity is in Second Normal Form and has no non-key attribute that is functionally dependent on another non-key attribute. Figure 06-13 depicts an entity named Employee with a key of Employee Number and non-key attributes of department number, start date, building number, and building name. Building name is dependent on building number and building name is duplicated for each employee.

This problem can be avoided by creating a Building entity and simplifying the Employee entity. The Building entity has a key of building number and a non-key attribute of building name. The new Employee entity continues to have a key of employee number and non-key attributes of department number, start date, and building number. Building name is no longer part of the Employee entity. Now building name exists once per building.

Figure 06-13: Third Normal Form

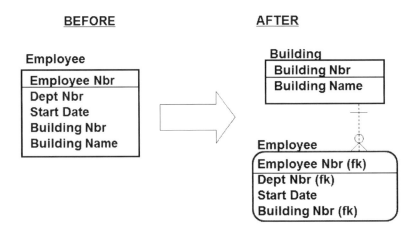

FOURTH NORMAL FORM

Usually, most normalization stops at the Third Normal Form. I recommend continuing to Fifth Normal Form, which results in a more consistent data model and database. The Fourth Normal Form occurs when an entity is in the Third Normal Form and has no merged independent, multi-valued facts.

In the Figure 06-14, the Employee Position Skill table contains position and skill, which are independent and should not be combined in the same entity. To correct this problem, we split the Employee Position Skill entity into the Employee Skill and Employee Position entities. This is in harmony with the normalization principle "The whole key and nothing but the key."

Figure 06-14: Fourth Normal Form

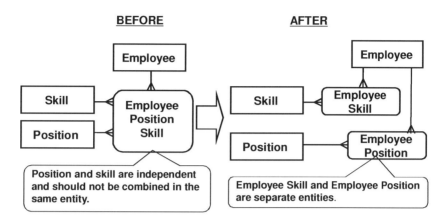

FIFTH NORMAL FORM

The Fifth Normal Form is a condition that occurs when an entity is in the Fourth Normal Form and has no interdependent attributes.

The Figure 06-15 example starts the same as for the fourth normal form. There are four entities: employee, skill, position, and employee position skill. The employee position skill table contains position and skill, which are independent and should not be combined in the same entity. In addition, we have requirements that we must know which skills apply to which position.

To correct this problem, six entities are created: employee, skill, position, employee skill, employee position, and position skill. The Position Skill entity shows which skills are required for which positions.

Figure 06-15: Fifth Normal Form

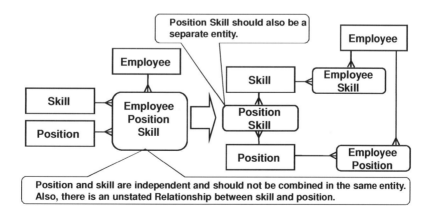

Summary: The Entity Relationship Model

The critical topics that you need to understand about the Entity Relationship Model (ERM) have been covered. This knowledge will help you to move ahead with logical data modeling. Here is a review of important ERM terms.

The first part of the Entity Relationship Model is the entity. An entity is a person, place, thing, or idea of interest to the business. It is a primary unit of data modeling. Think of entities as singular nouns.

The next concept presented was the attribute. An attribute is a characteristic of an entity or a relationship. It describes entities and relationships by containing data values.

Next is the relationship. A relationship is an association between entities. It represents business rules about the association and builds our understanding of the data. Data modeling focuses on binary relationships; that is, relationships between two entities.

Finally, you learned about the five levels of normalization, which is a data modeling process that organizes data so that it follows these principles:

- One fact in one place
- The whole key and nothing but the key
- A place for everything and everything in its place.

Normalization helps to produce logical data models that lead to effective and efficient databases.

REAL WORLD DATA MODELS

Data models for large complex systems tend to have hundreds of entities, which give them a difficult to understand appearance at the top level. Figure 06-16 shows what such a complex model might look like. Entities are so reduced in size that text is not visible. Do not despair or become intimidated. Instead, break the data model into understandable chunks such as subject areas and build understanding from there.

Figure 06-16: Real World Data Model

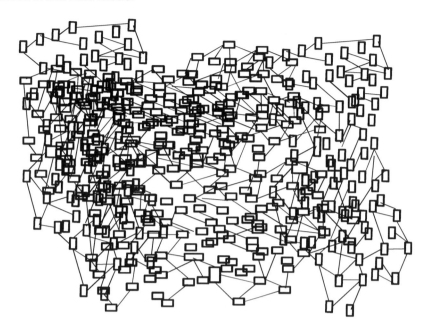

Learn More

Build your know-how in the area of data modeling using these resources.

Visit a Website!	Improve your data modeling using Steve Hoberman's Data Model Scorecard!
	http://www.stevehoberman.com
Read about it!	This book provides useful insights into the how and why of data modeling:
	Hoberman, Steve. *Data Modeling Made Simple: A Practical Guide for Business and IT Professionals, 2nd Edition.* Technics Publishing, 2009.
Try this software!	ERwin is a leading data modeling tool. Try the Community Edition for free, which allows up to 25 entities.
	http://www.ca.com/us/software-trials.aspx
	Oracle also offers a free data modeling tool called Oracle SQL Developer.
	http://www.oracle.com

Key Points

- Data Modeling enables visualization of data through graphical means – data design through pictures.

- There are three kinds of data modeling: conceptual, logical, and physical.

- Use of a prebuilt industry data model often saves time and money compared to creating data models "from scratch".

- Entity relationship modeling is a proven way to understand data and design databases.

- An entity, modeled as a rectangle, is an object of interest such as a person, place, thing, event, or abstract idea.

- An attribute is a characteristic of an entity and contains data values such as: order number, marital status, and skill level.

- A primary key is kind of attribute that identifies an entity, such as an order number.

- A relationship is an association between two entities, modeled as a line connecting the entities and described with a verb such as 'Places', as in "Customer Places Order."

- Normalization is a process of organizing data to avoid update anomalies by making sure there is one fact in one place.

- Data models can be created by adding progressive levels of detail. This starts with a Conceptual Model that contains only entities, and ends with a fully attributed and characterized Logical or Physical model.

Section 6B – Data Warehouse Modeling

It is now time to switch gears and focus on data warehouse modeling. When you have completed the following topics in this chapter you will be able to:

- Understand data warehouse modeling terms
- Apply data modeling to data warehousing and business intelligence
- Understand the canonical concept
- Design data staging and work areas
- Design data integration hubs and atomic data warehouses.

> *It (the Data Warehouse) not only serves as the integration point*
> *for your operational data, it must also serve as the distribution*
> *point of this data into the hands of the various business users.*
>
> Claudia Imhoff (Imhoff 2003)

Earlier in this chapter, you learned the basics of data modeling, which can be applied to a wide range of data modeling and database design situations. You are now ready to work with design patterns for data warehouses, where data is integrated and stored in preparation for delivery to the data mart.

Data warehouse modeling includes:

- Top Down / Requirements Driven Approach
- Time Phased / Temporal Data
- Operational Logical and Physical Data Models
- Normalization and Denormalization
- Staging / Landing Area – looks like source system
- Data warehouse / Backroom – uses normalized ERD stored in a common format
- Data Mart / Frontroom – uses dimensional modeling – the ROLAP star schema or the MOLAP cube.

Data is moved through a pipeline of databases and database areas from source systems to the data mart where the data is available for presentation and analysis. Data in each of the source systems has a format unique to those systems.

Figure 06-16: Data Flow Source to Atomic Warehouse

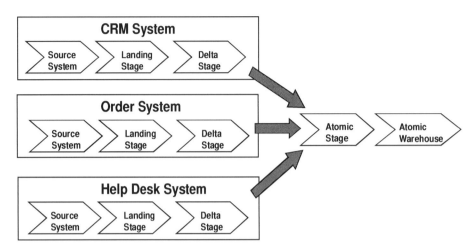

A canonical model is a model in which a common set of naming, definition, and value standards is applied. Data from multiple sources, each with their individual models, can be integrated by storing their data in a database with a canonical model. Each source system may have different names and code values for gender, for example. Names could include gender, gender_code, and sex. Some source systems might code these as alphabetic – 'M' and 'F', while others use '0' and '1'. The canonical model would take these two different representations and represent gender using a single common name like 'gender_code', and a common set of values, such as '01' and '02'.

There are several kinds of databases in a data warehouse, each of which has its own pattern of data model. Table 06-02 shows where each type of database fits in the architecture. More detailed discussions of each type follows.

Table 06-02: Databases and Areas within the Data Warehouse System

Term	Definition and Description
Source System	The database that supports a system or application from which data originates. Many source systems manage their data in a normalized manner.
Landing Stage	An area of a data warehouse system where data is first placed after extraction from a source system. The landing stage is a derived version of source system information.
Delta Stage	An area of a data warehouse system that is patterned on source data where only changed data is stored.
Atomic Stage	An area of a data warehouse system that is a simple integration point for data before it is placed in the atomic

Term	Definition and Description
	portion of the data warehouse. The atomic stage has the following characteristics: • **Narrow focus** – contains only required data elements • **Delta** – often contains only changed data • **Integrates** – unifies multiple sources in a single area • **Standardizes** – provides a common name, translates to common code and format known as the **canonical model** • **Simplifies** – reduces the complexity of loading the atomic warehouse via ETL.
Atomic Warehouse	An area of the data warehouse where data is broken down into low level components in preparation for export to data marts. The atomic warehouse is designed using normalization techniques, along with methods that make it fast to load. Recording of history is enabled.
Dimensional Stage	An area of the data warehouse where data is built up before inserting it into a dimensional data mart. Facts and dimensions are assembled here.
Data Mart	A data mart is the part of a data warehouse system where data is stored for presentation and user access. Early definitions of data marts specified that they were targeted to specific subjects and business processes. In practice, however, the data mart is a database that is organized into facts and dimensions that can cross subjects.

Source Systems

A source system is a database or application where data originates. Examples include: ERP systems, finance systems and manufacturing systems. These systems tend to manage specific entities, such as person or insurance policy, and enable:

- Efficient insert
- Efficient update
- Efficient delete
- Efficient retrieval.

Many source systems manage data in a normalized manner to promote high quality data with referential integrity, no data loss, and no conflicting data. An important goal is to provide a high degree of availability with limited stopping for batch activities. Systems must fit batch window SLAs (Service Level Agreements). The data warehouse system seeks to gather information from source systems without slowing down the source system.

The source system may also audit and log changes to data. Audits of database tables can include a record of the person who made the last change and the date/time of those changes. In some cases, a log of changes that include before and/or after images of the data may be available. The data warehousing system will work much more efficiently if it can extract only changed data, rather than all data.

See Chapter 9 for more information about Data Sources and Data Quality.

Landing Stage

The landing stage area of the data warehouse system is the location where data is placed, after it is extracted from the source system. Data is extracted once from the source and may be reused multiple times, thus avoiding loss of source system availability. The goals of the landing stage include:

- Providing a reliable and efficient copy of source data
- Rapid insertion of large sets of data
- Rapid identification of data changes
- Controls to detect and avoid data loss.

The landing stage contains tables that are matched one to one with source system tables. Following is an example developed using an ERP source system with the tables described in Table 06-03.

Table 06-03: Example ERP Source System Tables and Columns

Table Name	Column Names
Product	Product Code (Primary Key)
	Product Name
	Product Status Code
Customer	Customer Code (Primary Key)
	Customer Name
	Customer Status Code
Sale Item	Sale Id (Primary Key)
	Customer Code (Foreign key to Customer)
	Product Code (Foreign key to Product)
	Sale Amount
	Sale Date

Multiple source systems may feed a single landing area, so a naming convention is used to keep the source straight. In the sample data model in Figure 06-17, you can see that the base name of the ERP product landing stage table matches the source table name and the Customer table maps to the ERP customer landing table. Notice that 'ERP' is a prefix, showing that this data came from the ERP system. The sale item from the source maps to ERP_Sale_Item_Landing suffix. A suffix added to the name indicates a landing area.

We've also added an attribute to the end of the table for the landing checksum. Checksum is a computed value that helps to detect changes. When a row is added to the table, its checksum is calculated. If there are changes in a sale item, and the customer code changes, the system is going to be able to detect that change because the checksum of the updated record will differ from that of the original record.

Figure 06-17: Source System to Landing Stage

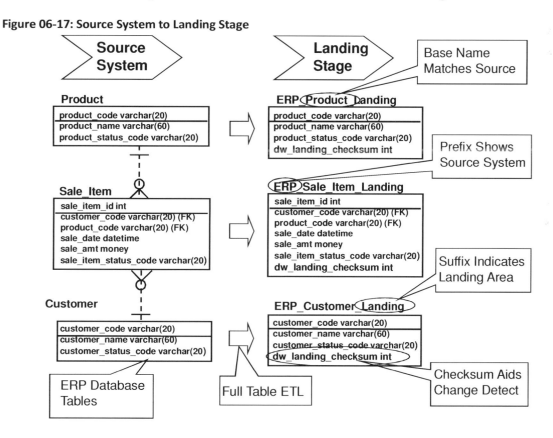

Delta Stage

The delta stage is part of the staging area of the data warehouse system. It is patterned on the data source, but only change data is stored. Figure 06-18 shows an example of the delta. The goal is to detect what data has changed as rapidly and efficiently as possible.

Data Change Detection is a capability that determines what changes in values have been made in a data store. There are several commonly used methods of determining when a change is taking place.

- Comparison of current and prior values – there was a particular value for last week, now there is a new value this week.
- Analysis of change dates in the source system – this is a good solution when the source system keeps consistent change dates.
- Changed Data Capture (CDC) – accesses database logs to identify changes, avoiding need to copy all data.
- Use of the checksum hash – avoids a column by column comparison, which improves performance and simplifies the comparisons.

Figure 06-18: Landing Stage to Delta Stage

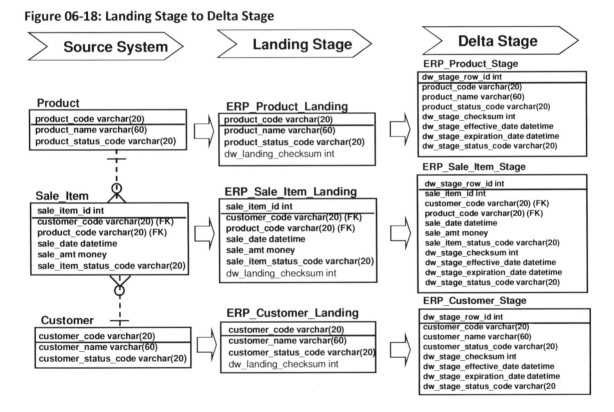

Change detection is important for a number of reasons. Trending analysis requires capture of change data. In order to know how things are changing and project the future, you are going to have to know what is changing. Regulatory compliance and audit also require a history of changes. In addition, it is helpful to know what was changed, when and by who in order to troubleshoot data problems.

Atomic Stage

The Atomic Stage is an area of a data warehouse system that is a simple integration point for data before it is placed in the atomic portion of the data warehouse. Goals and characteristics include:

- Enable rapid inserts of bulk data
- Provide a simple gateway to the Atomic Warehouse – reduce complexity of transformation from stage to Atomic Warehouse
- Support transformation and cleansing
- Enable a single cleansing, identify, and transform process, instead of duplicating these processes for each data source.

A single cleansing process is effective because it produces consistent results. It is efficient because it avoids duplication of effort in development and maintenance. Data is pre-processed and stored in canonical form before being moved to the Atomic Warehouse.

The atomic stage database design resembles the Atomic Warehouse tables without referential integrity and with natural keys, rather than surrogate keys. An example of the atomic stage is depicted in Figure 06-19, where versions of customer data from three systems are combined into a single canonical format.

Figure 06-19: Atomic Stage

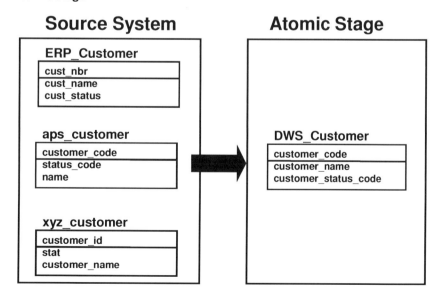

Support Tables

Supporting data is required to enable the data warehouse to operate smoothly. This data supports functionality including:

- Code Management and Translation
- Data Source Tracking
- Error Logging
- Control Total Checking.

A code is a way to substitute an identifier for a description and supports allowed values for data attributes. For example, the value 'FT' could be a code that represents the foot unit of measure. A challenge occurs when data from multiple data sources must be integrated and those systems have incompatible code values. Data source 1 could represent male gender as 'M', while data source 2 represents male gender as '1'. In the data warehouse, these disparate code values are resolved to a common set. Figure 06-20 depicts a data model that supports codes and code translation.

Figure 06-20: Code Management and Translation

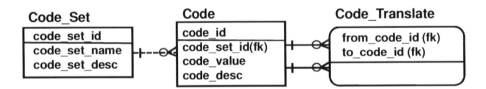

The tables that support code management and translation include:

- **Code_Set** – A group of symbols that represent assigned meanings. For example, EDW Gender Code, see Table 06-04.
- **Code** – An individual symbol that has a specific meaning within a code set. For example, 'M' or 'F'.
- **Code_Translate** – A cross reference between code values in different Code_Sets. For example, from 'M' to '01'.

Data source tracking, depicted in Figure 06-21, provides a means of tracing where data warehouse data is coming from:

- **Data_Source** – Identifies the name of the system providing input to the data warehouse. It contains one entry per system or interface.
- **Data_Process** – Identifies the loading process from a data source. Each data source may be loaded through multiple data processes.

- **Data_Process_Log** – Records the start and end date on which data processes were run.

Table 06-04: Code Management Example

Code_Set Table		
code_set_id	code_set_name	code_set_desc
100	EDW Gender	Gender Code for EDW
212	ERP Gender	Gender Code in ERP System

Code Table			
code_id	code_set_id	code_value	code_desc
10001	100	01	Male
10002	100	02	Female
10099	100	99	Unknown
21201	212	M	Male
21202	212	F	Female
21205	212	U	Unknown

Code_Translate Table	
from_code	to_code
21201	10001
21202	10002
21205	10099

Figure 06-21: Data Source Tracking and Logging

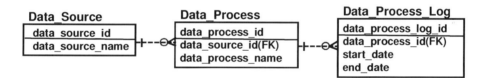

Message logging, depicted in Figure 06-22, provides a record of events that occur during the population of data warehouse data.

- **Message_Type** – A description of the kinds of messages recorded in the Error_Log. Severity_level_nbr indicates how serious the message is, ranging from informational to fatal.
- **Message_Log** – A recorded message associated with a data process. Notice that Message_Log is related to Data_Process_Log, which identifies the process for which the message was generated. Message_Log contains key values, the text of the message, and the type of message to better describe the log entries.

Figure 06-22: Message Logging

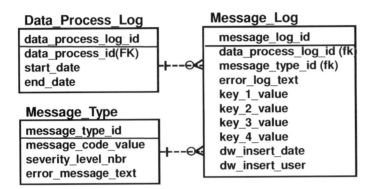

Controls, depicted in Figure 06-23, provide support for data quality in the data warehouse. This may be required as part of the data governance process and by financial auditors, as well. It introduces two new tables:

- **Control_Set** – A grouping of controls. For example, one set of controls may address comparison of record counts between source systems and the data warehouse. Another set of controls may test monetary amounts for reasonableness.
- **Control** – An individual control check. It describes the control by name and description, as well as specifying the control through minimum and maximum thresholds. A datatype code specifies the format of the data checked through the control. Count data is evaluated through the min_count and max_count columns. Monetary data is evaluated through the min_amount and max_amount columns. Percentages and rates are evaluated using the min_percent and max_percent columns. The message_type_id column specifies the kind of message to be logged when the control threshold is exceeded.

This control structure has proven itself to be very flexible and to support ongoing data quality in data warehouses and other analytical applications. Control checking is performed through custom programming or through data load configuration.

Figure 06-23: Controls

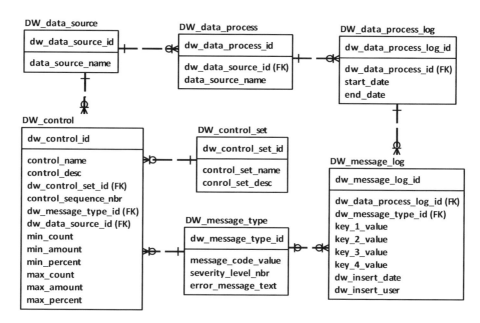

Atomic Data Warehouse

The Atomic Data Warehouse is the part of the data warehouse system where data is broken down into low level components and integrated with other components in preparation for export to data marts. The atomic warehouse is designed using normalization techniques along with methods that enable recording of history and make it fast to load and retrieve data. Expected functionality must:

- Act as a data hub, distribute information to the data warehouse and other targets.
- Accept, integrate, and cleanse data coming from multiple sources.
- Enable trace back to the source system; must show lineage of data.
- Support controls to ensure that data is complete and correct.

There are specific data modeling patterns that make for a successful and efficient atomic data warehouse. These data model patterns include:

- Use of an atomic data store with normalized structures.
- Split data entities into static and dynamic parts, where the entity containing the static part contains the logical key, and the dynamic part includes an effective date that supports tracking of history.
- Relationships between entities are modeled using associative tables with effective dating.

- Translation tables enable translation of codes from multiple sources to common values.

Figure 06-24 illustrates the use of static and dynamic data. A source system defines Product in a single table, where a product is identified by a code and described by a product name and product status code. The product code is the logical key of Product. In the atomic data warehouse, the product code is static and stored in a header table, while the product name and product status code are stored in a detail table. If the name or status of a product changes, a new row is inserted into the atomic data warehouse Product Detail table with a new effective date, thus maintaining a history of product name and status changes.

Figure 06-24: Tracking Change in Atomic Data

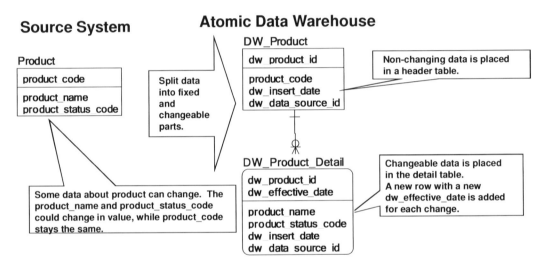

A history of relationships between entities is maintained through associative entities and effective dating. Figure 06-25 shows how a history of relationships is maintained between static entities DW_Product and DW_Sale_Item. DW_Product_Sale_Item is an associative entity that records a history of the relationship between the two entities. The effective_date specifies when the relationship started while the expire_date specifies when the relationship ended.

Specialized data warehousing attributes are added to each table to enable management of the system. Figure 06-26 shows a data model that includes these specialized data elements, which have a "dw_" prefix.

Figure 06-25: Associative Entity Tracks Relationships

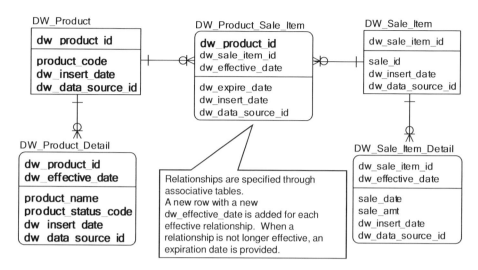

Figure 06-26: Specialized Data Warehousing Attributes

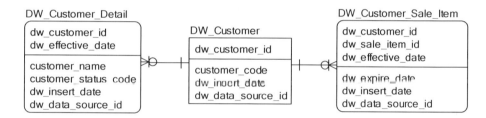

The meaning and usage of each of these specialized attributes are described in Table 06-05. "Audit attributes" track the dates when information was inserted or will expire.

Table 06-05: Specialized Data Warehousing Attributes

Attribute Name	Attribute Description
dw_xxx_id	Data Warehouse assigned surrogate key. Replace 'xxx' with a reference to the table name such as 'dw_customer_ id'.
dw_insert_date	The date and time when a row was inserted into the data warehouse.
dw_effective_date	The date and time when a row in the data warehouse began to be active.
dw_expire_date	The date and time when a row in the data warehouse stopped being active.
dw_data_process_log_id	A reference to the data process log, which is a record of the process that loaded or modified data in the data warehouse.

The completed Atomic Data Warehouse example is depicted in Figure 06-27.

Figure 06-27: Completed Atomic Data Warehouse Example

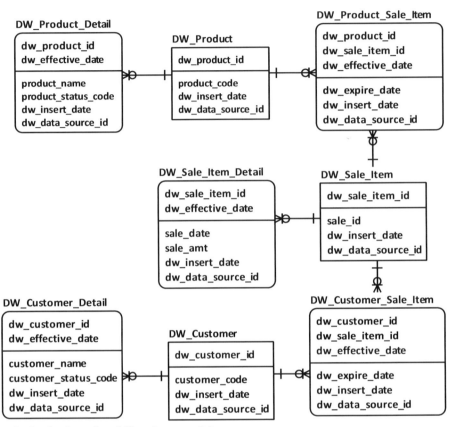

The example includes the following entities:

- DW_Product – The unchanging header entity for products
- DW_Product_Detail – The change tracking detail entity for products
- DW_Customer – The unchanging header entity for customers
- DW_Customer_Detail – The change tracking detail entity for customers
- DW_Product_Sale_Item – An associative entity that relates products to sale items
- DW_Customer_Sale_Item – An associative entity that relates customers to sale items.

Key Points

- Data staging areas contain intermediate data on the way from data sources to the data warehouse / data mart.

- Metadata is documentation about the data warehouse, including data entities, data attributes, and data mappings.

- The data warehouse is designed to support rapid data loading, retention of data relationships, and history tracking.

- An atomic approach, where data is organized in a normalized fashion and where relationships and changing data are isolated, is an effective way to model the data warehouse.

Learn More

Build your know-how in the area of data warehouse modeling using these resources.

Do It Now!   Design a data warehouse model to meet the requirements described in Table 06-06.

Table 06-06: Data Warehouse Problem

Entities

Entity Description	Fixed Attributes	Changeable Attributes
Branch	Branch Code	Branch Name Branch Status Branch Address
Account	Account Number Account Type Code Open Date	Account Status Close Date
Account Holder	Account Holder Id Tax Id Birth Date	First Name Last Name Income Level Code

Transactional Entities

Entity Description	Parent Entity	Attributes
Account Transaction	Account	Transaction Type Code Transaction Date Transaction Amount

Associations

Association Description	First Entity	Second Entity
Account Held at Branch	Account	Branch
Account Holder Owns Account	Account Holder	Account

Compare your results to Figure 06-28.

Figure 06-28: Data Warehouse Completed Problem

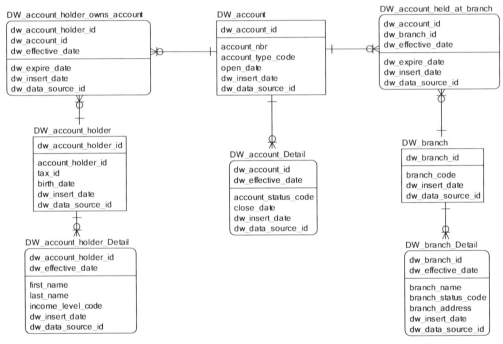

Read about it!   *These books show how to model the Atomic Data Warehouse and the Data Vault.*

Imhoff, Claudia. And Nicholas Galemmo and Jonathan G. Geiger. *Mastering Data Warehouse Design: Relational and Dimensional Techniques.* Wiley, 2003.

Linstedt, Daniel. *The Business of Data Vault Modeling.* Lulu, 2010.

Chapter 7
Dimensional Modeling

Dimension modeling is a logical design technique that seeks to present the data in a standard framework that is intuitive and allows for high-performance access.

Ralph Kimball (Kimball 2008)

When you have completed this chapter, you will be able to:

- Understand dimensional modeling terms
- Apply data modeling to business intelligence
- Design a data mart using dimensional modeling.

In Chapter 7, you learned to model the data as it is extracted, cleansed, and integrated in preparation for loading to the data mart. In this chapter, you will understand how to arrange data for delivery to the user – the people who analyze the data.

The following dimensional modeling topics will be explained:

- Top Down / Requirements Driven Approach
- Fact Tables and Dimension Tables
- Multidimensional Model / Star Schema
- Roll Up, Drill Down, and Pivot Analysis
- Time Phased / Temporal Data
- Operational Logical and Physical Data Models
- Normalization and Denormalization
- Model Granularity – the Level of Detail.

Areas that require specialized patterns are:

- Staging / Landing Area – looks like source system
- Data Warehouse – uses normalized ERD
- Data Mart – uses dimensional modeling – the ROLAP star schema or the MOLAP cube.

Dimensional Data Modeling

The best way to organize data is to meet the needs of its users. Business intelligence commonly performs analytic operations on data. These operations are described in more detail in Chapter 12, Business Intelligence Operations. They include the following:

- **Query by multiple criteria** – The analyst explores data and focuses the search on specific areas of interest. For example, the analyst may use sales territory and product as criteria for data selections.
- **Drill down** – The analyst explores data at a more detailed level. For example, the analyst may start analysis of sales figures summarized by sales territory, then drill down to the store level, and even further to individual sales transactions.
- **Roll up** – The analyst explores data at a summarized level. This is the reverse of Drill Down. For example, sales could be rolled up from the territory level to the region level.
- **Slice and dice** – The analyst explores data by focusing on a specific dimension, such as sales territories or products.

The "Dimensional Data Model" was popularized by Ralph Kimball and others in the 1980s to support business needs for analytical operations. This approach has stood the test of time and is the recommended way to organize data for business query and analysis.

The dimensional model provides a number of benefits including:

- **Maps to business process** – The measures correspond to business activities such as sales, manufacturing, and accounting.
- **Ease of query** – Data is organized so that analysts can easily query information, which enables operations like drill down and roll up.
- **Ease of modification** – The data is organized so that changes can be made to the database design, such as the addition of new attributes.
- **Efficiency of query** – Data is organized so that it can be accessed quickly by computer. For example, data is stored using surrogate keys, which enable highly efficient data access.
- **Support by query tools** – BI tools are designed to access data that is stored in dimensional format.
- **Understandable design** – The arrangement of data in the dimensional format is easy to understand because it builds on the well understood paradigm of cubes and analytical operations.

The basic terms describing the dimensional model are described in Table 07-01.

Table 07-01: Data Mart Basic Model

Term	Definition and Description
Data Mart	A data mart is a database in which data is stored to ensure good performance for presentation and user access. Early definitions specified that data marts were targeted to specific subjects and business processes. In practice, the data mart is a database that is organized into facts and dimensions that can cross subjects.
Fact	A fact is a set of measures. It contains quantitative data that are displayed in the body of reports. It often contains amounts of money and quantities of things. In the dimensional model, the fact is surrounded by dimensions which categorize the fact.
Dimension	A dimension is a database table that contains reference information to identify and categorize facts. The attributes serve as labels for reports and as data points for summarization. In the dimensional model, dimensions surround and qualify facts.
Hierarchy	A hierarchy is an arrangement of entities into levels where each entity has one parent and may have multiple children. A geographic hierarchy could have levels such as: continent, country, state, county, city and postal code.
Cube	A cube is a data structure organized into dimensions, measures, and cells. Cubes contain a set of detailed measures at the leaf-level, for each distinct combination of dimensions, plus aggregated measures for roll ups where one or more dimensions are removed from a hierarchy.
Metric	A metric is a direct, quantified measure of performance, such as revenue, cost, unit sales, and complaint count.
Cell	A cell is a set of measures associated with a distinct set of dimensions within a cube. Empty cells contain no data for a particular combination.

Star Schema

A Star Schema is a database that is optimized for query and analysis. It is a form of dimensional model consisting of facts and dimensions, where each fact is connected to multiple denormalized dimensions that are not further categorized by outlier dimensions. It is a straight forward dimensional model.

The two major table types of the Star Schema are the fact table and the dimension table. The fact table contains quantitative measures, while the dimension contains classification information. Each fact is surrounded by the dimensions that provide context to it, giving it the appearance of a star, as depicted in Figure 07-01.

Figure 07-01: Star Schema – A Fact Surrounded by Dimensions

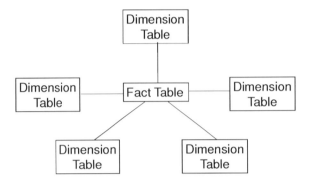

The Sales Order Fact with dimensions, shown in Figure 07-02, is a classic example. In this case, the Sales Order Fact includes the measures order quantity, and currency amount. Dimensions of Time Period, Product, Customer, Geo Location, and Sales Organization put the Sales Order Fact into context. This star schema supports looking at orders like a cube, enabling slicing and dicing by customer, time, and product.

Figure 07-02: Sales Order Star Schema

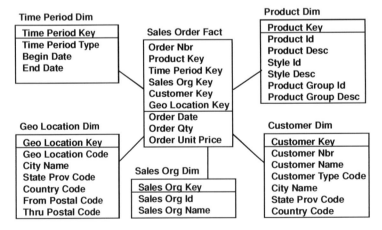

The Star Schema, fact tables with their associated dimensions, is oriented to describing and measuring business processes and answering critical questions. Figure 07-03 shows that dimensions typically answer descriptive questions such as:

where, when, why, how, who, and what. Facts answer quantitative questions such as how much and how many.

Figure 07-03: Star Schema is Oriented to Answering Questions

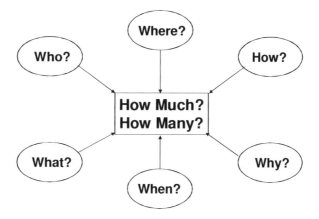

The order process is an example of what may be measured using a star schema. Use of business process analysis methods such as SIPOC (Suppliers, Inputs, Processes, Outputs, and Customers) is a great way to get a handle on the requirements for a star, as depicted in Figure 07-04.

Figure 07-04: Analytical Data Supports Business Processes

S	I	P	O	C
➢Consumer ➢Engineering ➢Order Entry ➢Admin	➢Product data ➢Customer data ➢Order request ➢Marketing data ➢Location ➢Users	➢Order create ➢Order update ➢Order cancel ➢Order ship ➢Order bill ➢Order search ➢Order view ➢Order print ➢Order analyze	➢Order confirm ➢Order info ➢Order items ➢Shipping info ➢Billing info ➢Data mart ➢Order changes	➢Consumer ➢Shipping Dept ➢Billing Dept ➢Marketing ➢Order Audit ➢Mfg Dept

Process   **Data**

Example Star Schema

Understanding the star schema requires a deeper dive. In the Figure 07-05 example, each table follows a naming convention with a prefix of "DM_" for Data Mart, a suffix of "_Dim" for dimension names, and facts have a suffix of "_Fact".

Each dimension has a primary key that uniquely identifies the dimension. This primary key, known as a surrogate key, is system generated and used in place of the business key of the dimension.

Surrogate keys, typically stored as integers, improve efficiency and increase performance. Database joins between facts and dimensions are faster with integers. Indexes on integers are compact and provide rapid access. Figure 07-05 shows surrogate keys for each of the dimensions – product, customer, sale item, and date. The DM_Product_Dim table has a primary key of dm_product_dim_id and a business key of product_code.

The primary key of the fact consists of one or more foreign keys that relate to dimensions. In this case, the primary key of the DM_Sale_Item_Fact brings together the product, customer, sale item, and date dimensions. This fact contains a single measure, the item sale_amt.

Figure 07-05: Star Schema DM_Sale_Item_Fact Example

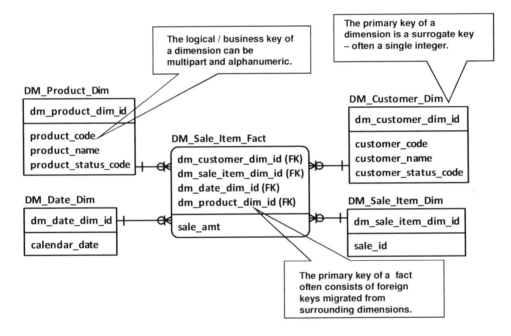

It is now time to go to the next level and explain both facts and dimensions in greater depth.

Facts – the Data Mart Measuring Stick

Facts contain quantitative measures about the subject of analysis, typically a business process. Facts focus on answering the questions of how much and how many. Figure 07-06 provides an additional example of a fact, in this case a Sales Order Fact. The name of the fact table should describe the business process and granularity of the fact.

The primary key of the fact table is made up of foreign keys from its surrounding dimensions. These dimensions specify the grain of a single fact. Keep in mind that not all foreign keys from dimensions have to be part of the fact primary key.

Of course, data is a critical part of facts. Keep in mind what you learned about data in Chapter 5, Data Attributes, when selecting measure data to be included with the fact.

Figure 07-06: Anatomy of a Fact

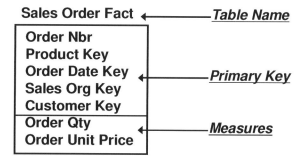

Granularity

The grain is the lowest level of detail of what is measured by a single occurrence of the fact. A fact with fine granularity might contain data about a single transaction or part of a transaction, while a coarse-grained fact might contain information that summarizes multiple transactions over a period of time. Selecting the appropriate grain for each fact is a critical design decision, and should be part of the design specification for each fact.

In the data mart, atomic data is detailed data at the lowest level of granularity – it cannot be broken down further. Transactional data, such as sales, shipment, and financial transactions, are common examples of atomic data. The advantages of data at a detailed grain are that it can answer very detailed questions and it can also be rolled up into summary information. Summary information has an aggregated grain, which provides faster summarized results and requires less storage than detailed grain information.

On the downside, a very detailed grain requires more storage and more time to summarize when querying. The down side of an aggregated grain is that details may not be available for further analysis (drill down). Creating aggregated grain (summary) tables may be a little risky unless it is very clear what aggregation is needed. Otherwise, time and space could be wasted creating unused summaries when the data is populated.

Fact Width and Storage Utilization

In most data marts, facts use most of the disk space because they naturally have far more rows than dimensions. Data models make it look like dimensions are equal in size to facts. This may be true in terms of the number of attributes per table, but it is not true in terms of the total disk space used. See Figure 07-07 to get this in perspective. To conserve disk space and improve performance, fact tables should be narrow, minimizing the number of attributes needed to provide the measures the business requires. Every attribute added to a fact table is costly because it is multiplied by the large number of rows that are stored in the table.

Figure 07-07: Disk Storage Model

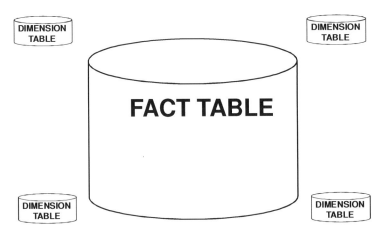

Mathematical Nature of Facts – Can it "Add up"?

The ability to summarize data is limited by the additive nature of the data, coupled with its grain. First, the properties of the data are examined without considering dimensions. This topic was first tackled in Chapter 5, which describes the types of data attributes – nominal, ordinal, interval, and ratio. The definitions and descriptions are repeated here in Table 07-02.

Table 07-02: Data Attribute Quantitative Categories

Term	Definition and Description
Nominal	Nominal data names and describes. It can be evaluated for equality or inequality, but it cannot be ordered, added, or multiplied. Nominal data is usually part of dimensions, not facts.

Term	Definition and Description
Ordinal	Ordinal data has sequence. Data can be ranked and evaluated as being equal to, less than, or greater than other ordinal data of the same type. Ordinal data cannot be added or multiplied. The following is a typical ordinal scale: 1 = Strongly Disagree 2 = Disagree 3 = Neither Agree or Disagree 4 = Agree 5 = Strongly Agree
Interval	Interval data is numeric without a "true zero", so the operations of division and multiplication are not applicable. Examples of interval attributes include time of day, credit scores, and temperatures measured in Celsius or Fahrenheit.
Ratio	Division and multiplication do apply to ratio data because ratio data does have a "true zero" in its scale. Examples of ratio attributes include time durations, counts, amounts, weights, and temperatures measured in Kelvin.

The terms describing the additive nature of attributes are described in Table 07-03.

A data mart can be composed of several types of facts. Each of these types is explained in the following pages:

- Event or Transaction fact
- Snapshot Fact
- Cumulative Snapshot Fact
- "Factless" Fact.

Table 07-03: Addition Related Terms

Term	Definition and Description
Fully-Additive	Fully-additive attributes can be summed across all dimensions of a fact table. These attributes are discrete numerical measures of performance. Fully-additive attributes often occur in facts that measure events. They contain information such as quantity shipped and dollars deposited.
Semi-Additive	Semi-additive attributes can only be summed across some of the dimensions of a fact table. These attributes tend to be point in time computed values such as inventory balance, account balance, and period to date activity.
Non-Additive	Non-additive attributes cannot be correctly summed for any of the dimensions of a fact. Examples of non-additive attributes include rankings, percentages, and unit price.

Event or Transaction Fact

The most commonly utilized fact type is the event or transaction fact. This type of fact captures events, with each event record in a single row of the fact table. The grain of the table is a single event such as a financial transaction, sale, complaint, shipment, or sales inquiry. Measures for event facts are generally additive across all dimensions, subject to the guidance just provided about the mathematical nature of measurements. Figure 07-08 shows an event fact. In this model 'txn' is an abbreviation for transaction and 'GL' is an abbreviation for general ledger.

Figure 07-08: Event Fact Example

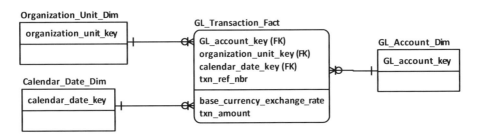

Event transactions are often at or near the atomic level. For example, a single sale may be broken into multiple sales transactions – one per line item. The dimensions associated with an event can be identified using the Kipling question model (Table 07-04 – who, what, when, where, why) and the measures by the Kipling Questions (how much, how many).

Table 07-04: Kipling Dimensional Questions

Term	Definition and Description
When	When did this event occur? What was the date and time of the event?
Who	Who played the roles of worker, customer, supplier, authorizer, etc.?
Why	Why did this event occur? This could include a reason code, as well as links to plans such as campaigns, projects, and budgets.
Where	Where did the event take place? This can be a geographical breakdown, as well as an organization breakdown.
What	What products or assets are associated with the event?
How	How did this event happen? What processes or procedures are associated with the event?

Snapshot Fact

A snapshot fact captures the status of something at a point in time. The snapshot fact captures quantities and balances effective on a specified date and is sometimes known as an inventory level fact or balance fact. The time dimension is used to identify the grain, such as monthly, quarterly, and yearly. Snapshot data is not additive across time; however, data is typically additive across the other dimensions. Examples of snapshot fact types include:

- Financial account balances
- Inventory levels
- Activity counts such as open issues.

Figure 07-09 shows a snapshot fact that contains general ledger balances. The balances are effective on a specified calendar date, for a specific account, and organizational unit.

Figure 07-09: Snapshot Fact Example

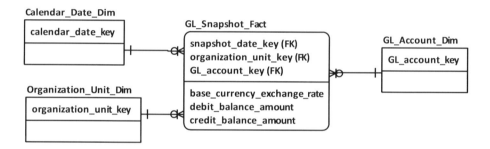

Cumulative Snapshot Fact

A cumulative snapshot fact is a variation of the snapshot fact with the addition of year to date (YTD) totals. Figure 07-10 shows an example of a cumulative snapshot fact.

Figure 07-10: Cumulative Snapshot Fact Example

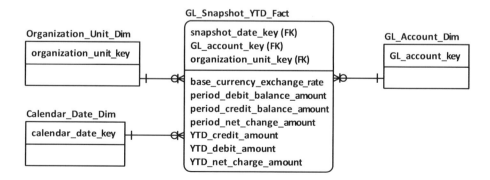

Aggregated Fact

An aggregated fact is a summary of information, such as atomic facts. The aggregations are arrived at by removing one or more dimensions from an atomic level fact. The additive properties of the measures must be recognized when building the aggregated fact data. Aggregation may include count, sum, minimum, maximum, mean, and median quantities. Aggregation analytical categorization such as:

- Sales by sales rep by month
- Shipments by product by facility by week
- Complaints by product by store by month
- Downloads by category by website by quarter.

Figure 07-11 shows an aggregated fact. In this case, revenues have been aggregated by month. In this model 'txn' is an abbreviation for transaction and 'GL' is an abbreviation for general ledger.

Figure 07-11: Aggregated Fact Example

"Factless Fact"

A factless fact tracks the existence of a set of circumstances as described by dimensions, rather than a measurement of amounts or quantities. This type of fact is helpful when describing situations such as events or coverage. Examples of factless facts include milestone occurrence, event attendance, and sales promotion. Figure 07-12 shows a factless fact.

Figure 07-12: Factless Fact Example

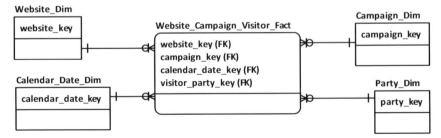

Dimensions Put Data Mart Facts in Context

Dimensions enable business intelligence users to analyze data using simple queries. Dimensions focus on the questions of who, what, when, and where. They contain attributes that describe business entities. Typical dimensions include:

- Time Period / Calendar
- Product
- Customer
- Household
- Market Segment
- Geographic Area
- Financial Account Structures.

Dimensions are used in the query process to select, group, and order data. The attributes of an entity can be independent or can be organized into hierarchies, often with three to five levels. For example, sales organization attributes could include region, district, territory, branch, and sales representative.

Getting the number of dimensions and attributes right is an important part of dimensional design. Most facts should be associated with two to fifteen dimensions. Too few dimensions tend to be not descriptive enough, while too many dimensions are a sign that the dimensions are not structured correctly and should be combined. Placing a large number of dimension keys on a fact table increases storage space and load time.

Effective dimensions are descriptive and contain rich information. Figure 07-13 provides an example of these rich dimensions. There are often numerous attributes, fifty to one hundred or more. Data is denormalized to reduce database joins, while providing rich descriptions. Much of the data in a dimension is descriptive and stored in character format. It often contains both code and expanded values, such as mfg_location_code and mfg_location_desc, to simplify and speed up queries.

When designing dimensions, it is important to understand dimension hierarchies and the navigation paths that data mart users are likely to use. Clues to this can be found by analyzing existing reports for data groupings and summarization levels. Dimensions are supported by source data, so apply data profiling to source data to make sure that it is correct and complete in the area of hierarchies.

Figure 07-13: Rich Dimensions

Product_Detail_Dim
product_detail_key
product_nbr
product_version_nbr
dm_effective_date
product_name
product_form_code
product_form_desc
mfg_product_desc
mkt_product_desc
mfg_status_code
mfg_status_desc
mkt_status_code
mkt_status_desc
uom_code
product_length
product_height
product_width
product_weight
make_buy_code
make_buy_desc
env_safety_code
env_safety_desc
mfg_unit_cost
pur_unit_cost
supply_chain_code
supply_chan_desc
mfg_location_code
mfg_location_desc
create_date
decommission_date
saleable_item_ind
mfg_lifecycle_phase_code
mfg_lifecycle_phase_desc
mfg_lead_time_days
pur_lead_time_days
mkt_product_family_code
mkt_product_family_desc
mfg_product_family_code
mfg_product_family_desc
more_attributes

Consumer_Detail_Dim
consumer_detail_key
global_consumer_nbr
dm_effective_date
first_name
last_name
middle_name
gender_code
ethnicity_code
spoken_language_code
income_band_code
income_band_name
lifestyle_grouping_code
lifestyle_grouping_name
residential_zip_code
residential_state_code
service_engagement_level_code
service_engagement_level_desc
social_media_group_nbr
social_media_group_desc
profitability_segment_code
profitability_segment_desc
print_responsiveness_code
print_responsiveness_desc
employee_ind
email_opt_in_code
telephone_opt_in_code
age_band_code
age_band_name
warranty_profile_code
warranty_profile_desc
returns_profile_code
returns_profile_desc
vehicle_profile_code
vehicle_profile_name
more_attributes

Zip_Code_Detail_Dim
zip_code_detail_key
zip_code
dm_effective_date
zip_3_code
region_code
region_name
city_name
state_postal_code
state_name
state_fips_code
lattitude_degrees
longitude_degrees
population_count
household_count
male_population_count
female_population_count
msa_code
msa_name
cbsa_code
cbsa_name
median_age
male_median_age
female_median_age
county_growth_rank
median_income_amt
land_and_water_area
congressional_district_name
more_attributes

Dimension Keys

There are two types of keys associated with dimensions, the surrogate key and the business key. The surrogate key is used as the primary key of the dimension, while the business key is used as an alternate key. Figure 07-14 shows a typical dimension with surrogate and business keys.

The surrogate key is typically a sequential integer without any business meaning. This key is used to join from the dimension to the fact. A single integer has been found to be very efficient and effective for database joins. In addition, fact table sizing decreases with the use of more compact integers, rather than longer text columns.

The surrogate key should be generated within the data mart. Keys from source systems should be avoided because they could change in the source system, resulting in a mismatch with the data mart. Use of smart keys, which have embedded meaning, should also be avoided.

The business key does include human identifiable information such as purchase order number, credit card number, and account code. It consists of one or more columns that identify a distinct instance of a business entity. An effective date may be part of a business key, as described in SCD Type 2. Figure 07-14 illustrates the use of a surrogate key (product_key) and a multiple column business key (product_nbr, product_ver_nbr, dm_effective_date).

Figure 07-14: Dimension Keys

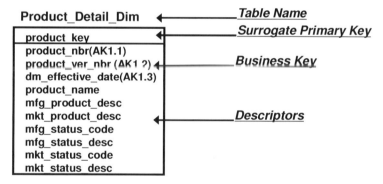

Data Modeling Slowly Changing Dimensions

At times, the data mart must handle changes to dimension. Ralph Kimball has identified the following slowly changing dimension (SCD) types that are widely recognized in data mart design:

- **SCD Type 0:** Data is non-changing – It is inserted once and never changed.
- **SCD Type 1:** Data is overwritten and prior data is not retained.
- **SCD Type 2:** A new row with the changed data is inserted, leaving the prior data in place.
- **SCD Type 3:** Update attributes within the dimension row. For example, both current customer status code and prior customer status code could be maintained.

SCD TYPE 0 – UNCHANGING DIMENSIONS

Slowly changing dimension type 0 is used when changes made to the source system should not result in any updates to the dimension and no maintenance of history is required. This can be used for static tables such as dates. In this case, rows are inserted once, but never updated.

SCD TYPE 1 – OVERWRITE

Slowly changing dimension type 1 is used when changes made to the source system result in an update to the dimension without maintaining a history of earlier values. This makes sense when source system changes are corrections or have no significance. Figure 07-15 shows the ***RatingCode*** in the data source has changed from "BBB" to "AAA". In the data mart, the ***RatingCode*** also changes from "BBB" to "AAA". The data mart shows only the current value and does not show the change.

Figure 07-15: SCD Type 1 Example

Data Source	Supplier Dim
	Supplier Key: 7843
Supplier Id: ZZ47845	Supplier Id: ZZ47845
Supplier Name: Zorn Office Supply	Supplier Name: Zorn Office Supply
Category Code: A1	Category Code: A1
Rating Code: ~~BBB~~AAA	Rating Code: ~~BBB~~AAA
First Use Date: 01/25/2001	First Use Date: 01/25/2001

SCD TYPE 2 – NEW ROW

Slowly changing dimension type 2 is used when changes made to the source system should result in saved history in the data mart. This is used when changes to the source system are true changes in meaning and significance. Typically, an effective date is part of the dimension table and the business key. A new row is inserted, with a new effective date, matching business key, and changed data. This approach preserves the earlier data. Figure 07-16 shows the ***RatingCode*** in the data source has changed from "BBB" to "AAA'. In the data mart, the existing row is expired by changing ***DWEndDate*** to "2004-04-09" and then inserting a new row with the changed value.

Figure 07-16: SCD Type 2 Example

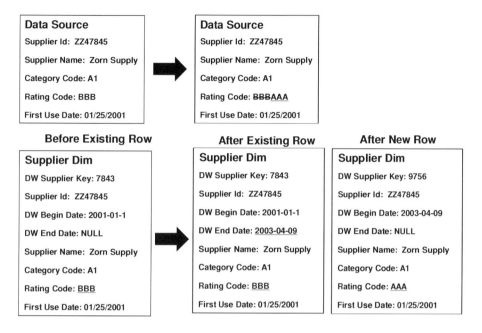

Figure 07-17: SCD Type 3 Example

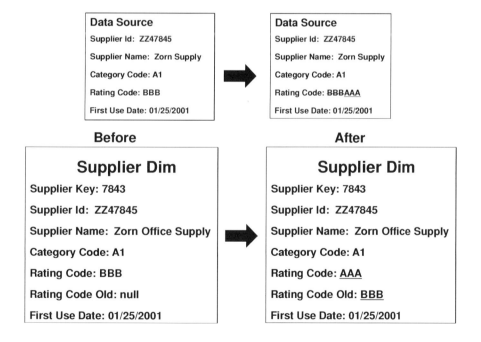

SCD TYPE 3 – NEW COLUMN

Slowly changing dimension type 3 is used when there is a transition of values in the source system. An example of this would be adding a new department name. SCD

Type 3 maintains current and old versions of the changing columns. An effective date that is specific to the updated column may also be included. Figure 07-17 shows an additional column, **RatingCodeOld**, which contains the prior value of **RatingCode**.

In this case the source system changes **RatingCode** from "BBB" to "AAA". In the data mart there is an update where **RatingCodeOld** is set to "BBB", the prior value of **RatingCode**, and **RatingCode** is set to "AAA". Note that only the most recent change is available. If the rating code changed again at a later date, Rating Code Old would become "AAA" and Rating Code would contain the new value.

Date and Time Dimension

Date and time dimensions are an important part of almost every dimensional model. I recommend that you establish date and time of day dimension tables rather than use hard coded date logic. A date dimension is often organized into days and accounts for days of the week, weeks, quarters, seasons, holidays, etc. Figure 07-18 shows example date and time dimensions. The date_key can be a smart integer key such as 20120103 (yyyymmdd) or non-smart key such as 140789 to represent January 3rd, 2012. Use of the smart date key avoids the need to join to the date_dim table for simple dates, however, an unknown date represented as 99999999 must be treated an exception. Smart keys could also be used for the time of day dimension such as 180403 (hhmmss) to represent 6:04:03PM.

Figure 07-18: Date Dimension and Time of Day Dimensions

Date Dimension

Date_Key
Calendar_Date
Absolute_Day_Nbr
Absolute_Month_Nbr
Absolute_Week_Nbr
End_Of_Month_Ind
Fiscal_Period_Nbr
Month_Day_Nbr
Quarter_Nbr
Week_Day_Nbr
Week_Day_Ind
Year_Month_Nbr
Year_Week_Nbr

Time of Day Dimension

Time_of_Day_Key
Time_HHHMMSS
Time_HH
Time_MM
Time_SS
Morning_Ind
Shift_1_Ind
Shift_2_Ind
Shift_3_Ind

The Time of Day Dimension captures the time during the day and is useful for gaining an understanding of business volume questions. For example, time of day could be captured for ATM transactions in a fact which references the time of day dimension to learn when peaks and valleys occur.

One Dimension – Multiple Roles

At times, one dimension may be related in multiple ways to the same fact. This often happens with the Calendar Date Dimension and the Party Dimension. Figure 07-19 shows an example of how a dimension may have multiple relationships to a fact. Project Snapshot Fact, could be related to a Calendar Date Dimension for snapshot date, start date and end date. A project could be related to Party Dimension for project manager and project sponsor.

Figure 07-19: Multiple roles for a Dimension

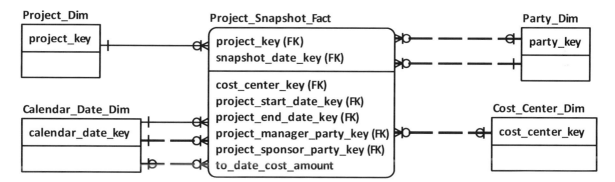

Snowflake Schema

The snowflake schema as shown in Figure 07-20 is an extension to a star schema, intended to reduce storage and duplication. Instead of all dimensions being directly associated with facts, it allows dimensions to be associated with other dimensions. This is a normalized approach that reduces duplication. It can make hierarchies explicit and is very flexible.

Unfortunately, the snowflake also has undesirable consequences. It can make it queries more difficult and complex, and slow performance because more joins are required.

Use of the snowflake to reduce storage cost is an advantage. Since dimensions often account for less than five percent of space, this advantage usually is of minor importance.

Figure 07-20: Snowflake Schema

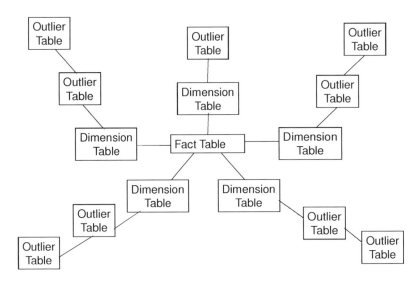

Dimensional Hierarchies

Dimensions are often used to express hierarchies, which are arrangements of entities that are organized into levels where each entity has one parent and may have multiple children. Some hierarchies have a fixed number of levels, while others have an open ended number of levels. Figure 07-21 shows two hierarchy examples, a calendar hierarchy and a sales hierarchy.

Figure 07-21: Dimensions Support Hierarchies

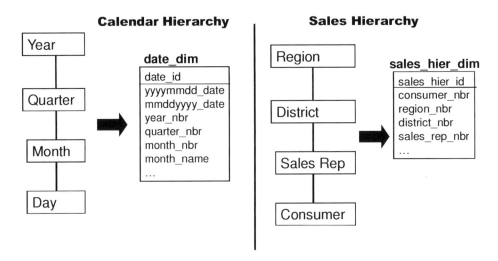

Figure 07-21 shows hierarchies that can be expressed through a single dimension with specific attributes. The sales hierarchy is broken into levels: region, district, sales representative, and consumer. A hierarchy where each level is filled in is known as a balanced or smooth hierarchy. The world is not always so simple. The layout of hierarchies can change over time.

A general purpose alternative is the hierarchy helper approach, as shown in Figure 07-22. The columns that make up a hierarchy helper are described in Table 07-05. This approach allows for a virtually unlimited number of levels, including ragged hierarchies, which are hierarchies that can have variable depth and missing intermediate levels. The drawback is that queries and loading are more complicated for this type of hierarchy.

Figure 07-22: Hierarchy Helper

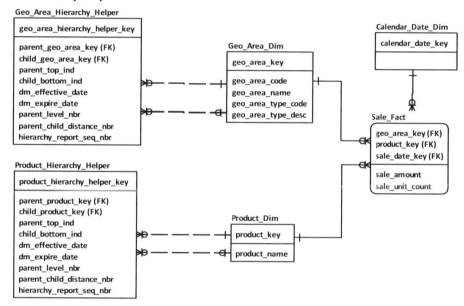

Table 07-05: Product Hierarchy Helper Attributes

Attribute Name	Attribute Description
product_hierarchy_helper_ key	The primary key of the product_hierarchy_helper table.
parent_product_key	Foreign key to the next higher level product dimension.
child_product_key	Foreign key to the next lower product dimension.
parent_top_ind	An indicator that specifies whether the parent is at the highest point of the hierarchy.
child_bottom_ind	An indicator that specifies whether the child is at the lowest point in the hierarchy.
dm_effective_date	Date when this helper relationship started to be effective.

Attribute Name	Attribute Description
dm_expire_date	Date when this helper relationship stopped being effective.
parent_level_nbr	The position of the parent product in the hierarchy with level 1 being the top of the hierarchy.
parent_child_distance_nbr	A count of the levels between parent and child products.
hierarchy_report_seq_nbr	The sequence in which this relationship should be included in hierarchy reports and displays.

Three patterns for expressing hierarchies are shown in Figure 07-23: star schema snowflake schema and hierarchy helper.

Figure 07-23: Hierarchy Example Comparisons

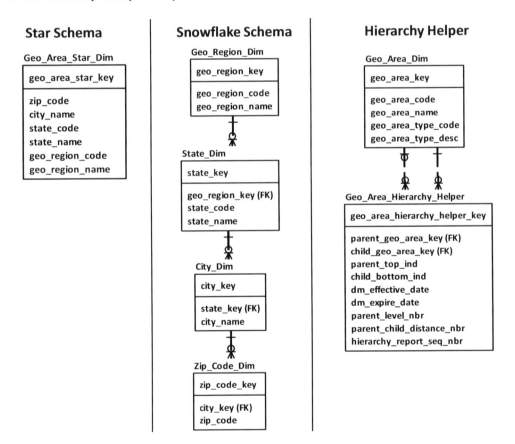

Bridge Tables Support Many to Many Relationships

A bridge table supports a many to many relationship between facts and dimensions. For example, a bridge table could show the percentage commission split between multiple sales reps (dimension) and a sale (fact) as shown in Figure 07-24.

Figure 07-24: Bridge Table Linking Fact and Dimension

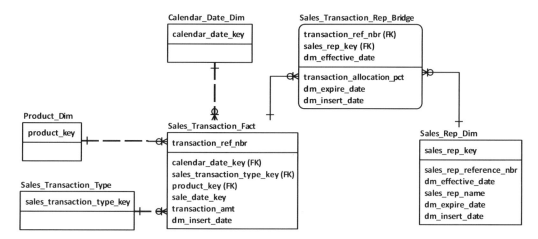

Degenerate Dimension

A degenerate dimension consists of a dimension key without a supporting dimension table. Operational control numbers such as transaction number, shipment number, and order number are added to a fact. This number provides valuable information and can be traced back to a source system. Figure 07-25 shows an example of the use of a degenerate dimension.

Figure 07-25: Fact with Degenerate Dimension

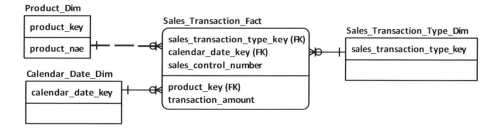

Profile Dimension

The profile dimension contains a cluster of related characteristics such as customer behavior or customer engagement. Figure 07-26 shows an example of profile dimensions. The behavior profile describes what an individual does, while the demographics profile describes who an individual is. Use of profiles enables discovery of patterns. In addition, it saves storage space because the profile data is stored less often than it would be if stored for each customer. The demographics and behavior profile dimensions could be directly related to the customer dimension or they could be related to customers via facts.

Figure 07-26: Profile Dimension

Behavior_Profile_Dim

behavior_profile_key
lifestyle_grouping_code
lifestyle_grouping_name
service_engagement_level_code
service_engagement_level_desc
social_media_group_nbr
social_media_group_desc
print_responsiveness_code
print_responsiveness_desc
email_opt_in_code
telephone_opt_in_code
warranty_profile_code
warranty_profile_desc
returns_profile_code
returns_profile_desc
more_attributes

Demographics_Profile_Dim

demographics_profile_key
gender_code
ethnicity_code
spoken_language_code
income_band_code
income_band_name
age_band_code
age_band_name
more_attributes

The clusters discovered through statistics and data mining are candidates to be rows in profile dimensions. Clusters are groupings of data points with a large degree of affinity. The data points within a cluster are closer to other members of the cluster and farther away from members of other clusters.

Clusters can be given names and may be used for customer analysis. Analytic data suppliers such as Acxiom supply customer life style information organized into clusters.

Junk Dimension

The junk dimension is a table that groups multiple unrelated attributes with the goal of reducing the number of dimensions which results in saving storage space and multiple joins. In addition, the junk dimension avoids placing miscellaneous descriptive information on facts. Figure 07-27 shows an example of a junk dimension.

Figure 07-27: Junk Dimension

Sales_Junk_Dim

Sales_Junk_Key
supply_chain_code
supply_chain_desc
social_media_group_nbr
social_media_group_desc
spoken_language_code
more_attributes

Specifying a Fact

What should be included when specifying a fact? I recommend developing and using a standard template that covers the basic factors of fact design. Figure 07-06 illustrates the specification of the Sales Shipment Transaction Fact.

Table 07-06: Fact Specification Template

Fact Name	Sales Shipment Transaction Fact
Business Process	Customer Order Fulfillment
Questions	How much of product X did we ship in May 2012?
Grain	Individual customer shipment transaction
Dimensions	Date, Customer, Product
Measures	Shipment quantity
Load Frequency	Daily
Initial Rows	55,000

The elements of the fact specification include:

- **Fact Name** – A fact name is a string that identifies and describes a fact in the data mart
- **Business Process** – The names of the business activities or tasks associated with the fact
- **Questions** – A list of questions that the fact will be used to answer
- **Grain** – A description of the level of detail or summarization represented by a single fact
- **Dimensions** – A list of the dimensions associated with the fact
- **Measures** – The quantitative characteristics associated with the fact such as counts and amounts
- **Load Frequency** – A specification of the timing of the population of the fact, such as daily, weekly, or hourly
- **Initial Rows** – The number of entries that will be populated in the fact table when it is first created.

Specifying Data Mart Attributes

Use of a template to define each attribute is also useful. Table 07-07 illustrates elements that are helpful in specifying the data attributes.

Table 07-07: Attribute Specification Template

Attribute Name	YTD Deposit Amount
Datatype	decimal(11,2)
Domain	money
Initial Value	zero
Rules	This amount is reset to zero at the start of each year.
Definition	The monetary amount that has been deposited in an account from the beginning of the current year until the present.

The attributes are described as follows:

- **Attribute Name** – An attribute name is a string that identifies and describes an attribute. Each attribute has a name, such as Account Balance Amount.
- **Datatype** – This is the format used to store the attribute. It specifies if the information is a string, a number, or a date. In addition, it specifies the size of the attribute. The datatype is also known as the data format. An example of a value is decimal(12,4).
- **Domain** – A domain is a categorization of attributes by function; for example Money.
- **Initial Value** – An initial value such as 0.0000 is the default value that an attribute is assigned when it is first created.
- **Rules** – Rules are constraints that limit the values that an attribute can contain. For example, "The attribute must be greater than or equal to 0.0000." The use of rules helps to improve the quality of our data.
- **Definition** – An attribute definition is a narrative that conveys or describes the meaning of an attribute. For example, "Account balance amount is a measure of the monetary value of a financial account such as a bank account or an investment account."

The meaning and usage of specialized data mart attributes are described in Table 07-08. "Audit attributes" track the dates when information was inserted or expired.

Table 07-08: Specialized Data Mart Attributes

Attribute Name	Attribute Description
assigned_key	A Data Mart assigned surrogate key. The convention followed in this book is the name of the assigned key includes the name of the table with the suffix removed. For example, the assigned key of Product_Dim is Product_Key and the assigned key of Campaign_Dim is Campaign_Key.
dm_insert_date	The date and time when a row was inserted into the data mart.
dm_effective_date	The date and time when a row in the data mart became active.
dm_expire_date	The date and time when a row in the data mart stopped being active.
dm_data_process_log_id	A reference to the data process log, which is a record of the process that loaded or modified data in the data mart.

The Big Picture – Integrating the Data Mart

To build an understanding of the enterprise requires linking our facts together to perform root cause analysis and enable drill across. This is accomplished by defining and sharing common dimensions between facts. These dimensions, known as conformed dimensions, are designed to mean the same thing when attached to multiple facts. Figure 07-28 shows example star schemas before they have been related using conformed dimensions.

Figure 07-28: Stars and Integration

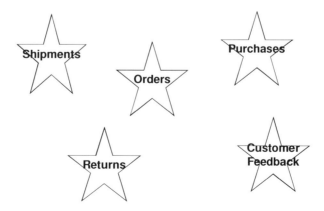

A conformed dimension is a consistently defined dimension that qualifies multiple facts. For example, a product dimension could qualify both a sale_fact and a customer_feedback_fact. A conformed dimension is used to link multiple facts, build federated data marts, and support drill across. Examples of candidate conformed dimensions include:

- Product Dimension
- Customer Dimension
- Geographic Dimension
- Date Dimension.

Data Warehouse Bus

Use of the Data Warehouse Bus, an innovation by Ralph Kimball, takes the conformed dimension to the next step. A data warehouse bus is a method of coordinating data marts by matching conformed dimensions to facts. This method promotes drill across. Figure 07-29 shows an example of a set of conformed dimensions, arranged in a bus-style that connects multiple facts.

Figure 07-29: Data Warehouse Bus Summary Data Model

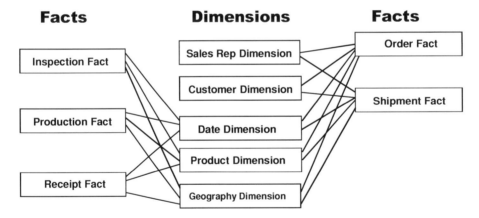

Another way to describe and document the data warehouse bus is through use of a table that relates the facts and dimensions as depicted in Table 07-09. This is the clearest and most compact way to describe and document the data warehouse bus. For example, the Inspection Fact is connected to the Date, Product, and Geography dimensions. In addition, the Date, Product and Geography dimensions are connected to all of the facts. It would make sense to implement these shared dimensions before implementing the Sales Rep and Customer dimensions, which are not shared.

Table 07-09: Data Warehouse Bus Table

Fact/ Dimension	Sales Rep Dimension	Customer Dimension	Date Dimension	Product Dimension	Geography Dimension
Inspection Fact			x	x	x
Production Fact			x	x	x
Receipt Fact			x	x	x
Order Fact	x	x	x	x	x
Shipment Fact	x	x	x	x	x

The data warehouse bus is an excellent design, planning, and communication tool. As a design tool, it helps in laying out the data mart – deciding on the specific dimensions needed to make the system produce good analytic results. As a planning tool, it enables determination of dependencies. It shows which dimensions must be in place to support which facts. In addition, it becomes easier and faster to implement facts as more dimensions are implemented. It is a matter of attaching existing dimensions, rather than creating new dimensions. Finally, it is a great communication tool. This straightforward chart is an understandable way to talk through the structure of the data mart with stakeholders.

The Bigger Picture – The Federated Data Mart

Organizations often have multiple data warehouses and data marts, which leads to an integration challenge. These data marts may have been acquired as turnkey systems, created for department and division applications, or through an acquired business. Benefits could be realized by integrating this data, but developing an overall data warehouse may be expensive and time consuming.

One answer is the federated data warehouse, which is a data warehouse system that uses virtual methods to consolidate multiple underlying data warehouse and data mart databases. It is used to produce a unified view of data and improve speed to market. The virtual method approach does not physically combine the data. Instead, data is related through a virtual schema which makes it appear as a single data warehouse to its users. This approach was introduced in Chapter 4, Technical Architecture. The database technology is further described in Chapter 11, Database Technology.

Data in the virtual schema is integrated through conformed virtual dimensions. This is based on matching logical keys between systems. For example, customer number can be used to integrate customer data.

Key Points

- The star schema, the key structure of the dimensional model, is where a fact table is connected to multiple dimension tables.

- A fact is a set of numeric measures, such as money and quantities of things.

- Dimension tables provide context in the form of descriptive data that is used as labels on reports or filters for analysis.

- A dimension that consistently qualifies a number of facts is called a conformed dimension. This supports analysis that requires linking of facts, plus reduces costs by reducing duplication.

- Slowly changing dimensions (SCDs) are dimensions where the logic key is constant and non-logical key data may change overtime. These SCDs are categorized into types one through three, with each type having its own approach to recording change.

Learn More

Build your know-how in the area of dimensional modeling using these resources.

Read about it!   There are numerous books that describe dimensional modeling. These are some of the best:

Kimball, Ralph and Associates. *The Data Warehouse Lifecycle Toolkit*. Wiley, 2008.

Adamson, Christopher. *Star Schema The Complete Reference*. McGraw-Hill Osborne Media, 2010.

Chapter 8
Data Governance and Metadata Management

The only things that evolve by themselves in an organization are disorder, friction and malperformance.

Peter Drucker

In this chapter you will learn how to successfully manage through data governance. This means getting the business engaged in managing the data, which includes:

- **Planning:** Creating data blueprints and roadmaps.
- **Organizing:** Determining the organization units, roles, and responsibilities required to manage the data. It can also include a communication plan.
- **Staffing:** Attracting and retaining the right people. This often means bringing existing employees to the team.
- **Directing:** Making the appropriate requests of the staff.
- **Controlling:** Ensuring that the requests are carried out in the requested quality manner.

Data governance is at the center of data architecture because it is needed to manage the other data architecture sub-domains. This is graphically depicted in Figure 08-01.

Figure 08-01: Data Architecture Sub-domains

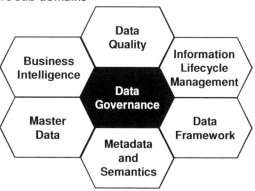

Five Steps to Data Governance (DG)

Data governance is the overall management of data and information. It is a critical element in the success of data warehousing and business intelligence efforts. A large percentage of DWBI efforts fail due to the lack of effective data governance.

A step by step approach is an effective way to establish a data governance program. In many ways, data governance is about managing change. It involves setting standards, determining policies and deciding on technologies that impact enterprise-level data management. The steps of data governance are outlined in Figure 08-02. Notice that this is an iterative process, where data governance reaches new levels of maturity over time.

Figure 08-02: Data Governance Steps

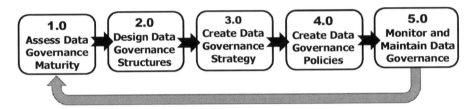

DG STEP 1.0 – ASSESS DATA GOVERNANCE MATURITY

The first step is to assess the maturity of current data governance. This means gaining an understanding of the effectiveness of maturity areas such as management oversight and strategy. Table 08-01 describes the areas to be assessed.

Table 08-01: Data Governance Maturity Areas

Management Oversight	Executive management recognizes that data and information are critical enterprise assets which must be managed.
Management Structures	Effective organizational structures are in place. One or more data governance bodies oversee the data-related rules, policies, and procedures of the enterprise.
Roles and Responsibilities	Data governance roles and responsibilities are defined and in place. See Figure 09-05.
Strategy	An overall plan is in place to increase the effective and efficient use of data for the enterprise. This plan being actively managed.
Policies and Procedures	Policies, procedures, and rules are defined and in place to manage data.
Technologies	Technologies such as metadata management and data quality tools are in place.
Controls	Data efforts are monitored to ensure that the data governance program is producing the desired results.

A heat map is a good tool for capturing the assessments. Table 08-02 shows the assessment areas and levels for data governance. Each area is assessed for both current state ("As-Is") and for desired future state ("To-Be"). The maturity level of these capabilities is evaluated using a scale divided into multiple levels, such as unaware, trailing, par, leading, and excelling. Table 08-03 describes these maturity levels.

Table 08-02: Data Governance Heat Map

Assessment Area	Level 1 Aware	Level 2 Trails	Level 3 Par	Level 4 Leads	Level 5 Excels
Management Oversight		As-Is		To-Be	
Management Structures	As-Is		To-Be		
Roles and Responsibilities		As-Is	To-Be		
Strategy		As-Is	To-Be		
Policies and Procedures		As-Is	To-Be		
Technologies		As-Is	To-Be		
Controls		As-Is	To-Be		

Table 08-03: Maturity Levels

#	Maturity Level	Description
5	Excels	The enterprise has established a capability that is a competitive advantage over peer enterprises, as determined through benchmarking and competitive intelligence.
4	Leads	The enterprise has a level of capability that is ahead of peer enterprises.
3	Par	The enterprise has a level of capability that is similar to peer enterprises.
2	Trails	The enterprise has some level of capability that is behind the level of peer enterprises.
1	Aware	The enterprise realizes that a capability exists and wants to pursue it.

DG STEP 2.0 – DESIGN DATA GOVERNANCE STRUCTURES

Data Governance is implemented using structures such as those described in Table 08-04. Three levels apply to data governance: top-level, strategic, and tactical. In this approach, Executive applies to the top-level; Data Governance Board applies to the strategic-level; and Data Governance Team, along with Data Owners, Data Stewards, and Data Stakeholders, applies to the tactical-level.

Table 08-04: Data Governance Structure and Role Descriptions

Executives	The executives of an enterprise provide top-level oversight and sponsorship of data governance.
Data Governance Board	The Data Governance Board is responsible for providing strategic-level guidance and promoting data governance throughout the organization. This board reviews and approves data related policies, programs, decision rights, and priorities.
Data Governance Team	The Data Governance Team is responsible for tactical-level work. Members include representatives of functional areas, plus data specialists such as data stewards and data architects.
Data Owner	Individuals who have management accountability for specific domains of data at a tactical-level. The data owner appoints one or more data stewards as guardians of the data.
Data Steward	Individuals who are guardians of specific data subjects at a tactical-level, including determining data requirements, definitions, naming, security, quality, and compliance.
Data Stakeholder	Parties who are impacted by data and therefore have a voice in its governance.

How much data governance is needed and how does it specifically apply to data warehousing?

DG STEP 3.0 – CREATE DATA GOVERNANCE STRATEGY

Data governance strategy means aligning data and information plans to support the vision, mission, objectives, and plans of the enterprise. The enterprise vision and mission captured through business architecture is made more actionable through data governance.

Data governance requires its own charter. This charter identifies data governance mission, vision, objectives and key programs. In support of these metrics, it is important that participants understand the vision and metrics of the data governance program.

DG STEP 4.0 – CREATE DATA GOVERNANCE POLICIES

Data governance policies and procedures document the approaches that will be taken to ensure data goals are met. This includes promoting data quality, data reuse, and data exchange. The data governance policies will facilitate decision-making rules and escalation of decisions.

DG STEP 5.0 – MONITOR AND MAINTAIN DATA GOVERNANCE

It is important to keep up the momentum once data governance is established. This is accomplished by executing the processes in an ongoing manner.

Metadata – "Data about data"

Data cannot become useful information and knowledge until it is understood and defined. The solution is metadata, which is often called "data about data". Metadata is your control panel to the data warehouse. It is any data that describes the data warehousing and business intelligence system, other than procedural programming code:

- Reports
- Cubes
- Tables (Records, Segments, Entities, etc.)
- Columns (Fields, Attributes, Data Elements, etc.)
- Keys
- Indexes.

It is often used to control the handling of data and describes:

- Rules
- Transformations
- Aggregations
- Mappings
- Data definitions
- Data models

- Data mapping specifications
- Taxonomies.

Metadata Management answers these questions:

- What is Metadata?
- How can Metadata be managed?
- How can Metadata be extracted from legacy systems?

The power of metadata is the ability to enable data warehousing personnel to develop and control the system without writing code in languages such as Java, C#, or Visual Basic. This saves time and money, both in the initial set up and ongoing management.

Defining data once through metadata and then re-using those data definitions can save much development and support time, while resulting in more consistent data warehousing solutions.

Metadata is typically created in tools such as the data modeling tool and the data integration tool. It may then be stored in the metadata repository that manages and coordinates this information.

Data Warehouse Metadata

Data warehousing has specific metadata requirements. Metadata that describes tables typically includes:

- Physical Name
- Logical Name
- Type: Fact, Dimension, Bridge
- Role: Legacy, OLTP, Stage
- DBMS: DB2, Informix, MS SQL Server, Oracle, Sybase
- Location
- Definition
- Notes.

Metadata that describes columns within tables includes:

- Physical Name
- Logical Name
- Order in Table
- Datatype
- Length
- Decimal Positions (if applicable)
- Nullable/Required
- Default Value
- Edit Rules
- Definition
- Notes.

How Can Data Warehousing Metadata be Managed?

Data warehousing and business intelligence metadata is best managed through a combination of people, processes, and tools. The people side requires that people be trained in the importance and use of metadata. Project team members need to understand how and when to use tools, as well as the benefits to be gained through metadata.

The process side incorporates metadata management into the data warehousing and business intelligence life cycle. As the life cycle progresses, metadata is entered into the appropriate tool and stored in a metadata repository for further use. Metadata can be managed through individual tools:

- Metadata manager / repository
- Metadata extract tools
- Data modeling
- ETL
- BI Reporting.

Metadata Manager / Repository

Metadata can be managed through a shared repository that combines information from multiple sources. The metadata manager can be purchased as a software package or built as a "home grown" system. Many organizations start with a spreadsheet containing data definitions and then grow to a more sophisticated approach.

Key Points

- Data governance is the overall management of data, including people, processes, and tools.

- The data governance chair leads the data governance council, which is the organization responsible for setting the direction for data for the enterprise or business unit.

- The data steward is the person who is a guardian of specific data subjects at a tactical level, including determining data requirements, definitions, naming, security, quality, and compliance.

- Metadata is critical to the success of data warehousing projects. It is information that describes and specifies data-related objects.

- Metadata includes a data dictionary that describes each data element, including its name, definition, data type, and usage.

  Metadata should be managed in a controlled Metadata Repository, which can be as simple as a spreadsheet or as complicated as a multimillion dollar software package.

Learn More

Build your know-how in the area of data governance using these resources.

Visit a Website!   Check out this website that focuses on Data Governance:

http://www.datagovernance.com/

Read about it!   These books show how to implement data governance successfully:

Fisher, Tony. *The Data Asset: How Smart Companies Govern Their Data for Business Success.* Wiley, 2009.

DAMA International. *The DAMA Guide to the Data Management Body of Knowledge (DAMA-DMBOK).* Technics Publications, 2010.

Chapter 9
Data Sources and Data Quality Management

Garbage in, Garbage Out.

Urban Wisdom

A data warehousing and business intelligence effort is only as good as the data that is put into it. The saying "Garbage In, Garbage Out" is all too true. A leading cause of data warehousing and business intelligence project failure is poor data quality.

In Chapter 8, you learned about Data Governance and Metadata Management. Data Governance needs to be in place to prioritize data quality efforts and to specify data quality rules.

This chapter will provide an efficient and effective workflow for obtaining the right source data and using it in a data warehousing and business intelligence project.

Managing data warehouse input sources includes a number of steps organized into two phases. In the first phase, the following activities are undertaken:

- Manage the Data Source Identification Process
- Identify Subject Matter Experts (SMEs)
- Identify Dimension Data Sources
- Identify Fact Data Sources.

Understanding Data Sources

Information provided by the data warehouse and business intelligence is only as good as its source data. Finding, understanding, selecting, and improving data sources are critical to the success of any data warehousing project.

A leading cause of data warehousing project failures is a lack of understanding of its data sources and poor data quality from them. I recommend gaining an understanding of the data by using data profiling tools. Data quality is achieved through data cleansing and data quality management approaches.

Data is pulled out of the data sources through data integration tools: EII (Enterprise Information Integration), ETL (Extract, Transfer and Load), and ESB (Enterprise Service Bus). Data integration tools move data into an Atomic Data Staging area and from there it is placed in the Atomic Data Warehouse.

Once data is integrated and stored, it is moved to an area where it is exposed to analysts and managers who are going to make use of it through business intelligence tools. Supporting this is the metadata that describes the whole process. System monitoring tracks what is happening as information is moved from place to place. In our overall architecture, the inputs are data sources that can be categorized as shown on Figure 09-01 including:

1. **Transactional systems** – This is a computer system that tracks business actions such as receipts, issues, or purchase orders. So you might have a purchasing system, a receiving system, or a bank account administration system that is actually managing the processes.

2. **Process-oriented systems** – Workflow systems move data from place to place using computer or manual means. Examples of process-oriented systems are shop floor control, claim processing, and order fulfillment. Tracking work from step-to-step generates a large volume of data.

3. **Specification systems** – These are computer systems that contain plans, settings, and rules, including assumptions, budgets, business rules, or organizational units. They describe how the organization works or should work. This is very critical to analytics in which plans/goals are specified and compared to actual results. Specification systems produce outputs that are going to be directed to specifically responsible parties, such as organizational units.

4. **Syndicated data** – This is data that is obtained from outside of the organization to enrich internal data. Examples of this are census data, which might be obtained from the federal government; consumer data, which can be obtained from research companies; and any syndicated data that can add value and be combined with our internal data.

5. **Big Data** – This is humongous, multi-terabyte volumes of data, often unstructured, and often obtained externally or through instrumentation. Instrumentation is an automated method of gathering information through measurement devices such as cameras, factory sensors, health monitors, smart phones, and gas meters. Instrumentation may provide an information stream at a faster rate than it can be stored and processed; therefore, it may need to be processed immediately without storing details.

Figure 09-01: Data Sources and Data Warehouse Architecture

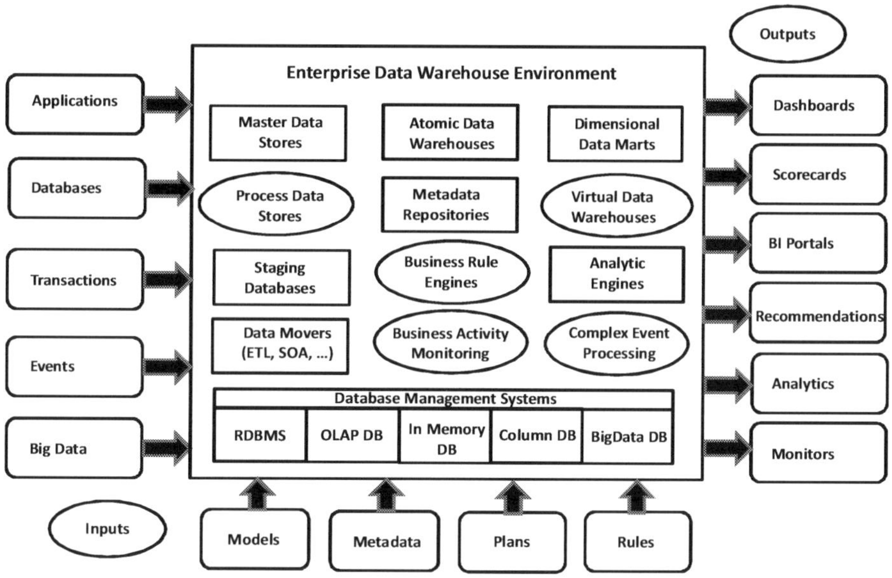

Modern applications have components that you need to understand to fit them into the data warehouse/data mart environment. A modern application often has these components:

- **Multi-tier** – It is organized into layers, such as a presentation layer, a business logic layer, and a data layer.
- **Application server** –The business logic for the application typically runs on an application server.
- **Main database** – The database where the results of online transaction processing are stored.
- **Reporting database** – A copy of the information in the main database used for BI and reporting.

Most organizations have many data sources from which data is culled by the data movers described earlier. Data is moved from the data sources into the data integration and storage area and, within that, the data staging area. The data staging area is a database that contains data pulled from the data sources in its raw format. Data can be integrated in specialized data stores, including Master Data Stores and Process Data Stores.

Identifying Data Sources

The source identification process is critical to the success of data warehousing and business intelligence projects. It is important to move through this effort quickly, obtaining enough information about the data sources by documenting the needed information without getting bogged down in excess detail.

Start with a list of the entities planned for the data warehouse / data mart. This can be managed with a spreadsheet containing the following columns:

- Entity Name
- Data Mart Role (Fact, Dimension, Bridge, etc.)
- Subject Area
- Data Source(s)
- Analyst Name(s)
- Subject Matter Expert(s)
- Status.

Complete the entity name, data mart role, and subject area entries. Assign an analyst to each entity to find data sources and subject matter experts.

DATA SOURCE QUESTIONS

Consider the following questions when determining the sources of and costs for data for the Data Warehouse:

- Where does the data come from?
- What processes are used to obtain the data?
- What does it cost to obtain the data?
- What does it cost to store the data?
- What does it cost to maintain the data?
- What are the sources for the dimension data?

DIMENSION DATA SOURCES FOR THE DATA MART

Dimensions enable business intelligence users to put information in context. They focus on questions of: who, when, where, and what. Typical dimensions include:

- Time Period / Calendar
- Product
- Customer
- Household
- Market Segment
- Geographic Area.

Master data is a complementary concept and may provide the best source of dimensional data for the data warehouse. As defined earlier, master data is data that is shared between systems. Master data is stored in a Master Data Store and managed by using a Master Data Management (MDM) system which includes data governance and well defined business rules. The benefits of this approach, when effectively executed, include:

- MDM data is less expensive. It costs less to access data from a single source (Master Data Store) than extracting it from multiple sources.
- MDM data is rationalized.
- MDM data is of high quality.

If a Master Data Store does not exist, consider creating one. It will have many uses beyond supporting the data warehouse and business intelligence.

If no Master Data Store is available, you will need to examine source systems directly and determine which system contains the data most suitable for your dimensions. If the data is not stored in a managed database, you may need to define the data locally, in a spreadsheet or desktop database, and then provide it to the data warehousing system.

Identifying Fact Data Sources for the Data Mart

The fact contains quantitative measures, while the dimension contains classification information. The data sources for facts tend to be transactional software systems. Table 09-01 provides examples of data sources for fact data.

Table 09-01: Example Fact Data Sources

System	Example Fact Data
Sales Order Entry	Sales Order Transaction
Customer Service Episode	Service Result
Accounts Payable	Payment Transaction
Sales Campaign	Sales Campaign Event

Larger enterprises may have multiple systems for the same kind of data. In that case, you will need to determine the best source of the data, the System of Record (SOR), as the source for the data warehousing.

DETAILED DATA SOURCE UNDERSTANDING FOR DATA WAREHOUSING

When the exact data sources have been identified, it is time to obtain a high level understanding of each data source. Consolidate the spreadsheets developed by data source in the identification phase, then create a new spreadsheet to track and control the details:

- Data Subject Name
- Obtain Documentation Date
- Define Input Date
- Profile Input Date
- Map Date
- Data Quality Date
- Save Results
- Analyst Name
- SME Name(s)
- Status.

This approach provides an effective workflow, as well as a project planning and control method. Due dates are assigned and actual completion dates and status are tracked. A deeper dive into understanding data sources will include:

- Obtaining Existing Documentation
- Modeling and Defining the Input
- Profiling the Input
- Improving Data Quality
- Saving Results for Further Reuse.

Obtain Existing Documentation

When seeking to understand a data source, the first thing to do is look at existing documentation. This avoids "re-inventing the wheel." If a data source is fully documented, data profiled, and of high quality, most of the job of data source discovery is complete.

Existing documentation may include:

- Data models
- Data dictionary
- Internal / technical documentation
- Business user guides
- Data profiles and data quality assessments.

Check through the documentation to assess its completeness and usefulness. Start a new documentation file if existing documentation is not available.

The data source analyst should study the existing documentation before engaging in any in depth discussions with the SMEs. This improves the credibility of the data analyst and saves time for the SMEs.

Model and Define the Input

A data model is a graphic representation of data structures that improves understanding. This section assumes that the data source is stored in a relational database that is modeled using typical relational data modeling tools.

If there is an existing data model, start with that. Otherwise use the reverse engineering capability of the data modeling tool to build a physical data model from the existing database or portion of interest of the existing database. Next, group the tables that are of interest into a subject area for analysis. Unless, a large portion of the data source is needed for the data warehouse, avoid studying the entire data source – stay focused on the current project.

For each selected data source table, define:

- Physical Name
- Logical Name
- Definition
- Notes.

For each selected data source column define:

- Physical Name
- Logical Name
- Order in Table
- Datatype
- Length
- Decimal Positions (if applicable)
- Nullable/Required
- Default Value
- Edit Rules
- Definition
- Notes.

Profile the Data Source

The actual use and behavior of data sources may not match the name or definition of the data. Sometimes this is called "dirty data" or "unrefined data" and may have problems such as:

- Invalid code values
- Missing data values
- Multiple uses of a single data item
- Inconsistent code values
- Incorrect values.

Data profiling is an organized approach to examining data to better understand it. This can be accomplished by querying the data using tools such as:

- SQL queries
- Reporting tools
- Data quality tools
- Data exploration tools.

One technique for code values such as gender code and account status code is to generate a listing of each value and the number of times it appears in the database. For example:

Table 09-02: Example Code Data

Code	Count	Notes
F	500	Female
M	510	Male
T	12	Transgender
Z	5	Other
NULL	1000	Missing

Other systems may represent female and male as 1 and 2 rather than F and T, requiring standardization when stored in the data warehouse. When data from multiple sources is integrated in the data warehouse, it is expected that the data will be transformed to one standard and integrated.

Statistical measures are a good way to better understand numeric information such as revenue amounts. These helpful statistics are described in Chapter 15:

- Mean (average)

- Median
- Mode
- Maximum
- Minimum
- Standard Deviation
- Variance.

Consistency within a database is another important factor to determine through data profiling. For example, a business rule states that the order table should only have orders for customers established in the customer table. Perform queries to determine if this is true.

Data Profiling and Data Quality

Data profiling may reveal problems in data quality. For example, it might show invalid values are being entered for a particular column, such as entering "Z" for gender when "F" and "M" are the only valid values.

By working with data owners to define the appropriate level of data quality, build steps into a data governance program to:

- Determine why there are data quality problems – do a root cause analysis
- Establish business rules to handle data quality problems as they enter the data warehouse
- Correct the data in the source system through manual or automated efforts
- Add edits or database rules to prevent the problem
- Change business processes to enter correct data
- Make data quality visible to the business through scorecards, dashboards and reports
- Save results for further reuse.

Correction of data may be required during the data warehouse population process, in addition to or instead of source system clean up. See Chapter 11, Data Integration, for methods to cleanse data in the data warehouse without impacting source systems.

The information gathered during the data source discovery process is valuable metadata that can be useful for future data warehousing or other projects. Be sure to save the results and to make them available for future efforts. This work can be a great step toward building an improved data resource.

Grey Data

Data, due to its nature, can vary in quality and completeness. "Grey data" is data that tends to be of lower quality and completeness. It is often unstructured, such as: web pages, free form text, emails, tweets, and other documents.

This "Grey Data" can be highly useful for analytics, yet it is not formatted or cleansed to the degree needed to load into a structured data warehouse or data mart. This data can be indexed to identify word patterns and frequencies. This index information can then be structured and added to the data warehouse for analysis. For example, indexing customer feedback can identify customer complaint trends.

Six Steps to Data Quality Management (DQM)

Data Quality Management is the discipline of ensuring that data is fit for use by the enterprise. It includes obtaining requirements and rules that specify the dimensions of quality required such as: accuracy, completeness, timeliness, and allowed values. It is part of a good Data Governance program. Figure 09-02 shows a sound approach to improving data quality.

Figure 09-02: Data Quality Steps

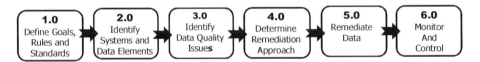

DQM Step 1.0 – Define Goals, Rules, and Standards. The DQM team, under the direction of Data Governance, specifies rules that define data quality, as well as standards for the review of quality.

DQM Step 2.0 – Identify Systems and Data Elements: The DQM team determines which systems and data elements should be analyzed for data quality.

DQM Step 3.0 – Identify Data Quality Issues. Data is examined and compared to the rules for correct data. Problems such as the following may be found:

- Missing data values
- Inaccurate data
- Mismatched data.

The issues are prioritized and critical issues are selected to be remediated.

DQM Step 4.0 – Determine Remediation Approach. Methods are selected to correct data problems and to prevent them from happening again. For example, some data may be corrected through automation, while other data must be manually updated. To prevent the problems from recurring, new edits may be added to the user interface that is used to maintain the information.

DQM Step 5.0 – Remediate Data. The approach determined in Step 4 is then put into action – data problems are corrected and prevented from happening again.

DQM Step 6.0 – Monitor and Control. Successful data quality requires ongoing effort, rather than a one-time cleanup effort followed by inaction. Controls are put in place to monitor quality – comparing data content to the rules for the data. People responsible for data quality are rewarded for improvements in data quality.

Key Points

- The data warehouse and business intelligence depends on data sources for success. Lack of clean data leads to the "garbage in, garbage out" syndrome.

- The first phase of data acquisition is identifying data sources.

- Data can be obtained from transactional systems, process oriented systems, specification systems, and from syndicated data.

- The second phase of data acquisition is drilling into the details of each data source.

Learn More

Build your know-how in the area of data quality using these resources.

Visit a Website!	The International Association for Information and Data Quality (IAIDQ) is a professional organization that is a great educator on the subject of data quality.
	http://www.iaidq.org/

Get Research!

Search the web for research reports (filetype=pdf):

- Forrester Wave Data Quality
- Gartner Magic Quadrant Data Quality

Read about it!

These books describe how to implement data quality successfully:

Maydanchik, *Arkady. Data Quality Assessment.* Technics Publications, 2007.

Olson, Jack E. *Data Quality: The Accuracy Dimension.* Morgan Kaufmann, 2003.

Chapter 10
Database Technology

Database: the information you lose when your memory crashes.

Dave Barry, Claw Your Way to the Top

When you have completed this chapter you will be able to:

- Understand relational database features and functions
- Understand relational database terms
- Understand Big Data and Data Warehouse Appliances
- Augment data access using Federated Databases
- Improve performance using In Memory databases
- Improve performance using Column Oriented databases
- Understand OnLine Analytical Processing (OLAP) databases.

In Chapter 9, you learned about data sources and data quality management. There are many categories of data sources, including transactional systems, process oriented systems, specification systems, and data syndicators. By using the six steps to Data Quality Management, you positioned yourself to avoid the "garbage in, garbage out" syndrome.

Relational database systems are great for managing structured data, such as that produced through transactional business systems. The data modeling techniques described in Chapters 6 and 7 of this book apply to relational databases. This chapter starts with relational database, then goes beyond that to Big Data, which is data that is unstructured and huge in size.

Relational Databases

Which relational database should you choose for the staging, data warehouse, and data mart databases that make up the data warehousing system? In addition, which version and feature set are the best choices? The following are points to consider when making these choices.

First, look at your goals and objectives. Requirement factors to consider when evaluating database technologies and supporting infrastructure include:

- **Organization standards** – Organizations may standardize on a limited number of database systems and vendors in order to manage their software portfolios. The data warehousing effort may need to use an organization standard database rather than a non-standard database, unless the standard database does not meet requirements.

- **Scalability** – The ability to start small and grow. A proof of concept (POC) may have good performance with a low volume of data, but not perform well when greater volumes of data are loaded or accessed.
- **Portability** – The ability to carry to solution to different hardware or software platforms. In general, a solution based on industry standard SQL has greater portability.
- **Volume of data stored** – The amount of data stored is a key driver for the database platform required. Make sure the database you select will comfortably accommodate the end-state volume you anticipate plus some, to account for extra growth.
- **Volume of data loaded / changed** – Volatility, the frequency that data changes or new data arrives, should be considered. Bulk load or dedicated servers for load are options to support greater volumes and volatility.
- **Number of users** – The number of people who access the data is a key driver to the level of database horsepower needed. You will need to know how many users are likely to access the system at the same time. Consult database vendor guidelines to learn about the software and hardware configurations required to support database workloads.
- **Analytics requirements** – The kinds of analytic operations are also a critical driver. Determine whether analytics will access large volumes of data or if they will access limited volumes of data in a single operation. Large volumes of data benefit from Massive Parallel Processing (MPP) architectures while limited volumes of are not effective for MPP.
- **Availability of pre-packaged data models** – Data models may exist that support a particular analytic subject such as finance, insurance, manufacturing or human resources. Those models may require use of certain database systems and so influence which database system to use. For example, Teradata provides an insurance model which is only used with Teradata databases.
- **Availability of tools** – Productive use of a database may require use of add on tools such as Data Profiling and Extract Transform Load (ETL) tools. Make sure that the database selected is compatible with other tools that may be utilized.
- **Availability of trained personnel** – The successful data warehouse requires people who are capable of supporting the underlying technologies. This includes both employees and trained professionals in the market place.

- **Existing database and hardware used** – The data warehouse may be more economical if existing assets, including database software and hardware, are re-used. In particular, a new data warehouse could be placed on an existing database server until data volumes and usage require that it be moved to its own database server.
- **Relationships and contracts with vendors** – Organizations may already be working with database vendors. For example, if a site software license enables new uses for a low cost or no additional cost, there is a great advantage in using that software.
- **Best of Breed vs. Total Product Line** – The "Best of Breed" approach of software acquisition favors acquiring each piece of software based on its individual capabilities and performance. This can be a problem, because each best of breed software component may be sourced from a different vendor and not integrate well with other tools. In contrast, the "Total Product Line" approach favors acquiring an integrated suite of products from a single vendor. This avoids productivity difficulties of integrating dissimilar software products.

Performance features to consider when evaluating and tuning database management systems include:

- **Table / index partitioning** – Database performance can be improved by breaking the data into physical chunks called partitions. so that some queries may require access to only a single partition, rather than an entire table. Databases might be partitioned by date of insert, for example. Determine if partitioning is available for the databases you are evaluating.
- **Fast drop / create index** – Indices enable rapid lookup of information, but have the drawback of slowing database loads. One way to speed up loading of the data warehouse is to drop indices, load data and then re-create the index. I recommend evaluating how fast indices can be dropped and then recreated.
- **Fast data import and bulk load** – Database management systems often include a database utility program that quickly loads large volumes of data into a database. See Chapter 12, Data Integration, for more information.
- **Data replication** – Data replication is the term for the automatic copying of all or part of a database to another distributed database. This enables data to be available for data warehouse access without slowing down the source of the data. This is typically accomplished using database software, rather than ETL software.
- **Change data capture (CDC)** – Changes are detected in the data source and then made available to the data warehouse and other data targets. This ETL

feature can greatly increase efficiency and responsiveness because it focuses on a small volume of changes, sometimes called "deltas", rather than processing a full set of data. This technique works very well when data is needed in near real-time, rather than with overnight delays.

- **Efficient full text search** – Unstructured text is increasingly important for use in analytics. Full text search features give databases search engine-like capabilities. Understand how much effort will be involved in making the unstructured text searchable.
- **High availability (HA)** – Databases are made continually available through HA features such as system monitoring and rapid recovery.
- **High data compression for archive** – Data storage costs can be reduced by using a data compression feature, which squeezes data into a smaller space.
- **Federated data access** – Data distributed in multiple data stores can be made to appear like a single data store to users. This approach is described further in this chapter.

Consider these financial factors in the Total Cost of Ownership (TCO) when evaluating database options:

- Software base license costs
- Infrastructure costs (See Chapter 4 for infrastructure architecture.)
- Trained people costs
- Financial viability of vendor
- Startup costs.

There are a number of relational databases that you may want to consider. The following databases and their respective vendors are market leaders that you are likely to evaluate:

- DB2® from IBM Corporation
- Informix® from IBM Corporation
- MySQL® from Oracle Corporation
- Oracle® from Oracle Corporation
- SQL Server® from Microsoft Corporation
- Teradata® from Teradata Corporation.

Big Data – Beyond Relational

Big Data is data that is so voluminous that it cannot be managed using traditional databases such as relational databases. This data is typically unstructured and consists of text, images, video, and audio. Big Data is flourishing in the Internet era, where data volumes are growing exponentially to the petabyte and exabyte level (see Table 10-01). Examples of unstructured data that have Big Data levels of volume include:

- Web pages
- Documents
- Email messages
- Tweets
- Instant messages
- Regulatory filings
- Voice recordings
- Instrument readings such as electric meters.

Table 10-01: Infrastructure Terms

Term	Description
Gigabyte (GB)	1,000,000,000 characters
Terabyte (TB)	1,000,000,000,000 characters
Petabyte (PB)	1,000,000,000,000,000 characters
Exabyte (EB)	1,000,000,000,000,000,000 characters

Successful management of Big Data has been a critical success factor for modern high tech companies such as Google, Facebook, Yahoo, Amazon, and Twitter. It is vital to the IBM Watson computer that amazed the world by defeating human Jeopardy champions. Big Data requires a platform that provides:

- Massively parallel processing with data searching
- High scalability
- Fault tolerance and self-healing
- Support for billions of rows of data
- Access to publicly available data.

On top of these high performance capabilities, the Big Data system must also be economical. Accessing petabytes and exabytes of data cannot cost billions of dollars. The Big Data platform treats data differently from the way relational databases treat transactional data. Big Data is built on:

- Open source software (avoids software license fees)
- Cheaper storage using less expensive disks
- Computer clusters
- Commodity hardware
- Cloud technology.

The software that provides the foundation for much of Big Data is Hadoop, an open source offering of the Apache Software Foundation. Hadoop is based on Map Reduce technology pioneered by Google. This technology breaks up data access requests, maps those requests to servers, and launches work to be performed. When work is complete the technology reduces the multiple answers into a single result. A master task follows up with worker tasks and will assign a new worker task if results are not returned. This makes the system both high performing and fault tolerant at the same time. Hadoop is strong on reading data, but it is not targeted toward dynamically maintaining data. Hadoop is associated with other open source projects listed in Table 10-02.

Table 10-02: Hadoop and Related Projects

Software	Description
Hadoop	Hadoop is an umbrella project of the Apache Software Foundation. It includes or is related to many projects listed in this table.
Hive	A SQL-like interface to data stored in HDFS (Hadoop File System). It was developed by Facebook.
HBase	A column oriented database that supports Hadoop access. It is modeled on Google BigTable. It supports hundreds of columns per table.
Map Reduce	A Google-originated technology that brings performance to Hadoop. Map breaks a problem up and assigns parts to worker nodes. Reduce brings data back together for the results. The Google-provided research papers were used by an Apache project to create Hadoop.
HDFS	Hadoop File System modeled on Google Distributed File System.
Pig	Data-flow oriented language that supports routing data and simple integration with Java. It is modeled on Google Sawzall.
Zookeeper	Distributed locking service modeled on Google Chubby. It is a distributed consensus engine.

Federated Databases

Federated databases, also called virtual databases, are a way to make data that is distributed across multiple databases look to users like a single database. Users can issue queries against the federated database and have results that span databases returned. This avoids the need to copy data to the data warehouse and data marts through ETL or other means. Benefits of this approach include:

- Fast setup
- Data is current because there is no delay in copying data
- No SOA service code is required
- Existing SQL skills can be used to access the data.

The federated data approach is useful when it is desirable to work with operational data that must be up-to-date. Dashboards often need this type of immediate data, for example. Another use is to provide drill down details and root cause analysis. The data warehouse or data mart may contain summary and trend information but lack supporting details. Use of federated databases is a practical way to obtain that information at a low cost. This approach can also be used to develop low cost Proof of Concept (POC) demonstrations without developing expensive ETL.

Set up is required to define the distributed schema. This schema requires identifying the supporting databases, along with the underlying tables and columns. The servers that provide the data are autonomous and distributed. The databases may be homogeneous, such as all IBM DB2, or can be heterogeneous, such as a mix of DB2, Oracle, and Microsoft SQL server. The databases and servers are linked to each other so that they can communicate and coordinate queries. This communication tends to include common protocols such as ODBC and JDBC.

The leading RDBMS products such as Microsoft SQL Server include this capability. With SQL Server there is a capability called "Linked Servers", which enables a database server to communicate with other database servers and to reference tables on those servers. Queries issued on the SQL Server can then cross multiple servers and joins can be made between tables on multiple servers. SQL Views that make it appear to the user that data is available as part of the local database can be constructed.

There are also issues to consider with this solution:

- Inefficient queries and high data traffic volume
- Interference with operational system performance
- Mismatch between data in the federated databases.

Queries that cross databases may be slow and inefficient due to a lack of optimization. For example, a join of tables that cross databases may result in an expensive table scan, which means that all rows in a table are accessed, rather than just the required rows with the data associated with the query. Furthermore, excess data may be pulled across the network, resulting in delays to the query and to other network traffic.

One or more of the source systems in the federated database may be production systems that are required to deliver good performance to their immediate users. It is undesirable to slow down mission critical systems to support analytics queries. This problem can be overcome by creating a replicated copy of the source database and using it in the federated database, instead.

The multiple databases that participate in a federated database may not match up due to differences in data content, datatypes, or SQL syntax. In database A, gender codes may have values of 'M' and 'F', while in database 'B' similar codes have values of '1' and '2', respectively. Views are one way to reconcile these differences.

There are federated database software packages which address these issues and correct these kinds of problems. These software packages include data discovery and comparison tools that help to develop schemas. In addition, they provide distributed query optimizers, which improve cross database query efficiency.

Federated databases can provide great benefits for relatively low cost, so they should be considered as part of the EDW technical architecture.

In Memory Databases

In Memory Databases (IMDBs) store their data in main memory rather than on disk drives in order to improve performance. This makes sense, because the access of data on the hardware file system is the main factor that slows overall performance. Facebook has improved its performance through the use of a custom In Memory Database that supports over 300 million users.

IMDBs are also known as Main Memory Databases (MMDB) and act as fully cached databases. Databases that store data on disks are known as "on disk" databases.

IMDBs are available from leading database vendors. For example, these vendors have acquired this technology:

- Oracle acquired TimesTen in 2005
- IBM acquired SolidDB in 2008.

The lowering cost of main memory is making it realistic to store multi gigabyte or even terabyte databases in main memory. The ways to improve performance that enable standard databases to avoid disk drive delays include:

- Use RamDisk, which makes main memory act like a disk drive
- Use Solid State Disk (SSD) to store data
- Use faster disk (15,000 RPM+)
- Increase memory so that the SQL optimizer caches more data
- Configure database caching parameters to cache more information in main memory.

Column Based Databases

Another way to improve performance for analytics is the column based database. Most databases are row based, which means that all data for a specific row is retrieved at the same time, even when a limited number of columns are required. The column based DBMS stores data in columns rather than in rows. Retrieval can be reduced to a few columns, which saves input/output load.

The SQL used to define and access columnar databases is the same as the SQL used to define and access other relational databases. It is the underlying data storage and access that is different and in many cases more efficient.

Advantages of column based databases for analytics include:

- Reduced CPU time
- Faster response time
- Rapid joins
- Rapid aggregation
- Parallel access, which improves performance
- Reduced disk space, which reduces the need for indexes and supports better data compression.

Column oriented databases are useful for multi-terabyte databases with intensively read-only data. This type of database does not do well for:

- Frequent database updates
- Retrieval of many columns from the same row, such as SELECT *.

Examples of column based databases include:

- MonetDB®

- Sybase IQ®
- HP Vertica®.

Data Warehouse Appliances

A Data Warehouse Appliance is a vendor-provided solution that includes software and hardware packaged to support analytics. Consider using a Data Warehouse Appliance for multi-terabyte data warehouses. A number of the major data warehousing vendors have acquired or developed data warehouse appliances, for example:

- IBM has acquired Netezza®
- Oracle has developed Exadata®
- SAP® has acquired Sybase®
- Microsoft has acquired DataAllegro®, resulting in the SQL Server 2008 Parallel Data Warehouse Appliance
- EMC® has acquired Greenplum®
- Teradata has long provided off-the-shelf database machines.

The data warehouse appliance may include predefined data models and data warehousing applications. Vendors offer analytic solutions aimed at supporting specific vertical industries, such as: retail, banking, insurance, and telephone. Other solutions support functional areas such as finance and human relations.

Appliances are often less expensive than assembling a data warehouse solution using separately acquired components for multi-terabyte solutions. The total package can often be acquired and start producing business benefits sooner than do-it-yourself analytics. The databases require less DBA support than usual relational databases because they are self-tuning. In addition, disk space and cost is reduced through data compression. However, appliances may be overkill for small gigabyte scale data warehouses.

Most data warehouse appliances share a number of architectural features that support Massively Parallel Processing (MPP). Systems tend to be delivered in two or more racks. One rack contains controlling computers and the other racks contain disk arrays. Adding more disk space typically requires adding a rack or half rack at a time rather than a single disk at a time. Figure 10-01 depicts the architecture of a typical data warehouse appliance.

Figure 10-01: Data Warehouse Appliance Architecture

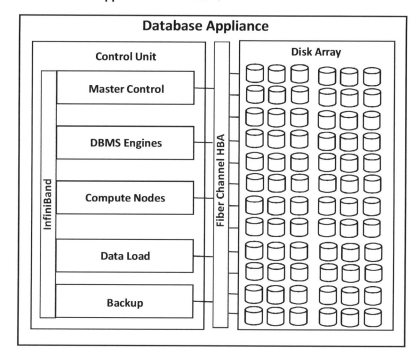

Each of the data warehouse appliance components is further described in Table 10-03.

Table 10-03: Data Warehouse Appliance Components

Component	Description
Control Unit	The Control Unit is the chassis that houses the Data Warehouse Appliance.
Master Control	The Master Control is a computer that coordinates the resources of the Data Warehouse Appliance.
DBMS Engine	The DBMS Engine component is a server that provides database access capabilities. This server is supported by multiple CPUs with multiple cores.
Compute Nodes	The Compute Node components support calculations such as statistical and data mining models. The Compute Nodes enable number crunching to occur at the same time as other data access.
Data Load	The Data Load component is a server that specializes on populating the Data Warehouse Appliance with data. This dedicated server provides rapid loads while enable the system to continue to perform well for query and analytics.

Component	Description
Backup	The Backup component is a server that specializes in making backup copies of data. This enables the system to continue to conduct backup.
InfiniBand	An ultra-high-speed network is used to communicate between data warehouse appliance components inside the Control Unit.
Disk Array	A group of disks that is managed as a unit. This supports massive parallel searches for data. In addition, the disk array is not shared with other applications and so provides high performance.
Fiber Channel HBA	A high speed network optimized for use in connecting to disk drives.

Examples of Data Warehouse Appliances include:

- Exadata from Oracle Corporation
- Netezza from IBM Corporation
- Parallel Data Warehouse (PDW) from Microsoft Corporation
- Teradata Appliance from Teradata Corporation.

OLAP Databases

If you want to analyze data, then On-Line Analytical Processing (OLAP), which structures data into cubes, is often the best way to organize the data. OLAP organization provides several benefits.

When you have completed this section you will be able to:

- Explain OLAP terms
- Identify cases where OLAP should be used
- Understand limitations of OLAP.

Entities in OLAP databases are organized as cubes, which are multidimensional structures consisting of dimensions and measures similar to the star schema described in Chapter 8. A cell is the points where dimensions intersect and contains the measures for that intersection. Dimensions provide the context for analysis that are used for labels on reports and selection criteria for queries. Dimensions answer questions like:

- Who (customers, employees, partners, ...)

- When (year, quarter, month, ...)
- What (products, contracts, ...)
- Where (state, zip code, territory, ...)
- How (method, process, formula, ...)

Cells supply quantitative information called measures. Cells answers questions like:

- How many (customer count, inventory count, ...)
- How much (revenue amount, budget amount, ...)

Cell data is available in both atomic and aggregated form. An atomic measure is one that is stored at the lowest level, such as an individual sale or a single receipt of goods. The benefit of atomic data is that it supports detailed analysis and can be summed as needed. The drawbacks of atomic data are that it takes more space to store and it requires time to aggregate into totals for analysis.

Aggregated data is a summation of atomic data. For example, sales by quarter and rejects by month are aggregations. The benefit is that query and analysis time are reduced. OLAP includes built in aggregation by dimensions and subsets of dimensions. This, in turn, supports analytic data exploration activities, including roll up, drill down, and pivot, through special database commands.

The downside of OLAP is that aggregation can be expensive. Time is required to build the aggregations and storage is required to save the aggregations.

ROLAP USES SQL FOR BUSINESS INTELLIGENCE

Relational OLAP (ROLAP) uses commonly available relational databases to support multidimensional analysis. Data is stored in fact and dimension tables rather than in cubes. The advantages include:

- Use of widely available technology
- Availability of skilled personnel.

Unfortunately, ROLAP has some disadvantages, including:

- Lack of built in cube operations
- Inefficient handling of empty cells ("sparse" data)
- Expense in pre-computing aggregates.

Relational database vendors address some of the problems through the "Materialized View", which includes predefined joins and aggregations. This works well when the joins and aggregations can be anticipated, but falls down when the need for aggregation cannot be predicted. MOLAP was created to address those problems.

MOLAP BUSINESS INTELLIGENCE BENEFITS

Multidimensional OLAP (MOLAP) addresses the problems of multiple aggregations, sparse data, and effective cube handling. Data is stored in a proprietary cube format rather than in relational tables. Cube operations such as aggregation are pre-calculated which saves query time. It provides these benefits:

- High scalability
- Controlled aggregations
- Data compression
- Distributed calculations
- Cubes that can be partitioned and distributed.

The Multi-Dimensional eXpressions (MDX) language created by Microsoft has become a defacto OLAP standard. An industry group, XMLA.org, promotes this approach. Examples of systems that implement MDX include:

- Microsoft SQL Server Analysis Services (SSAS)
- Pentaho Business Intelligence Platform.

Learn More

Build your know-how in the area of database technology using these resources.

Visit a Website!	Each of the major data warehouse database vendors provides one or more websites – search for vendor name plus data warehouse:

- IBM Corporation
- Microsoft Corporation
- Oracle Corporation
- Teradata Corporation

Get Research!	Search the web for research reports (filetype=pdf):

- Forrester Wave Data Warehouse
- Gartner Magic Quadrant Data Warehouse
- GiGaom Big Data 2011 Preview

Read about it!	These books provide an update on database technology:

Zikopoulos, Paul. *Understanding Big Data.* IBM – McGraw-Hill, 2011.

Key Points

- Relational databases can be used to support data warehouses and data marts. They can support multi-terabyte databases with appropriate infrastructure and design.

- Choice of relational database technology will have a great impact on the cost and performance of a data warehousing and business intelligence solution.

- Advanced technologies such as Data Warehouse Appliances, In-memory Databases, Columnar Databases and OLAP Databases can improve performance.

- Non-functional requirements for database technology often include scalability, reliability, and portability.

- Functional requirements may include the availability or support of business-specific solutions such as an industry data model or analytic application.

- Extending use of an existing database technology is often a good choice. For example, if SQL Server from Microsoft is used for many business applications, it could also be a good choice for the data warehouse and business intelligence project.

Integration: An infrastructure for enabling efficient data sharing across incompatible applications that evolve independently in a coordinated manner to serve the needs of the enterprise and its stakeholders.

John G. Schmidt and David Lyle – Lean Integration

Stocking the data warehouse with data is often the most time consuming task in making data warehousing and business intelligence a success. In the overall scheme of things, data integration often requires about 70 percent of the total effort.

Integrating data for the data warehouse includes:

- Making data integration architecture choices
- Data mapping
- Extracting data to staging area
- Applying data cleansing transformations
- Applying data consistency transformations
- Loading data.

Before starting the data integration step for the data warehousing and business intelligence project, it is important to determine the business requirements. See Chapter 3, Data Warehousing Business Architecture and Requirements, for more information. Also, the data sources and targets must be defined. See Chapters 10 to understand this.

In Chapter 10, Database Technology, you became familiar with database technology. You learned about: relational databases, NoSql Databases, federated databases, in memory databases, and OLAP databases. This data can be used as input to the data integration process.

Data Integration

Data integration is a technique for moving data or otherwise making data available across data stores. The data integration process can include extraction, movement, validation, cleansing, standardization, transformation, and loading. There are multiple approaches to data integration; your choice of approach depends upon how fresh the data that is stored in the data warehouse and data marts must be. The degree of data freshness is often referred to as "latency". Each degree of latency can be achieved with specific data integration techniques:

- **Daily or higher** – load in batch mode using Extract Transform Load (ETL) tools. The batch is typically run during off hours to avoid impacting transactional systems.
- **Hourly or more frequently** – load using a mini-batch pulling only changed data, using ETL. Changes are "trickled" from data sources to the data warehouse.
- **15 minutes and more frequently** – load using a micro batch, pushing using a data publishing interface. Change Data Capture (CDC) detects changes. An Enterprise Service Bus (ESB) may be involved rather than an ETL tool.
- **Sub-second** – make available in near real-time. CDC detects changes. Data is pushed using ESB. Organizing data through a federated database approach as described in Chapter 10 a method that may support sub-second response time.

Most data warehouses started out with a latency of daily and have been loaded using ETL, which will be the focus of the rest of this chapter. Please keep in mind that ETL is not the only way that data warehouse data can be integrated. ETL has a prominent place in data warehousing and business intelligence architecture. Selecting the right ETL tools is critical to the success the data warehousing and business intelligence project. Should your company acquire a top-of-the-line specialized ETL tool suite, use lower cost Open Source ETL, or use "Tools at Hand" such as Microsoft Access®? See the ETL Tool section of this chapter for a description of these options, along with their pros and cons.

Data Mapping

A Data Map is a specification that identifies data sources and targets, as well as the mapping between them. This design step must be completed before data integration can be implemented. The data map specification is created and reviewed with business Subject Matter Experts (SMEs) who understand the data.

There are two levels of mapping, entity level and attribute level. Each target entity (table) will have a high-level mapping description (see Table 11-01) and will be supported by a detailed attribute level mapping specification (See Table 11-02).

Table 11-01: Target Table Definition

Target Table Name	dw_customer
Target Table Description	High-level information about a customer such as name, customer type, and customer status.
Source Table Names	dwprod1.crm_cust dwprod1.ord_cust
Join Rules	crm_cust.custid = ord_cust.cust.cust_nbr
Filter Criteria	crm_cust.cust_type not = 7
Additional Logic	N/A

Then for each attribute the attribute level data map specifies:

- **Source Table Name** – identifier for the source table, file, spreadsheet, or similar source
- **Source Column Name** – identifier of a specific source column, field, property, or attribute
- **Source Datatype** – format of the source data item, such as string, number, or date
- **Target Table Name** – identifier for the target table
- **Target Column Name** – identifier of a specific target column, field, property, or attribute
- **Target Datatype** – format of the target data item, such as string, number, or date
- **Transformation Rule** – a description of how data should be transformed when going from source to target, such as copy, aggregate, look up, calculate, or concatenate

Table 11-02: Source to Target Mapping

Source Data			Target Data			Transform Rule
Table Name	Column Name	Data Type	Table Name	Column Name	Data Type	Copy Aggregate Substring Concatenate
product	product_id	int	dw_product	product_id	int	copy
product	category	char(8)	dw_product	product_category_code	char(8)	copy
product	description	varchar(200)	dw_product	product_desc	varchar(200)	copy
product	stat	char(2)	dw_product	product_status_code	char(2)	copy

Extracting Data to Staging Area

Data is first extracted from the source system and placed in a staging area. This staging area is typically formatted like the source system. Keeping data in the same format as the source makes the first extract simple and avoids bogging the source system down.

You most likely will want to process only changed data to avoid the overhead of reprocessing the entire set of data. This could be done by extracting data based on date/time information on the source system, mining change logs, or by examining the data to determine what changed. Data model patterns for this approach are described in Chapter 7, Data Warehouse Modeling.

- **Tip 1:** Make sure the source system date/time information is consistently available. Use data profiling to validate.
- **Tip 2:** Store a copy of the prior version of the data in the staging area so that it can be compared to the current version to determine what changed.
- **Tip 3:** Calculate check sums for both current and prior versions, then compare check sums rather than multiple columns. This speeds up processing.
- **Tip 4:** Add a source system prefix to table names in the staging area. This helps to keep data logically segregated.

Applying Data Transformations

Data is now ready for transformation, which includes cleansing, rationalization, and enrichment. The cleansing process, sometimes called "scrubbing", removes errors, while rationalization removes duplicates and standardizes data. The enrichment process adds data. Before starting data transformation efforts, it is important to diagnose and understand problems. See the Data Profiling topic in Chapter 10, Database Technology, for guidance. This chapter assumes that data errors that could be cleaned and / or prevented at the source have already been cleaned or corrected.

Transformation can be performed between extract and load for ETL or after extract and load for Extract Load Transform (ELT). With ETL, transformation is done "on the fly" as data is moved from staging to data warehouse or from data warehouse to data mart. With ELT, transformation takes place in typically in work tables dedicated to transformation.

There are tools that will scrub and standardize party information like Social Security Number (SSN), names, addresses, telephone numbers, and email addresses. This software can also remove or merge duplicate information ("de-duping").

Techniques available include:

- Audit
- Correct At Source
- Specialized Software (Address Correction Software)
- Substituting Codes and Values.

Use the techniques described in Table 11-03 to address specific data issues.

Table 11-03: Dealing with Data Issues

Data Issue	Explanation and Correction Procedure
Missing data	Data elements may be not present (NULL) in the input data, which can cause problems with data mining and statistics. This may be managed by seeking out more complete input, dropping data with missing values, or plugging data by adding default values or derived values.
Wrong granularity of data	The level of detail of the data may not be sufficient to provide the basis for aggregation. Correcting this problem may require going back to data sources and pulling more detailed information, or the level of granularity along the data warehouse pipeline may require a change. See Chapter 8, Dimensional Modeling.
Data Anomalies a.k.a. Dirty Data	Numeric data may be inaccurate. For example, a child's birth weight might be recorded as 81 pounds instead of 8.1 pounds. Reasonableness checks could be used to detect these problems and certain patterns can be used to correct them. Also, audits of source data could correct data at the source, such as an audit of inventory levels.
Non-integrated Data	Data for the same entity, such as a person, is not integrated. For example, it may not be recognized that different names (T. Jones, Tom Jones, Thomas Jones) represent the same person. Data matching techniques can be used to resolve entity identities and enable integration of the information.

Data Issue	Explanation and Correction Procedure
Dummy Data	There may be dummy data in columns, like "111111111" for SSN. This could happen in the source system when users try to get around data checks, such as when users are required to enter SSN but lack the correct value. These values should be treated as missing data.
Meaning Embedded in Identifiers and Descriptions	A data field could have multiple pieces of information within it. For example, a telephone number may contain country code, area code, exchange and extension. If it is important to the business, extract the pieces of data and store them in separate attributes.
Conflicting Data	Data is internally inconsistent. For example, postal code does not match city and state. This data may be corrected using postal software.
Inconsistent Codes	Codes such as those specifying gender, may differ from data source to data source, leading to problems when analyzing the data. For example, in one system gender code may be specified as "M" and "F", while in another system it is specified as "1" and "2". Correct this problem by transforming data to common and consistent values.
Inconsistent Formats	Formats of data such as product numbers, telephone numbers, zip codes, and social security numbers may be inconsistent. Some data could be separated by dashes, spaces, brackets, or other characters. Decide on a consistent format and then use the formatting features of ETL or other tools to put data into the consistent format.

Loading the Data

The ability to rapidly load data is critical to the success of data warehouse efforts. There are both widely applicable load techniques and load techniques specialized for the atomic data warehouse, data mart, data mart dimensions and data mart facts. Each of these areas is explained in the following pages.

Some techniques improve the performance of loading data under many situations. Consider these methods for improving data load performance:

- Turn off database logging to avoid the overhead of log insertions
- Load using a bulk load utility to avoid database logging overhead
- Utilize integer primary keys to improve join and index efficiency
- Drop relational integrity (RI) / foreign keys – restore after load is complete
- Drop indexes and re-build after load to avoid time to index data while loading
- Partition data leaving data loaded earlier unchanged
- Load changed data only – use "delta" processing
- Avoid SQL Update with logging overhead – possibly drop rows and reload using bulk loader
- Do a small number of updates with SQL Update, then use bulk load for inserts
- Use Cyclic Redundancy Checksum (CRC) to detect changes in data rather than the brute force method of comparing each column
- Detect changes in data through Change Data Capture (CDC) – better than brute force or CRC
- Divide SQL Updates into groups to avoid a big roll back log being created
- Use an ETL tool that supports parallelism to improve ETL performance
- Use an ETL tool that supports caching to improve ETL performance
- Use RAID technologies to improve disk storage efficiency and reliability
- Use fast disk and controllers – 15,000 RPM or Solid State Disk (SSD) to improve data access performance
- Dedicate servers and disk to business intelligence – do not share with other applications
- Use stored procedures to move data within the same database to avoid ETL network traffic overhead
- Use multiple servers to support BI, such as a database server, an analysis server, and a reporting server
- Use a server with large main memory (16 GB +) – this increases data caching and reduces physical data access
- Use a server with multiple processors / cores to enable greater parallelism.

LOADING THE ATOMIC DATA WAREHOUSE

The atomic data warehouse is organized in a normalized, relational format that facilitates rapid loading. Data is stored in three categories of tables, static, associative, and detail, which are loaded in that same sequence. Chapter 7, Data Warehousing Modeling, explains how to design the atomic data warehouse. This approach is very flexible and reduces contention and load time for the data warehouse.

1. **Insert Static Data** – Static data is data that does not change over time, such as the logical key of an entity. This data is inserted once into the atomic data warehouse and not updated thereafter. Data that is in the input but not yet in the atomic data warehouse must be inserted. Matching is performed on the logical key of the input and data warehouse entities. Static data must be loaded before associative and dynamic detailed data can be loaded.
2. **Insert Associative Data** – Associative tables relate two or more static tables. Data is inserted into the table along with an effective date. This enables the associative table to provide history.
3. **Insert Dynamic Detailed Data** – Dynamic data provides a history of changes to data. Each inserted dynamic detail row is subordinate to a static data row or associative data row. It includes an effective date, so as new rows are inserted a history of changes is maintained.

LOADING THE DATA MART

Loading the data through efficient and effective methods is the subject of this section. When loading the data mart, dimensions are loaded first, followed by facts. Dimensions are loaded first so that the primary keys of the dimensions are known and can be added to the facts.

Make sure that the following prerequisites are in place:

- Data is stored in the data warehouse and ready to load in the data mart
- Data maps have been created for moving data from the data warehouse to the data mart(s)
- Grain is determined for each dimension and fact.

LOADING DATA MART DIMENSIONS

There are specific prerequisites that must be in place for dimensions:

- Dimensions have surrogate primary keys
- Dimensions have natural keys
- Dimensions have needed descriptive, non-key attributes.

A maintenance strategy is determined for each dimension based on the Slowly Changing Dimension (SCD) pattern:

- **SCD Type 1:** Overwrite
- **SCD Type 2:** Insert new row – partitions history
- **SCD Type 3:** Columns in changed dimension contain prior data.

Some dimensions are loaded once at the beginning of the data mart project such as:

- Calendar Date
- Calendar Month
- US State
- US Zip Code.

For each dimension, document the information specified in Table 11-04 and place in a data mart detailed design document.

Table 11-04: ETL Dimension Load Specification

Dimension Name	Date_Dim
Description	Dates of the year
Grain	A single day
Primary Key	Date_Key (generated integer)
Natural Key	YYYY_MM_DD_Date
Descriptive Attributes	Multiple date formats are stored, plus week, month, quarter, year, and holidays. Both numeric dates and spelled out dates are included.
Maintenance Strategy	The date dimension is loaded once at the beginning of the dart mart project. It may require updates to correct problems to change attributes such as: company_holiday_ind.

LOADING DATA MART FACTS

Data mart facts consist of 3 types of columns:

- Primary Key
- Alternative Identifiers
- Measures.

In the data warehouse, there will be natural keys that can be joined with dimensions to obtain dimensional keys. For example:

Table 11-05: ETL Fact Load Specification

Fact Name	Purchase_order_snapshot_fact
Description	A point in time view of a purchase order line item.
Grain	Single purchase order line item.
Primary Key	purchase_order_nbr line_item_nbr effective_date
Alternative Identifiers	effective_date_id product_id facility_id
Fully Additive Measures	order_qty received_qty rejected_qty accepted_qty
Partially Additive Measures	account_balance_amt inventory_balance_amt
Maintenance Strategy	Insert new snapshot monthly until purchase order is closed

ETL Tools

The selection of tools for ETL is critical to successful data warehouse projects. At a high level, there is a choice between programmer-written applications and off-the-shelf tools. There is also the selection of Commercial Off The Shelf (COTS) versus Open Source, and the option of using "Tools At Hand".

ETL tool functions include:

- Data extracting
- Database utility management
- Extract management
- Extract job scheduling
- Activity recording
- Activity reporting
- Extract building
- Metadata management.

Factors to consider when selecting a tool include:

- **Business requirements** – There may be business requirements, such as the need to audit data sources, that must be supported by ETL functionality.
- **Security requirements** – Data may require security protection while it is being moved. For example, Non-Public Private Information (NPPI) may need to be encrypted and/or hidden.
- **Data latency requirements** – Data may need to be provided immediately or on a delayed basis. The ETL tool must support your data timeliness needs.
- **Data volume** – Make sure that the ETL product can handle the volume of data that is expected.
- **Staff skill sets** – There are advantages to selecting an ETL tool that is in wide use so there is a pool of trained personnel who can work with it.
- **Organization standards** – Organizations may standardize on a limited number of software suppliers to better manage their software portfolios.
- **Solution complexity** – Consider if your organization is seeking to simplify their solution portfolios by using fewer different software packages. Existing tools will be favored, rather than acquiring new tools.
- **Technology of data sources and data targets** – The ETL tool must be able to connect to the required data sources and targets. Some ETL tools have predefined mapping for industry standard data such as ACORD formatted data for the insurance industry.
- **Data quality level of data sources** – The ETL tool or related tools may require the ability to cleanse data to correct data quality problems before loading.
- **Budget** – The amount of money available to invest in current and long term use is an important factor. A limited budget points to the use of existing tools or low-cost open source tools.
- **Schedule** – Some projects have a tight timeline, which does not allow for time to evaluate new tools or the learning curve required to train in new tools. This could be offset by new tools that support rapid development.

PROGRAMMER WRITTEN ETL APPLICATIONS

Programmer written applications may be useful because they provide capabilities beyond standard tools. They are good for complex logic that off-the-shelf solutions may not provide. In addition, existing development staff is often skilled in development languages such as SQL, COBOL, C#, Java, and PERL. Table 11-06 shows some of the pros and cons of this approach.

Table 11-06: Pros and Cons of Programmer Written ETL Applications

Factor	Pro	Con
Budget	Additional software licensing fees are avoided.	More development labor may be required.
Metadata	Comments can be embedded in the application.	Metadata is not automatically included.
Performance	Standard languages have low overhead.	Standard languages may not support parallelism in processing like COTS ETL tools.
Skill Sets	Current staff tends to have skills in language use.	Data warehousing requires specialized techniques for populating facts and dimensions that staff must learn.
Solution Complexity	New tools are not introduced to the environment.	Total solution may consist of many "moving parts" that must be managed and maintained.
Vendor Relations	Standard languages are available from multiple vendors, avoiding vendor lock-in.	Vendor support is not available.

DATA WAREHOUSING ETL TOOLS AT HAND

Your organization may already have tools that could be used to perform ETL functions. Desktop tools like Microsoft Access® and Excel® include data movement functionality. Database software like Microsoft SQL Server and Oracle include ETL functionality that is competitive with COTS Dedicated ETL Tools.

Table 11-07: Example ETL Tools At Hand

Vendor	Software	Description
Microsoft	Access	Provides an import and export capability for both flat files and databases. Jobs can be built using macros. Data can be transformed using SQL and Visual Basic scripting language. It is suitable for small scale systems or proof of value demonstrations.
Microsoft	SSIS	SSIS is included as part of SQL Server 2005 and 2008. It has features competitive with COTS Dedicated ETL Tools. Many file types and database types are supported.

Fast load utilities are included with many databases, such as those described in Table 11-08.

Table 11-08: Example Fast Load Utilities

Vendor	Software	Description
IBM	DB2 Bulk Loader	Provides rapid loading of IBM DB2 databases
Microsoft	SQL Server BCP	Provides rapid loading of Microsoft SQL Server databases.
Oracle	Oracle Data Pump	Provides rapid loading and unloading of Oracle databases.
Sybase	BCP	Provides rapid loading of SYBASE Adaptive Server databases.

COTS DEDICATED ETL TOOLS

If you are part of a large organization with a sufficient budget, Commercial Off The Shelf (COTS) software is probably the way to go for the bulk of ETL work. Here are some toolsets that you should consider:

Table 11-9: Example COTS Dedicated ETL Tools

Vendor	Software	Description
IBM	DataStage	Multi-platform software enables visual specification of ETL. Integrates with suite of products including data quality and metadata management. Supports numerous data sources, including IBM mainframe legacy databases.
Informatica	PowerCenter	Flexible software supports numerous data sources and targets. Design through point and click visual approach. Many transformations are built in. Supports both batch and real time. Large product family with many options and components.
SAS	ETL Studio	Graphical software enables development of ETL applications. Over 300 transformation types along with numerous source and target types.

OPEN SOURCE ETL

Open Source ETL tools have been steadily improving and are in use by many organizations, large and small. The tools are graphical and metadata driven. They tend to be a bit simpler than the COTS Dedicated ETL Tools. The base systems are available without licensing fees. Support and other services are available for a fee.

Table 11-10: Example Open Source ETL Tools

Vendor	Software	Description
Jitterbit	Jitterbit	Graphical system supports real-time and batch integration. Strong support for web services and XML. User and vendor community supplies JitterPaks, specialized interfaces to systems such as salesforce.com and SugarCRM.
Pentaho	Data Integrator	Visual development of ETL. Supports many database and file formats. Integrates with other products in Pentaho suite.
Talend	Talend Open Studio	Combines graphical design with a metadata-driven approach. This product and approach are very flexible.

Key Points

- The data warehouse is loaded through a process of Extracting, Transforming, and Loading.

- Picking the right ETL tool and approach is critical to a successful data warehouse and business intelligence project.

- The first step is to build a list of requirements and decision criteria. These factors guide the choice of ETL tool.

- Developing ETL using programming languages like Java and C# may appear advantageous, but there are many drawbacks.

- An enterprise may already have "tools at hand" that could be used for ETL, rather than acquiring a new tool. This approach could be useful in proof of concept projects.

- High-end Commercial Off The Shelf (COTS) software provides strong ETL functionality along with excellent support.

- Open Source ETL is another option to consider because it provides functionality that is starting to rival high-end COTS software, while keeping software costs low.

- Designing, building, and testing data integration is often the most time consuming task in data warehouse projects, often consuming 70 percent of the total effort.

- Architectural choices can greatly influence the efficiency and effectiveness of ETL.

- Data mapping is the process of documenting the movement of data from data source to data target at both the entity and attribute level.

- Use of a well-structured data mapping template can speed up the data mapping process and avoid errors.

- Data is usually first extracted to a staging area where changes can be identified.

- The data transformation process can improve data quality through a data cleansing process, sometimes called "scrubbing".

- Data transformation can also make data more consistent by translating it to common code values.

- The data mart is loaded through a series of steps including: loading new dimensions, updating existing dimensions and loading facts.

Learn More

Build your know-how in the area of data integration using these resources.

Get Research!

Search the web for research reports (filetype=pdf):

- Gartner Magic Quadrant Data Integration

Read about it!

These books provide an update on database technology:

Kimball, Ralph. *The Data Warehouse ETL Toolkit*. Wiley, 2004.

Schmidt, John G. *Lean Data Integration*. Addison-Wesley, 2010.

Chapter 12
Business Intelligence Operations and Tools

Some people try to find things in this game that don't exist but football is only two things – blocking and tackling.

Vince Lombardi

In Chapter 11, you gained an overall appreciation for Extract, Transform, and Load (ETL). You learned how data is loaded into the data mart so that it can be accessed for BI Operations. This chapter is organized into two sections:

- Section 12A – Business Intelligence Operations
- Section 12B – Business Intelligence Tools

Section 12A – Business Intelligence Operations

After studying section you will be able to:

- Discuss applications that slice, dice, drill down, and roll up
- Document data exploration requirements
- Link data mart design to supported operations.

BI operations enable exploration and understanding of data. The BI operations slice, dice, drill down, roll up and pivot are summarized in Table 12-01.

Table 12-01: BI Operation Summary

Technique	Action	Description
Slice	Query a specific set of dimensions.	Focus analysis by specifying values for one or more dimensions.
Dice (like Pivot)	Present data from a different perspective.	Change the dimensions used in a query.
Drill-down	Seek the detailed data that supports summarized data.	Shift analysis from an aggregated level to a detailed level.
Roll-up	View data about the current level of detail that is summarized.	Zoom out from a detailed level to an aggregated level.
Pivot (like Dice)	Present data from a different perspective.	Change the dimensions used in a query.

SLICE AND DICE

Slice and dice are data warehousing operations that enable analysts to gain perspectives on the data stored in star schemas and cubes. The very words "slice and dice" give a picture of analyzing data from many levels and perspectives. Figure 12-01 provides an example of a cube with dimensions of location, product, and time.

Figure 12-01: Slice and Dice Operates on Cubes

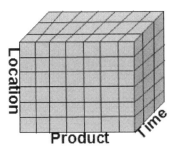

Slicing is an operation used to analyze dimensional data where the number of dimensions is reduced in order to focus on a single area. In Figure 12-01 slicing could be performed by examining product sales over time, not considering the location dimension.

Dicing is another kind of analytic operation. Dicing is used to analyze dimension data by which the cube is rotated by looking at different dimensions to provide a different perspective.

ROLL UP

The Roll Up analytical operation is performed by navigating up a dimensional hierarchy to a more summarized level. The data is aggregated by removing one or more dimensions or hierarchy levels. In other words, data is summarized.

Figure 12-02 shows a roll up example. In this case, web site visits are rolled up from the monthly level to the quarterly level. In the date hierarchy, quarters are at a higher level than months and contain months.

There are many possibilities for roll ups. For example, in a Geographic roll up, totals could be rolled up from city, to state, to region, to country. Organizational units such as team, department, division, and business unit are often rolled up.

Roll ups are useful for trend analysis and performance analysis. A roll up by product line along a time dimension can show trends in customer product preferences. A roll up by business responsibility area can identify performance "all stars", as well as those who may need help in reaching objectives.

Figure 12-02: Roll Up Example

Roll Up

Page Visitors	20xx			
In 1000s	Q1	Q2	Q3	Q4
Home page	200	240	310	312
Order page	140	210	280	294

Visitors in	20xx		
1000s	Jan	Feb	Mar
Home page	50	70	80
Order page	35	45	60

DRILL DOWN

Drill down is the opposite of roll up. Drill down is an operation for navigating down a dimensional hierarchy to lower, more detailed levels. Finer grained data is obtained by adding a dimension or hierarchy levels.

An example of drill down is illustrated in Figure 12-03. In this example, the analyst starts by looking at web page visits totaled by quarter. Then the analyst drills down from quarters to months. Further drill downs could go to daily or hourly levels. Beyond hourly levels, drill down could include individual visits – a very granular level of detail.

Figure 12-03: Drill Down Example

Drill Down

Page Visitors	2xx			
In 1000s	Q1	Q2	Q3	Q4
Home page	200	240	310	312
Order page	140	210	280	294

Visitors in	20xx		
1000s	Jan	Feb	Mar
Home page	50	70	80
Order page	35	45	60

Drill down tends to follow hierarchical levels, ending with detailed instances or events. Retail sales drill downs, for example, could start with country and then drill down to region, state, district, and store. Drill down from the store level could go to individual sales transactions.

Drill downs are useful for root cause analysis. By looking at finer levels of detail, the analyst seeks to determine why something is happening.

PIVOT

Pivoting is another kind of analytic operation. Pivoting is used to analyze dimension data by which the cube is rotated by looking at different dimensions to provide a different perspective. It is like dicing, as depicted in Figure 12-04. The labels are supplied by data mart dimensions, while the quantities are supplied via a data mart fact.

Figure 12-04: Pivot Example

Pivot from Product Line To Region

Quarter/Product Line	Desks	Chairs	Bookcases
20xx-Q1	10	30	5
20xx-Q2	13	35	7
20xx-Q3	10	40	10
20xx-Q4	15	35	10

Quarter/Region	East	Central	West
20xx-Q1	20	10	15
20xx-Q2	25	20	10
20xx-Q3	20	25	15
20xx-Q4	25	20	15

BI OPERATIONS TIPS AND TRAPS

The ability to query depends on the store of data provided in the data mart. This data is structured into dimensions and facts that contain both detailed (atomic) data as well as aggregated data. Use the Tips and Traps information in Table 12-02 to improve the success of BI operations for your data warehousing projects. These considerations are basic to creating a system that is responsive to data warehouse users who want to explore data and perform analytic functions in the data mart using query tools.

Table 12-02: BI Operations Tips and Traps

Tips (Do This)	Traps (Don't Do This)
• Design data mart and cubes to support basic analytic functions • Provide detailed data to support roll up • Provide rich hierarchies to support roll up • Obtain query tools that support basic analytic functions	• Focus on fixed reports rather than data exploration • Fail to provide conformed dimensions • Fail to provide hierarchies

Key Points

- Core BI Operations are the building blocks of BI.

- Slicing is an operation used to focus analysis on a specific area by reducing the number of dimensions. For example, slicing could be used to examine a geographic area or sales region.

- Dicing is an operation that enables analysis from a different perspective by rotating a cube to access it by a different dimension. For example, the analysis perspective could be change from a product perspective to a customer segment perspective.

- Drill-down is an operation for navigating down a dimensional hierarchy to a lower, more detailed level. For example, drill-down could provide greater detail by analyzing data at a sales transaction level instead of a customer sales total level.

- Roll-up is an operation for navigating up a dimensional hierarchy to a more summarized level; data is aggregated by summarizing it at successively higher levels. For example, zip code sales could be rolled up to a state level, which could be rolled up to a country level.

- Designing the data mart with the appropriate facts and dimensions makes a more effective BI environment.

Section 12B – Business Intelligence Tools

How many times do I have to tell you, the right tool for the right job!

Montgomery Scott ("Scotty")
Chief Operations Officer, Star Ship Enterprise

When you have completed the remainder of this chapter, you will be able to:

- Understand the types of business intelligence tools
- Explain the characteristics of BI tools
- Determine which type of BI tool fits the needs of your organization.

In the first part of this chapter, you learned about BI Operations including slice, dice, drill down, and roll up. Now it is time to learn about tools that can be used to carry out these operations so you can visually analyze and present data. This chapter will help you sort through numerous tools available for analyzing and presenting data. Business intelligence tools break down into these categories:

- Interactive Query and Analysis Tools
- Reporting Tools
- Data Visualization Tools
- OLAP Tools
- Data Mining Tools.

INTERACTIVE QUERY AND ANALYSIS TOOLS

Query tools enable the exploration of data through a user friendly exploration interface. These tools typically:

- Are interactive
- Are ad hoc
- Are driven by spontaneous user questions
- Display lower volumes of data.

They provide views of data that follow familiar patterns:

- Spreadsheet
- Drill down
- Roll up
- Pivot.

Examples of query tools include:

- Microsoft Access and Excel
- Microsoft ProClarity
- Business Objects BusinessQuery
- Cognos Report Studio and Query Studio
- SAS

These tools should display information graphically and enable production of scorecards and dashboards. See Chapter 18 for recommendations concerning the presentation of data.

REPORTING TOOLS

Reporting tools produce outputs that can be stored and reviewed. Often reports are produced on a time schedule such as monthly. Reporting tools are typically:

- Less interactive
- Less ad hoc
- Reporting a view of data (header and detail)
- Driven by pre-established user questions
- Displaying moderate volumes of data.

Examples of reporting tools include:

- Microsoft Access
- SAP Crystal Reports
- SolutionsIQ Managed Reporting Environment
- Microsoft SQL Server Reporting Services.

DATA VISUALIZATION TOOLS

This new and growing area enables users to better understand data through easy to use visualization tools. Examples of data visualization tools include:

- QlikTech Qlikview
- Tibco Spotfire
- Tableau.

DATA MINING AND STATISTICAL TOOLS

Data mining and statistical tools are used by specialized analysts and driven by the search for patterns. Analytic methods are used such as:

- Associations and Clusters

- Decision Trees
- Fuzzy Logic
- Genetic Algorithm
- Naive Bayes
- Neural Networks
- Regression Models
- Sequential Clusters
- Time Series.

In addition to these methods, mathematical techniques such as linear regression, probability, and optimization algorithms are used. Examples of statistics and data mining tools include:

- R Foundation for Statistical Computing R Open Source Analytic System
- SAP/Business Objects BusinessMiner
- SAS Institute SAS and Enterprise Miner
- IBM Cognos SPSS.

The patterns and rules discovered through data mining and statistics can be used to improve decision-making and to forecast the results of those decisions. Chapters 13 and 14 describe statistical analysis and data mining, respectively.

EVALUATING BI TOOLS

Selecting the right BI tool for the right purpose is an important element of BI success. First, review the requirements. Will the BI tool be used for reporting, data exploration or analytics? Who is the audience for the BI tool? Next, identify candidate tools that may satisfy the requirements using examples listed earlier in this chapter and through research. Determine which questions to ask about each BI tool. Table 12-03 presents BI tool evaluation topics.

Table 12-03: BI Tool Evaluation

Evaluation Area	Feature
Administration	Performance monitoring tools
	Audit trail reports
	Report locking and check-out
	User management
	Metadata management
	Easy install and configuration
Architecture	Operating system platform
	Web based output viewer – reports, dashboards, ad hoc queries
	Web based designer
	Portlet support
	64-bit processing support
	Multi-tier architecture
	Microsoft Office integration
Development Environment	'Drag and drop' report, query and analytics design
Reporting Capabilities	Multi-level totals
	Built-in functions
	Ad Hoc query
	Prompted reports – users can specify criteria for reports
Interactive Query Capabilities	Basic operations: drill down, roll up, slice, dice and pivot
Analytic Capabilities	Scorecard analysis
	Trend discovery
	Predictive modeling
Security	Security groups with subject filters
	Data level security
Data Sources	Adapter for DB2
	Adapter for flat files
	Adapter for JDBC and ODBC
	Adapter for Oracle
	Adapter for SQL Server 2005/2008/2012
	Adapter for XML
	Native adapters versus generic adapters
Costs	Software licensing plans and costs
	Data source adapter costs
	Software maintenance costs
	Training costs
	Additional costs

Finally, rate the tools using the criteria you have identified. You can learn about BI tool characteristics through analyst reports, discussion with BI tool users, Requests for Proposal (RFP) and hands on use of the tools. Invite members of your BI team to share their experiences with the tools.

Key Points

- Selecting the right BI tool for the right purpose is an important element of BI success.

- Interactive query and analysis tools enable exploration of data through a user friendly interface. These tools include support of core BI operations: slice, dice, pivot, drill down and roll up.

- Reporting tools produce outputs that can be saved and reviewed. Often these tools are run on a scheduled basis.

- Data mining tools are used to find patterns in data that support root cause analysis and improved decision-making.

Learn More

Build your know-how in the area of business intelligence operations and tools using these resources.

Get Research!	Search the web for research reports (filetype=pdf):
	• Aberdeen Business Intelligence
	• Forrester Wave Business Intelligence
	• Gartner Magic Quadrant Business Intelligence
Read about it!	This book provides insights into the use of Business Intelligence:
	Howson, Cindi. *Successful Business Intelligence: Secrets to Making BI a Killer App.* McGraw-Hill Companies, 2008.

There are lies, damn lies and statistics.

Mark Twain

When you have completed this chapter you will be able to:

*   Understand and discuss basic statistics
*   Understand and calculate mean, median, and mode
*   Use statistics to describe data
*   Appreciate the use of statistics for evaluation and prediction.

In Chapter 12, you became aware of business intelligence operations for exploring data – slicing and dicing, drilling down, and rolling up. In addition, you were introduced to BI tools. Now it is time to apply statistics, the branch of mathematics that helps us to analyze and organize data, especially numeric data.

In this chapter, you will take a baby step toward becoming a "quant", the people who can apply mathematics to data to describe and understand it. The aim is to be understandable; after all this is *Data Warehousing and Business Intelligence Made Simple*! If you have studied, but forgotten basic statistics, this will be a refresher for you.

Statistics is the application of mathematics to understanding and predicting data. There are two main branches of statistics – descriptive statistics and inferential statistics. Descriptive statistics address collecting, summarizing, and presenting data. Inferential statistics are used to draw conclusions about data and to make predictions. As you will see in Chapter 16, data mining can be divided into the same high-level branches as statistics.

Collecting Data

Statistics are geared toward analyzing moderate-sized datasets, in contrast to data mining, which is oriented toward analyzing huge datasets. A great strength of statistics is its ability to use smaller sets of data called samples to understand and apply toward larger sets of data. Smaller sets of data are less costly to collect than data about an entire population and require less computing power to analyze.

Earlier chapters of this book have provided much guidance about data definition, data modeling, data governance, and data quality. All of these disciplines are helpful in obtaining and conditioning data for statistical analysis. See Figure 10-01 of Chapter 10, Database Technology, for ways to deal with data issues.

Statistical analysis often starts with the selection of an area of study. In descriptive statistics, this means selecting a subject, and in inferential statistics, it means creating a hypothesis to be tested.

The overall universe of subjects to be studied is known as the population. Unfortunately, populations can be very large, which makes data analysis expensive and time consuming. The answer is to collect and analyze data from a subset of the population known as the sample. The concept is that what is true in the sample is likely to hold true in the larger population.

The hypothesis is compared to the "Null Hypothesis", which says that a condition or event occurs totally by chance or is unrelated to the factors under study. The probability that something occurs totally by chance is called the "p factor." Suppose a hypothesis proposes that a marketing campaign will increase sales of a product. An experiment that includes a randomly selected control group and a randomly selected test group can be run.

The control group does not experience the marketing campaign, while the test group does experience it. This sampling and comparison process could be performed using a data mart that contains a record of customers, marketing campaigns, and sales transactions. A function that pulls information in a random fashion and filters for outliers is a good way to select information for analysis. Outliers, sometimes called anomalies, are data elements with extreme values that can distort the results of statistical analysis.

Use of a sample to understand or make predictions about a population is subject to error. The confidence level and its inverse, the margin of error, are ways to quantify the probability that a sample-based conclusion is incorrect. Table 13-01 provides definitions of the terms that have used in this section.

Table 13-01: Statistics Definitions

Term	Definition
Control Group	A group of subjects who are not given an experimental treatment but participate in all other aspects of an experiment in order to rule out other shared factors. For example, pharmaceutical control group participants are given a placebo.
Outlier	A data value that is widely separated from other data values in a population or sample. These outlier data values can distort statistical analysis.
Statistics	Statistics is the application of mathematics to understanding and predicting data.
Probability	Probability is the branch of mathematics that addresses the relative frequency that events are likely to take place. Probability also refers to the relative frequency itself and is expressed as a fraction or percentage.
Hypothesis	An assertion that something is true, such as data properties of a population or the results of a treatment. Statistics are used to test the validity of hypotheses.
Population	The complete universe of data elements under study, such as the complete population of the United States.
Sample	A portion of a population selected for statistical analysis.
Null Hypothesis	A proposition which says a condition or event occurs totally by chance or is unrelated to the factors under study.
P Value	Evidence that the Null Hypothesis is true.
Confidence Level	The probability that a statistical result is correct. It is the opposite of the margin for error.

Descriptive Statistics

A summary description of data can help one to better understand it. This section shows three ways to summarize data – the mean, the median, and the mode.

The mean is the most widely used measurement of central tendency and is also known as the arithmetic average. The mean is computed by summing the values and dividing by the number of values. The mean is most representative when the data does not have extreme values, known as outliers, because these extreme values can distort the mean.

Figure 13-01: The Mean

```
Set 1: 3, 4, 5, 6, 7
Compute: ( 3 + 4 + 5 + 6 + 7 ) / 5 = 25/5 = 5
Set 2: 3, 4, 5, 6, 12 (Skewed by outlier)
Compute: ( 3 + 4 + 5 + 6 + 22 ) / 5 = 30/5 = 8
```

The median, sometimes called the "middle value", is a way to express central tendency without being skewed by extreme values. To determine the median of a set of numbers, first put the numbers in sequence from lowest to highest. If there is an odd number of numbers, select the middle number. If there is an even number of numbers, add the middle two numbers and divide by two.

Figure 13-02: The Median

```
Set 1: 3, 4, 5, 6, 7 (an odd number of numbers)
Compute: ( 3 4 5 6 7 ) = 5
Set 2: 3, 4, 5, 6, 7, 8 (an even number of numbers)
Compute: ( 3 4 5 6 7 8 ) = (5+6) / 2 = 5.5
```

The mode is the value or values that occur most often in a set of data. This measure can be used for both quantitative and qualitative data. To determine the mode(s) count the instances of each value in the set, then select the most frequently occurring value(s). There could be multiple modes or no modes.

Figure 13-03: The Mode

```
Set 1: 3, 4, 5, 5, 6, 7 (a single mode)
Compute: 5 is the mode. It occurs twice.
Set 2: 3, 4, 5, 5, 6, 6, 7 (multiple modes)
Compute: 5 and 6 are the modes. They both occur twice.
Set 3: 3, 4, 5, 6, 7, 10 (no mode)
Compute: No number occurs more often than any other number.
```

The measures of mean, median, and mode can differ for the same set of data. Table 13-02 shows an example of this.

Table 13-02: Summary Statistics Comparison

Data	Summary Statistics
$3,000,000	• **Mean:** ($5,000,000/5) = **$1,000,000**
900,000	
500,000	• **Median:** = middle value of ordered data = **$500,000**
300,000	
300,000	• **Mode:** Most frequent value = **$300,000**
Total $5,000,000	

Measures of Dispersion

How widely dispersed or varied is a set of data? Measures of dispersion or variation provide the answers to this question. This section provides five measures of variation, including range, interquartile range, variance, and standard deviation.

The most straight forward measure of variation is range. It is the spread between the smallest and largest values in a data set. To compute range, subtract the smallest value from the largest value. Table 13-03 shows an example of the range calculation. The advantage of the range is that it is easy to calculate and understand. Its limitations include that it gives greater weight to outliers and does not show how data is distributed within the range. Minimum and maximum are, by nature, outliers.

Table 13-03: Range Calculation

Data	Range
100	
2,000	• **Range:** 5,700 − 100 = 5,600
3,200	
5,700	

The interquartile range is a measurement of variation that avoids distortion by outlier values. To compute interquartile range, first order the data and determine the quartiles. Then subtract the lower boundary of the second quartile from the upper boundary of the third quartile. Notice that the interquartile range calculated in Table 13-04 is less than the range calculated in Table 13-03.

Table 13-04: Interquartile Range Calculation

Data	Interquartile Range
100	
2,000	• **Interquartile Range:** $3{,}200 - 2{,}000 = 1{,}200$
3,200	
5,700	

In many cases, data is distributed in a symmetrical fashion around the mean and can be plotted to show a "bell curve", where more data is close to the mean and less data is far away from the mean. In Figure 13-04, outer distribution is more widely distributed than the inner distributions. The distance which each measure is from the mean is a deviation. The standard deviation (σ) is a statistic that illustrates how closely the measures track to the mean.

Figure 13-04: Variance

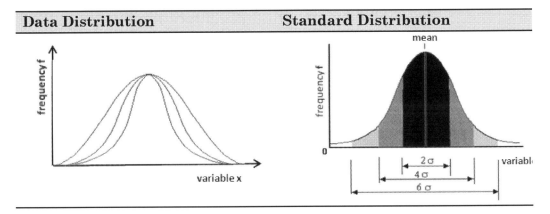

In this example, the data that is one standard deviation on either side of the mean (2σ) covers 68 percent of the data. Data that is two standard deviations from the mean (4σ) covers 95 percent of the data, and data three standard deviations from the mean (6σ) covers 99 percent of the data. A larger standard distribution indicates more widely spread data and a flatter curve. The methods used to calculate standard deviation and variation will be explained next.

Variance is closely related to standard deviation. Table 13-05 is an example of the variance calculation. To compute variance, perform the following steps:

1. Calculate the mean by summing the sample and dividing by the sample size
2. For each sample, calculate the square of the difference between the sample and the mean (These differences are deviations.)

3. Sum the calculations from step 2. (This is the sum of the squared deviations.)
4. Divide the sum from step 3 by the sample size minus 1.

Table 13-05: Variance Calculation

Data	Variance
100 2,000 3,200 5,700 11,000	Formula: $S = \sigma^2 = \dfrac{\Sigma(x - \bar{x})^2}{n - 1}$ n = number of samples

- Step 1: Mean = 11,000 / 4 = 2,750
- Step 2: (2,750-100) = 2,650 squared = 7,022,500
- (2,750-2000) = 750 squared = 562,500
- (2,750 – 3,200) = -450 squared = 202,500
- (2,750 – 5,700) = -2,950 squared = 8,702,500
- Step 3: Sum of squares = 16,490,000
- Step 4: Variance = (16,490,000 / 3) = 5,496,667

Now that variance is calculated, standard deviation can also be calculated. To compute standard deviation, first compute the variance, then calculate its square root, as depicted in Table 13-06. The reverse is also true. Standard deviation equals the square of the variance.

Table 13-06: Standard Deviation

Data	Standard Deviation
100 2,000 3,200 5,700 11,000	Formula: $\sigma = \sqrt{\dfrac{\Sigma(x - \bar{x})^2}{n - 1}}$ n = number of samples

- Step 1: Variance = 5,496,667
- Step 2: Standard Deviation = sqrt (5,496,667) = 2,344

Inferential Statistics – Regression Models

A regression model predicts average outcome based on one or more inputs known as covariates. The model is built by examining samples of inputs and known outputs. For example, one might build a model with inputs of: gender, age, and education level to predict annual income.

The analyst performs a hypothesis comparison:

- **Null Hypothesis.** The outcome is related to the input(s) only by chance.
- **Linear Hypothesis.** The outcome has a linear relationship to specified input(s).

A graphic view could show outputs plotted as a line compared to inputs. Figure 13-05 shows alternative scenarios. In the first scenario, the null hypothesis is supported. Distribution of the covariates does not align with the outcome. In the second scenario, there is a high correlation between covariates and the outcome. A line can be drawn which projects the mean outcome for each set of equal covariates.

Regression models are not limited to using a single covariate to predict a single outcome based on a linear relationship. Multivariate regression can predict an outcome based on multiple inputs. In addition, there are non-linear models.

Regression models have many applications. Ian Ayres, in his book *Super Crunchers*, has pointed out numerous successful uses of regression models such as selecting baseball players, extending credit offers, including in marketing campaigns, and diagnosing illnesses. This is why data experts with statistics skill are in high demand.

Figure 13-05: Linear Regression Scenarios

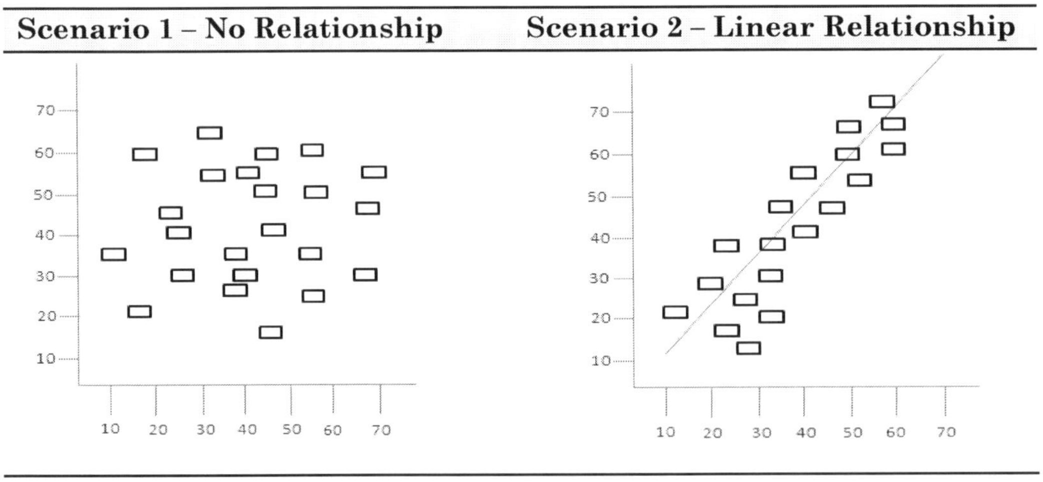

R and Octave Open Source Software

You definitely need to know about the R system. It is a widely used open source software that is available for free download. The system is an implementation of the statistical language known as S. If you take a college course about statistics or data mining, you are likely to use R. Check out this website: http://www.r-project.org/

R is also gaining in use in the greater statistics and data mining community. Commercial software like SAS, SPSS, and Teradata can now work with R which validates its importance. Numerous solutions have been developed using R which can applied to applications like actuarial analysis, river flood forecasting and marketing optimization.

GNU Octave is another popular open source system that enables mathematical analysis. The language resembles the commercial Matlab language and can be used to generate great visualizations. Download Octave from this website:

http://www.gnu.org/software/octave/

Learn More

Expand your knowledge of statistics. These resources can help.

Visit a website!   The StatTrek website provides great tutorials to help you to learn about statistics.

http:/www.stattrek.com/

Read about it!   This book provides a good introduction to the use of statistics in business:

Thurman, Paul W. *MBA Fundamentals Statistics*. Kaplan MBA Series, 2008.

Key Points

- Descriptive statistics addresses collecting, summarizing, and presenting data.

- Inferential statistics provides conclusions about data and makes predictions.

- Statistics work with subsets of data populations called samples.

- The statistician tests hypothesis about a population using control and test groups.

- Probability is used to determine the level of confidence that a statistical finding holds true for an entire population.

- Measures of central tendency provide an overall understanding of a set of data including mean, median, and mode.

- Measures of dispersion describe the degree of variation in a set of data.

- Range is the spread between the largest and smallest values in a set of data.

- Standard deviation and variance describe the variability of data compared to the mean. The larger the standard deviation and variance, the wider the distribution.

- Regression models are tools of inferential statistics that can be used to make predictions.

- Linear regression analysis identifies a linear relationship between covariates and outcomes, so for a given set of covariates it can infer an outcome.

*With a BlackBerry full of information about hitters on hand, he
searches for clues, patterns, anything that will help him
through the next inning, all the while beseeching pitchers who
wander by to share any tidbit they have picked up.*
Jorge L. Ortiz, USA TODAY, 10/12/2005 writing about Roger Clemens

After studying this chapter you will be able to:

- Understand major data mining terms
- Use data mining best practices
- Avoid data mining traps.

In Chapter 13, you gained an understanding of Statistics. You learned about the branches of statistics, including descriptive and predictive statistics. The use of controls and sampling carry over to data mining.

In this chapter, you will advance your knowledge in the area of data mining and analytics. Data mining is a set of techniques for analyzing large volumes of data. It is useful for uncovering previously unknown patterns or knowledge. This differs from BI, which seeks to provide 100% correct answers based on known data.

The term Data Mining is sometimes mistakenly used to refer to all data querying – this is not true. Data querying without analytics is not data mining. In addition, data mining is much more open-ended than data querying and BI, yet builds on many of the same disciplines, including statistics, database technology, algorithms, and machine learning. Figure 14-01 illustrates the dependency of data mining on related disciplines and concepts.

Figure 14-01: Data Mining and Related Concepts

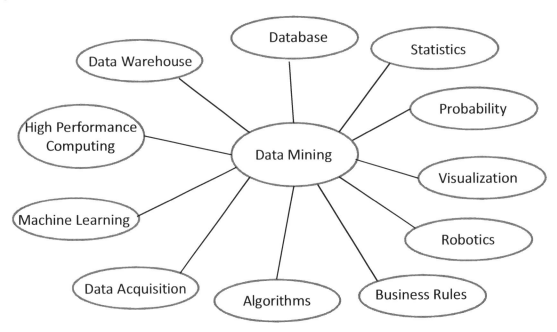

The two approaches to selecting the scope of data are directed and undirected. Directed data mining is often predictive in nature, while undirected data mining is descriptive in nature. Table 14-01 defines data mining terms.

Table 14-01: Data Mining and Analytics Terms

Term	Definition
Data Mining	Data mining is the application of analytical methods to huge volumes of data to find new and useful patterns or knowledge.
Optimization Analytics	The use of analytic methods such as data mining and statistics to make decisions ("next best action") with the best outcomes. For example, optimization analytics may recommend the most profitable price to offer to an auto insurance customer.
Predictive Analytics	The use of analytic methods such as data mining and statistics to anticipate future outcomes. For example, predictive analytics may provide insights into future demand for a product or the buying habits of a customer.

Directed Data Mining is very specific. It aims to provide an understanding of a particular data topic, like response to a marketing offer or credit worthiness. It is Predictive Data Mining that forecasts the direction and properties of targeted data using a large volume of data as input.

In contrast to directed data mining, Undirected Data Mining seeks to provide an understanding of patterns in data without the goal of learning about a specific target field. It is Descriptive Data Mining that aims to understand a set of data which, in turn, represents real world entities such as customers or investments. Data that depicts the subject area is presented in understandable and useful forms.

Predictive Data Mining

Predicting the future and recommending courses of action are critical decision support functions achieved through data mining. Activities of data mining that are predictive in nature include:

- **Classification** – dividing entities into predefined classes such as good credit risks and poor credit risks.
- **Estimation** – surmising unknown current values such as net worth based on known values.
- **Prediction** – anticipating future values such as customer lifetime value based on a set of known values.
- **Recommendation** – proposing the actions that will result in the best predicted result.

Use of predictive models is a hallmark of predictive data modeling. A predictive model is a depiction of how something functions. It can translate input data into a prediction that applies to reality such as those described in Table 14-02.

Table 14-02: Input Data and Predicted Attributes

Input Data	Predicted Attribute
Customer Profile Information such as payment history	Offer credit – Yes or No Or Credit Score
Student Profile Information such as grades, honors, and activities	Offer college admittance – Yes or No Or college admittance ranking
Baseball player profiles such as batting average, birth date, weight, health history	Recruiting priority score
Bridge characteristics – age, materials, construction technique, and inspection results	Bridge repair / replacement score

The predictive model is developed using multiple sets of input data:

- **Training Set** – a set of data that contains attributes along with the predicted attribute. Data mining analysis builds models that can determine the predicted attribute using the training attributes.
- **Validation Set** – a set of data that tests the predictive models, enabling the selection of the most effective model.
- **Test Set** – a set of data that tests the performance of the model.

Predictive data mining may require the development and comparison of multiple models in order to find the one that produces the best practical results. After the predictive model is developed, it can be used repeatedly to analyze data that represents real world situations. For example, it may be used to flag activity as potentially fraudulent, as shown in Figure 14-02.

Figure 14-02: Fraud Detection Model

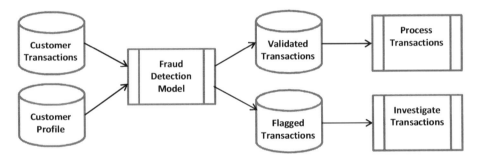

Descriptive Data Mining

Descriptive data mining seeks to find interesting patterns in data. Data mining activities that are descriptive include:

- **Description and profiling** – describing distinguishing characteristics of groups of entities such as customers.
- **Clustering** – grouping entities into mutually exclusive groups where members of each group are similar to each other and different from other groups.
- **Affinity Grouping** – placing entities into groups with similar associations. For example, Market Basket Analysis (MBA) identifies products that are frequently purchased together.
- **Outlier analysis** – discovery process that identifies anomalies, which are data points outside the range of other data points in the same set. In other words, finding exceptions.

Clusters

Clusters are groupings of data points with a large degree of affinity. In other words, data is being categorized. This means that data points within a cluster are closer to other members of the cluster and farther away from members of other clusters. Figure 14-03 depicts an example of obvious clusters.

Figure 14-03: Clusters

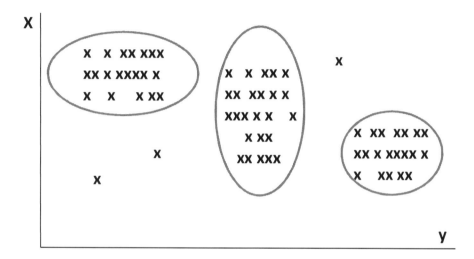

Clustering a small set of data with two dimensions is usually straightforward. When there is a large sample size or population with dozens to thousands of attributes, it becomes more difficult and requires the use of statistical algorithms. These algorithms use measures of distance to determine how far apart or close together the data points are.

Applications of clustering include:

- Customer analysis
- Cataloging of astronomical objects
- Grouping books and music into genres.

The ability to cluster books has given Amazon a competitive advantage. The display of book titles that are related leads to more sales and is a service to customers.

Predictive Data Mining – Decision Trees

A decision tree is a structure that enables large collections of inputs to be classified into homogeneous groups through a series of choices called nodes. The tree is processed from left to right or top to bottom, with the first node called the root node, nodes secondary to the root node called child nodes, and nodes at the bottom called leaf nodes. Figure 14-04 depicts a generic decision tree. The leaf nodes are where the final group/value is determined.

Figure 14-04: Decision Tree

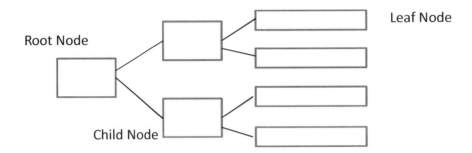

Decision tree algorithms have been available since the late 1970s. These algorithms include ID3 (late 1970s), C.4.5 (1980), and Classification and Regression Trees (CART – 1984). Developing a decision tree requires providing a set of training data to a software package which determines the appropriate set of rules that results in the desired classification.

The strengths of decision trees include their understandability, applicability to practical problems, and their generation of business rules that can be applied to further sets of data. The weaknesses of decision trees include output of a single discrete attribute, so they are not suited to generating a series of actions or continuous values.

Consider using decision trees when the desired output is a discrete value and input data can be described by multiple attribute value pairs. The final group/value can correspond to a decision, such as grant credit, place an order, or hire a baseball player.

Predictive Data Mining – Neural Nets

A neural net is a flexible predictive analytics tool that mimics the learning of the human brain. A neural net model accepts a large collection of known inputs and produces an output that may be continuous-valued. The net is processed from left to right, with inputs entering on the left and the final result output to the right. The model includes nodes referred to as neurons, and flows of data known as edges. Each node transfers inputs to an output using an algorithm, along with weights assigned to the inputs. Figure 14-05 shows a simple neural net model.

Figure 14-05: Neural Net

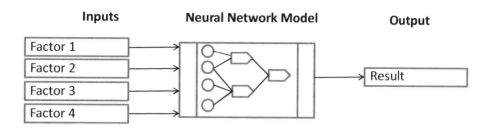

One way that neural nets learn is through a process called backward propagation. This is a feedback loop which enables the neural net to adjust the weights assigned to inputs. This powerful technique enables neural nets to produce surprisingly perceptive outputs.

The strengths of neural nets include the ability to handle many cases, the ability to handle poorly structured problems, and have easy implementation. Consider using neural nets when the desired output can be continuously valued and a high quality training data set is available.

The weakness of neural nets is that they are not easy to understand. The workings are hidden in a black box which does not make for intuitive explanations of how outputs are generated. This makes it difficult to evaluate the quality of neural network results.

Data Mining Tips and Traps

> *It's not so much how busy you are, but why you are busy. The bee is praised; the mosquito is swatted.*
>
> Marie O'Connor

Obtaining good input data is critical to building a successful predictive model. By studying this book, you have learned much about data – data definition, data modeling, data governance, and data quality. All of these disciplines are helpful in obtaining and conditioning data for data mining. Data Issues that are particular traps in data mining are described in Table 14-03. Also, see Table 10-01 of the Data Sources chapter for additional ways to deal with data issues.

Table 14-03: Dealing with Data Issues Specific to Data Mining

Data Issue	Explanation and Correction Procedure
Outliers	Outliers are extreme data values that are far from the average. These outliers can distort the predicted outputs. If necessary, avoid this by examining the outliers and removing them from the training data set.
Data is a Synonym of Predicted Attribute	Suppose we want to predict income level using data mining? It would not make sense to include gross income as an input, but if it's available, the model will use this factor to predict the outcome. It is not telling us anything that we do not already know.
Noise	Data that is not going to be a factor in determining the results is noise. For example, social security number is not a factor in credit worthiness, so it should not be part of the training data set. In general, unique identifiers are not helpful in data mining or statistical analysis.

Learn More

Expand your knowledge of data mining using these helpful resources.

Visit a website!	KDNuggets™ – is a great data mining and analytics resource: http://www.kdnuggets.com/
Read about it!	I recommend these books on Data Mining: Pang-Ninq and Michael Steinbach and Vipin Kumar. *Introduction to Data Mining – First Edition.* Addison Wesley, 2005. Celko, Joe. *Joe Celko's Analytics & OLAP in SQL.* Morgan Kaufmann, 2006.
Get Research!	Search the web for research reports (filetype=pdf): • Aberdeen Executive Intelligence • Forrester Wave Predictive Analytics • Gartner Magic Quadrant Business Intelligence
Try this software!	RapidMiner is a leading open source platform that provides integrated data mining capabilities. This product is both powerful and easy to use. Models are developed through a rapid prototyping approach and can include predictive analytics, reporting, and ETL. This product is in use by major organizations in numerous countries: http://www.rapid-i.com
	Excellent tutorials are available at the product website and at youtube.com.

Key Points

- Data mining addresses large volumes of data versus the data samples addressed by statistics.

- Data mining can be used to discovery previously unknown patterns and knowledge.

- Descriptive data mining aids in understanding a set of data.

- Predictive data mining infers the future and may recommend courses of action.

- A training set of data is used by data mining analytics to build predictive models.

- Obtain high quality input data. Avoid garbage data – "garbage in, garbage out" is all too true.

- Remove outlier data, which can distort results.

- Do not include synonyms of the predicted attribute, otherwise you will predict what you already know.

- Descriptive data mining enables better understanding of data and the reality that it represents.

- Clustering enables classification of entities such as customers into groups with a large degree of affinity.

- Decision trees classify collections of inputs through a series of choices that resemble a tree.

- Neural nets mimic the human brain to learn and solve problems.

It is a capital mistake to theorize before one has data. Insensibly one begins to twist facts to suit theories, instead of theories to suit facts.

Sherlock Holmes

When you have completed this chapter you will be able to:

- Understand analytic applications
- Architect at a high level, an analytic application such as risk analysis, actuarial analysis, and investment analysis.

In Chapter 14 you learned about data mining. This powerful approach is used to describe existing data, as well as make predictions using large volumes of data as input. Data mining builds upon methods used for statistics that were described in Chapter 13.

In this chapter, you will see how these techniques can be added to a technical architecture to produce practical results. Much of my experience is in the financial services area, which gives me grounding for financial portfolio analysis, risk analysis, and actuarial analysis. My experience shows that these approaches also apply to marketing, manufacturing, retail, supply chain, and other types of analysis.

Analytical Application Example Architecture

The example analytical application follows a proven pattern. Data is gathered from multiple input sources; stored in a central data store; data is processed through number crunching models; and finally, the resulting data is output. Figure 15-01 depicts the overall process. This process is systematic and repeatable, which is suitable for the heavy duty decisions that an enterprise relies upon, such as pricing its products or hedging its risks.

Figure 15-01: Analytical Application – Architected Data Flow

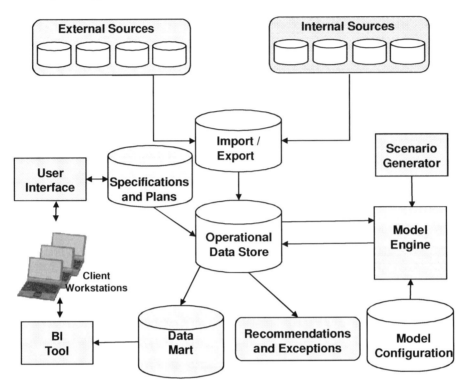

Each component in the analytical application has a specific role. Inputs to the application include external sources, internal sources, specifications and plans, scenarios, and model configuration parameters. Core data is stored in an Operational Data Store (ODS), with additional data stored in an import/export database, specifications and plans database, and data mart(s). Outputs include data mart updates, recommendations, and exceptions. Each of these components merits additional consideration.

External Sources	Sources of data from outside the enterprise, such as:
	• Census data
	• Customer surveys
	• Customer lifestyle profiles
	• Financial instrument prices
	• Economic indicators

Internal Sources	Sources of data from inside the enterprise, such as: • Customer data • Customer accounts • Product data • Organization and employee data • Transactions and events • Financial assets and liabilities • Inventory • Work centers • Employees
Import / Export	A staging database that contains the data accepted from internal and external sources. This area may have controls to ensure that the data is clean and complete. Control levels may include: • Row counts • Amount hash totals • Data element edits • Cross system consistency checks Data may also be staged for output through the import/export database.
Specifications and Plans	The Specifications and Plans database contains data that drives the process. Examples of data stored in this database include: • Plans and budgets • Calculation rules • Interest and other rates • Organizational hierarchies • Products • Sensitivities • Control rules This approach is better than creating a maze of uncontrolled spreadsheets or hardcoding values in calculations. Workflow controls and edits assure that this data is correct.
Specifications and Plans User Interface	The Specifications and Plans User Interface is a set of screens that enables users to maintain and view the Specifications and Plans Database. It supports a workflow for maintaining and publishing the data, as well as edits to improve the quality of the data.

Operational Data Store (ODS)	The Operational Data Store (ODS) is the integration and control point for the data. It is modeled in a normalized form and includes both current and historical data. Major inputs come from the Import Export database and the Specifications and Plans database. Data is exchanged with the model engine as it is computed. Data is output to the Data Mart for reporting and analysis. Recommendation and exception data may be sent elsewhere for action.
Model Engine	The Model Engine is the part of the analytical application that performs calculations. This is where number crunching happens and input is transformed into useful output. The model engine calculations can be based on a number of models and approaches, including: • Statistics • Data mining • Monte Carlo simulation • Custom models. For analysis based on Monte Carlo simulation methods, multiple scenarios are processed based on a combination of scenarios and system data. Use of repeated randomized cycles is called a stochastic approach. It differs from the deterministic approach which returns a single known answer. Calculations often require extensive computing horse power, so high performance computing methods may be required: • Multi CPU and core computers • Cloud computing • Hadoop / Map Reduce computing • Grid computing • Super computing and mini super computing. In-memory models perform faster than models that require data access. All data is prepared and provided to the Model Engine, which performs analysis on a slice of the data. The Model Engine may be executed many times in a single run.
Model Configuration	Model Configuration contains definitions and parameters for running the models. An off-the-shelf model can yield competitive advantage when provided with your organization's distinct data and parameters.

Scenario Generator	The Scenario Generator outputs "what if" situations and randomized analysis based on input parameters. For example, it might output varying economic conditions such as interest rates or unemployment rates. Changing an input data value to an extreme level is called a shock. It might also generate scenarios that cover all possible permutations and combinations.
Data Mart	A Data Mart is a database that is part of the analytic application where data is stored for presentation and user access. This data mart is organized into facts and dimensions specific to the analytical application.
Recommendations and Exceptions	Recommendations are a critical output of a system. For example, an investment hedging system will output recommendations for investments to be bought and sold. In insurance, the recommendation may be to provide reserves to meet obligations to policy holders. Exceptions are warnings about problems such as input data that has failed controls and conditions that require investigation.
BI Tool	BI Tools enable query and display of data from the data mart.

How long will an analytical cycle take? Analytical cycles can be very lengthy and require many weeks to complete. Factors that impact analytic cycle time include:

- **Number of business entities.** Analysis could require calculations for each financial account, product, fund, insurance policy, etc. If there are millions of business entities, cycle time will increase. Compression is a technique used to reduce the number of business entities. Using statistical techniques, entities are profiled to determine common characteristics. Then the model is run for the reduced number of entity profiles. This technique speeds processing, but may result in less accurate results.
- **Number of scenarios.** Each scenario is an alternate set of inputs to the analysis, resulting in a run for a business entity. Each scenario multiplies the calculations required. To reduce the number of scenarios, analyze inputs to the scenario generator. Random generation often results in fewer scenarios than scenarios generated to cover every possible permutation and combination.
- **Time required for calculation of each business entity scenario combination.** The length of time required to execute a unit of work has a multiplier effect. The complexity of the model, the performance of the computers used, and the use of memory are factors that determine calculation

time. Performance can be improved by optimizing the model algorithm, using faster computers, and using main memory rather than disk to hold and access data.

- **Number of calculation nodes.** Each calculation node works on one or more chunks of the problem. Increasing the number of nodes decreases the overall time the analytical cycle will take by breaking the work into more chunks. Methods of organizing the calculation nodes include, multicore computers, multi CPU computers, grids and clouds. Analytics often requires computer power for a short time rather than continuously. This can make a good case for cloud computing, where resources can be obtained and returned dynamically.

A high-level view of the time required for analytic calculations is:

Time = (Entities x Scenarios x SingleScenarioTime) / CalculationNodes

Key Points

- Common building blocks are used for many analytic applications.

- The calculation engine is where the number crunching happens.

- Use of controls can improve results through better data quality.

- A specifications and plans database provides better data management than distributed spreadsheets.

- The scenario engine produces alternatives for analysis.

- Controlling the number of scenarios and business entities should reduce the time required.

- Increasing the number of nodes reduces the elapsed time for analytical processing.

Chapter 16
Presenting Data: Scorecards and Dashboards

If it doesn't matter who wins or loses, then why do they keep score?

Vince Lombardi

After studying this chapter you will be able to:

- Align the presentation with requirements
- Select the presentation type most appropriate to your needs
- Understand scorecard and dashboard terms
- Determine requirements for your scorecards and dashboards
- Design your scorecards and dashboards
- Understand data visualization graphics – the building blocks of reports, scorecards, and dashboards
- Apply techniques to mobile devices – smart phones and tablets.

In Chapter 15, you became familiar with the components of analytic applications. The data resulting from analytic applications can be used as input to data presentations on scorecards, dashboards, reports, and charts.

KPIs (Key Performance Indicators) are the primary data that will drive presentations. Therefore, before starting to specify scorecards and dashboards, it is necessary to define a library of KPIs. Each KPI library entry will include the information specified in Table 16-01. Designing dashboards and scorecards is a matter of pulling together the KPIs required for each job role.

Table 16-01: KPI Library Information

Characteristic	Description
KPI Name	A KPI name is a string that identifies and describes a KPI. Each KPI has a unique name, such as Customer Retention Percent.
Datatype	This specifies if the KPI is stored as a string, a number, or a date, and its size. The datatype, also known as the data format, has a value such as decimal(12,4). Most KPIs are numbers.
Definition	A KPI definition is a narrative that conveys or describes the meaning of a KPI. For example, "Customer Retention Percent is a percentage of customers that continue to buy each year."

Characteristic	Description
Responsibility Level	Categorize the KPI as one or more of the following: • **Operational** – detailed information needed by supervisors to monitor operations • **Tactical** – department information needed by managers to improve processes • **Strategic** – enterprise information needed by executives to carry out strategy
Responsible Business Roles	Identify the job roles that are measured by the KPI. This includes identification of drill down levels responsible for levels of the KPI.
Targets and Priority	Specify target levels of the metric for each business role, as well as the priority level for each role. Rules that specify notifications and alerts that should be generated when the KPI deviates from target should also be specified.
Align to Enterprise Scorecard Categories	Relate the KPI to strategic categories, such as those proposed in the Balanced Scorecard (BSC): • Customer Satisfaction • Financial Performance • Organizational Learning • Production and Innovation
Frequency of Review	Specify how often the KPI should be reviewed and analyzed. Operational data should be reviewed multiple times during the day, tactical data daily or weekly, and strategic data monthly or quarterly.
Data Calculation and Sources	Specify the data that makes up the KPI, calculations and where the data should be obtained. Include sources of drill down details.
Presentation Type	Select the appropriate presentation type for the KPI such as: • Bar Graphs • Broken Line Graphs • Pie Charts • Histograms • Gauges • Reports • Trees See the Presentation Types section of this chapter for guidance on choosing presentation type.

An effective process can lead to better scorecards and dashboards. Figure 16-01 depicts a step-by-step process for designing and building dashboards and scorecards.

Figure 16-01: Dashboard and Scorecard Building Steps

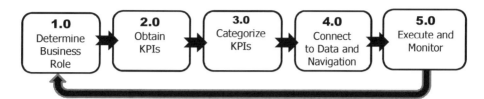

Follow these steps to design and build a scorecard or dashboard for a given business role:

- **Step 1.0 – Determine Business Role.** Examine job duties of the user and classify the role. This classification should match a job role in the KPI Library. Strategic job classifications require a scorecard, while tactical and operational roles require a dashboard.
- **Step 2.0 – Obtain KPIs.** Select KPIs from the KPI Library that match the business role targeted by the scorecard or dashboard. Select KPIs based on priority and business input.
- **Step 3.0 – Categorize KPIs.** Group KPIs by category. For example, a Balanced Scorecard has categories for customer satisfaction, financial performance, organizational learning, and innovation.
- **Step 4.0 – Connect to Data and Navigation.** Build the scorecard or dashboard. Data will be presented using the presentation type determined from the KPI library. Include secure navigation to the display to enable the scorecard owners to access the display and drill down to details. Connect each KPI to the appropriate data source described in the KPI Library.
- **Step 5.0 – Execute and Monitor.** Begin using the scorecard and/or dashboard. Monitor to ensure that business needs are being met.
- **Repeat as needed to refine outputs and KPIs.**

Scorecards

In this section, you will see how to design and produce BI scorecards. A scorecard is a report or display that shows the performance of one or more individuals or organizations for a specific time period. It typically contains multiple scores based on multiple measurements with weighted rankings between those measurements. Scorecards are aimed toward executives who have strategic concerns.

The idea is to measure progress toward goals and to support performance management, which is a set of management and analytic processes. Performance management is used to control and improve organizational performance, which is the accomplishment of goals through execution of tasks that are measured and compared to goals. Other names for this are Business Performance Management (BPM), Corporate Performance Management (CPM), and Enterprise Performance Management (EPM).

Scorecards can be delivered as static outputs on PDFs or other fixed media, or they can be delivered through a dynamic medium like the web. There are great benefits to scorecards:

- Scorecards communicate and promote alignment with enterprise goals
- Executives quickly see key pieces of information
- Interactive scorecards enable drill down for analysis of root causes and accountabilities.

Scorecards include scores that are calculated from one or more KPIs. There are target values for each score; the difference between the target and actual score is a variance. Symbols are often included rather than numeric scores. For example, one set of symbols indicates if the score is on target, in danger of going off target, or is off target. Another set of symbols shows trends and indicates whether performance is better than, equal to, or worse than the prior period. Figure 16-02 includes an example of a scorecard that ranks a number of performers.

Figure 16-02: Scorecard Ranking Example

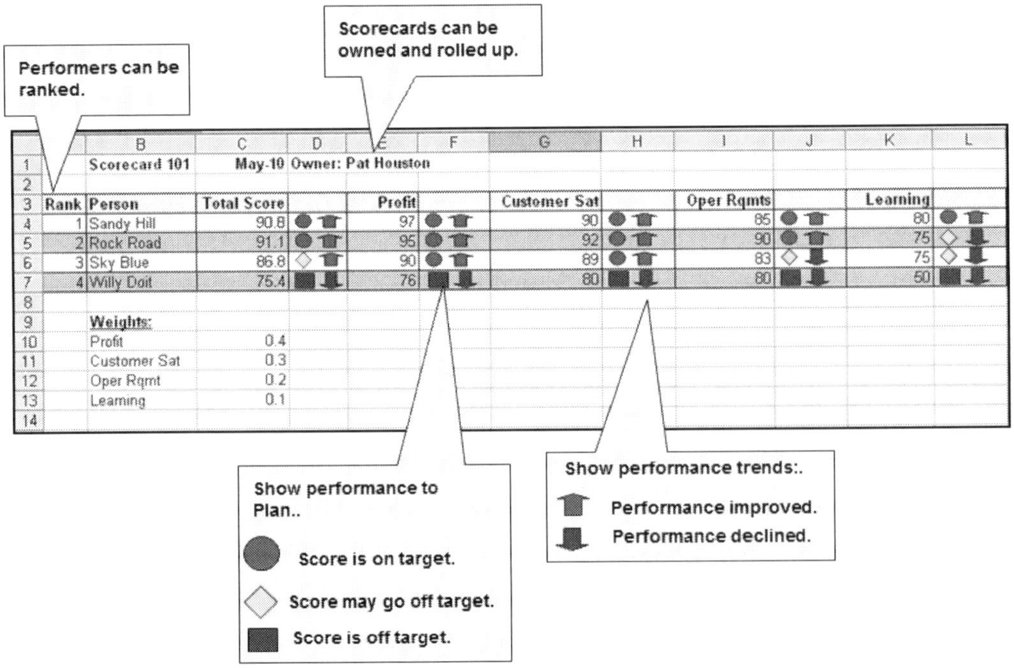

The Balanced Score Card (BSC) is a management approach that evaluates the overall performance of an organization. Information provided by the scorecard enables management to make effective decisions which lead to actions that improve scorecard results. It combines multiple factors (financial performance, customer satisfaction, organizational learning, and production and innovation) to produce scores that can be included in scorecards. BSC was originated by Robert Kaplan and David Norton in 1992 (Kaplan 1996). Objectives, measures, targets, and strategies are determined for each of these BSC aspects. Figure 16-03 shows an example of a Balanced Score Card.

Figure 16-03: Balanced Scorecard Example

First Place Toys Balanced Scorecard
20xx - First Quarter

Perspective	Objective	Measurement	Target 20xx	KPI 20xx	Variance
Financial	Maximize Returns	ROE	15%	12%	3%
Customer	Provide Great Service	Consumer NPS	95	87	-8%
Internal Process	Fast production	Order to delivery cycle time	12 Days	10 Days	2 Days
Learning and Growth	Well trained workforce	Percent employees certified	60%	65%	5%

The individual scores in the scorecard are calculated using metrics along with weighting factors that yield a comparative score. Table 16-02 depicts an example set of calculations for computing BSC scores from metrics.

Table 16-02: Scorecard Calculations

Calculated Item	Calculation
ProfitScore	(ActualProfitAmount / TargetProfitAmount)*100
CustomerSATScore	(Net Promoter Score * NetPromoterWeight) + (Returns * ReturnsWeight) + (Repeat Business * Repeat Business Weight)
ProductionScore	(InventoryTurns * Inventory Turns Weight) + (MfgLeadTime * Mfg Lead Time Weight)
LearningScore	(Training Event Count * Training Event Weight) + (Test Score Average * Test Score Weight) + (Step In Count * Step In Count Weight) + Employee Engagement Score
TotalScore	(ProfitScore * ProfitWeight) + (CustomerSATScore * CustomerSATWeight) + (ProductionScore * ProductionWeight) + (LearningScore * LearningWeight)
Rank	Order TotalScore in descending order The highest TotalScore is a rank of 1, etc.

OBTAINING SCORECARD DATA

Scorecard data is often obtained from data warehouse systems, taking advantage of the data integration and aggregation available there. Data is often strategic in nature and summarized to monthly, quarterly, and annual levels, which supports trending and period to period comparisons.

Figure 16-04: Big Picture – The Data Warehouse System

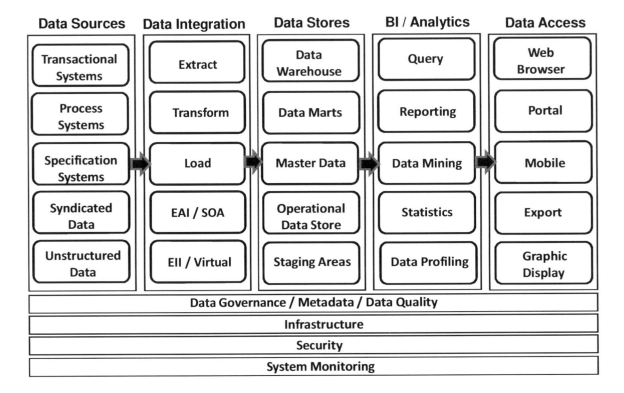

Scorecards may link to more detailed data to enable analysis of root causes. Those data displays may include data in more dynamic databases, such as an ODS, ERP, or CRM system.

SCORECARD TIPS AND TRAPS

There are a number of practices to emulate and to avoid. Table 16-03 shows both Tips and Traps to guide you in the right direction.

Table 16-03: Scorecard Tips and Traps

Tips (Do This)	Traps (Do Not Do This)
• Keep it balanced – include multiple factors – financial, customer, and internal process, as well as learning and growth • Align with strategy and objectives • Develop summary financial metrics such as Earned Value Added (EVA) and Return on Net Assets (RONA) • Include customer satisfaction measures like returns and lost business • Include team and individual performance • Include competitor or benchmark data as a comparison	• Rolling out without quality input data • Choosing unrealistic or non-aligned objectives • Failing to provide timely and accurate data • Using the same metric in multiple ways • Forcing unhealthy competition within the organization • Ignoring unintended obligations

Scorecard Key Points

- A Scorecard is a report or display that shows the performance of individuals or organizations for a specified time period in the form of scores.

- A Scorecard that evaluates performance using multiple balanced factors (financial performance, customer satisfaction, organizational learning, and production and innovation) is known as a Balanced Scorecard (BSC).

- A Score is calculated from multiple KPIs using weighting factors. This calculation often includes a comparison to targets and the calculation of variances.

- Scorecards can be created and stored using multiple technologies, including paper and pencil, spreadsheets, specialized scorecard tools, and data warehouses.

- Some enterprises rank people and organizations based on their scorecard results as a motivational tool. Getting a high rank can result in being rewarded, while a consistently low rank can result in corrective action.

- Adding a drill down capability to scorecards is a way to analyze and possibly discover the root causes of high and low performance.

Dashboards

Not everything that counts can be counted;

not everything that can be counted counts.

Albert Einstein

A dashboard is a display of indicators that show the current status of key metrics in a graphic format that resembles aircraft control panels with charts and gauges. Figure 16-05 shows an example. Dashboards:

- Support an individual or single job function
- Focus on immediate action
- Provide a large amount of information on a single page
- Often use graphics
- Tend to be near real-time
- Tend to support operational and tactical BI.

Figure 16-05: Dashboards Track Business Processes

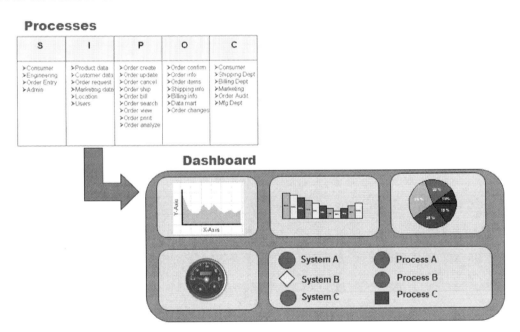

OBTAINING DASHBOARD DATA

Dashboard data may be obtained from a variety of sources including data mart, ODS, PDS, MDM Hub, and source system, as depicted in Figure 16-06. Data is often tactical or operational in nature and enables detailed views. This supports the details required to monitor and manage operations.

Figure 16-06: Dashboards May Need Near Real-time Information

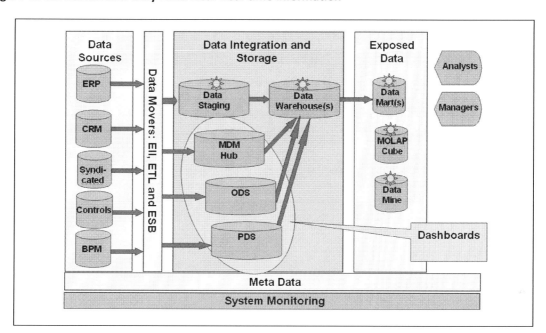

DASHBOARD TIPS AND TRAPS

Table 16-04 shows both Tips and Traps to guide you to best practices when building dashboards.

Table 16-04: Dashboard Tips and Traps

Tips (Do This)	Traps (Do Not Do This)
• Keep visuals simple	• Providing the wrong level of detail
• Consolidate to the most critical KPIs	• Failing to link to root cause detail
• Design KPIs and prove out using a spreadsheet	• Providing too many KPIs
• Manage change of KPIs	• Using the wrong data source(s)
• Catalog KPIs	• Choosing the wrong BI tool
• Validate and automate data sources	• Attempting a "do all" dashboard on the first try
• Build dashboards through an iterative approach	• Failure to test enough
• Support drill down to detail	• Entering data manually
• Identify trends	

Dashboard Key Points

- Start with requirements – what questions need to be answered?

- Every report is not a dashboard (define dashboard).

- Every output need not be a dashboard.

- Explain dashboards by showing diagrams with rectangles and questions answered.

- Keep it simple – avoid adding extraneous data.

- Keep it visually simple – avoid shading, fancy borders, and extra labels.

- Position the most important information in the upper right to draw attention to it.

- Support drill down – enable click on the display to obtain more detail.

- Excel is often used to display dashboard data.

Data Visualization Graphics Types

Statistical results are often presented graphically to enable people to visualize those results. Not only are results graphically displayed in reports, dashboards, and scorecards, they are also used to communicate in media like television, internet, newspapers, and books. Useful graphic types include:

- Bar Graphs
- Broken Line Graphs
- Pie Charts
- Histograms
- Gauges
- Trees.

Bar graphs are very effective for presenting data because they are easy to create and understand. The bar chart is two dimensional. One axis is labeled with data category names while the other axis is labeled with measurement amounts. Bar charts can be arranged horizontally or vertically. Additional data can be communicated using multiple and divided bars, as illustrated in Figure 16-07.

Figure 16-07: Bar Graphs

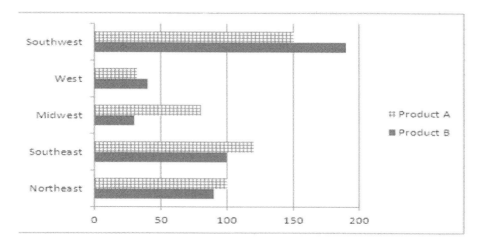

Broken line graphs show trends by connecting data points with lines. These graphs are arranged in two dimensions, like the bar graph, and are useful for illustrating trends. Multiple sets of measures can be depicted using different colors or line patterns like shading as seen in Figure 16-08.

Figure 16-08: Broken Line Graph – Sales by Product Example

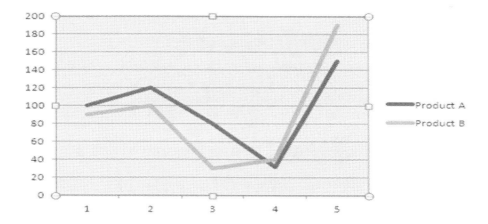

Pie charts show how a whole is divided into categories within a circle. The percentage of each category is represented by its size. Categories are sequenced by size and labeled. Each percentage point is represented by 3.6 degrees in the circle. Figure 16-9 shows sales divided between regions using a pie chart.

Figure 16-9: Pie Chart

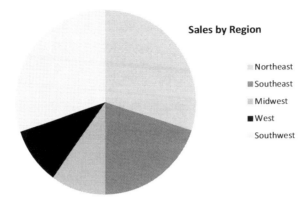

Histograms are commonly used to represent frequency distributions. They are bar graphs without space between the bars. Labels can indicate both absolute and relative frequency, as illustrated by Figure 16-10.

Figure 16-10: Histogram

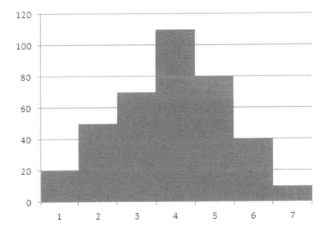

Gauges are used to show progress toward goals or performance within tolerance levels. Progress bars and speedometers are examples of gauges. Figure 16-11 shows an example of this.

Figure 16-11: Gauge of Daily Production Level

Trees are used to depict hierarchies and to enable drill down navigation. Trees may be placed on the left side of a display to enable navigation to desired information. Trees are presented so branches can be expanded and hidden. Figure 16-12 shows an example sales organization hierarchy represented through a tree structure.

Figure 16-12: Sales Organization Tree Example

- SalesRegions
  - MidwestRegion
  - NorthwestRegion
    - Territory1A
    - Territory1B
  - SoutheastRegion
  - SouthwestRegion
  - WestRegion

Mobile Device Considerations

The use of mobile devices to communicate business intelligence information is a revolutionary change. Increasingly business intelligence users expect to receive and use information on mobile devices. This in turn has an impact on the design of user friendly information displays.

Obviously screens are smaller than those of desktop and laptop computers. Mobile users intuitively touch and point at information desired as they explore data. These considerations should help you to design better scorecards, dashboards and other displays for mobile devices:

- Display the most important information in the upper right of the screen
- Break displays into multiple pages rather than trying to fit more items on a page than can be accommodated by mobile devices
- Avoid storing data on the mobile device to help mitigate security concerns
- Establish predefined drill paths and filters to easily navigate data

- Identify the mobile computing audience and determine requirements — different audiences may require different capabilities
- Obtain feedback from mobile users about display usability
- Consider HTML5 for designing mobile device displays because it can support many more devices than native apps.

Graphic Presentation Key Points

- Graphic displays help people turn data into information.

- Bar graphs are useful for displaying changes over time or for multiple categories for multiple groups. The groups can be rendered as separate bars or as stacked bars.

- Broken line graphs illustrate trends by connecting data points with lines. Different colors and line patterns can be used to depict multiple groups.

- Pie charts depict how a whole, rendered as a circle, is composed of categories, rendered as pie slices.

- Histograms illustrate frequency distributions as a bar graph with no spaces between bars.

- Gauges illustrate progress toward goals or measurement of KPIs using familiar symbols such as speedometers, progress bars, and traffic signals.

- Trees depict hierarchies and support drill down, often using the familiar directory folder paradigm.

- Keep it consistent — select a limited set of chart styles with consistent labels, colors, and symbols to make graphics.

- Design for mobile device users. Data must be structured to fit into a smaller footprint and to be easily navigated.

Learn More

Expand your knowledge of data presentation, including dashboards, scorecards, and portals.

Visit a website!

Chandoo.org provides numerous tutorials that show how to create dashboards and scorecards using Microsoft Excel:

http://www.chandoo.org

Balanced Scorecard Institute provides education and best practices toward building balanced scorecards:

http://www.balancedscorecard.org

Read about it!

Try these books:

Tufte, Edward. *The Visual Display of Quantitative Information.* Graphics Press, 2001.

LaPointe, Patrick. *Marketing by the Dashboard Light.* National Board of Advertisers, 2005.

Chapter 17
Business Intelligence Applications

The great strength of computers is that they can reliably manipulate vast amounts of data very quickly. Their great weakness is that they don't have a clue as to what any of that data actually means.

Stephen Cass, IEEE Spectrum, Jan 2004

After reading this chapter you will be able to:

- Identify opportunities for using BI in your organization
- Explain examples of successful analytics applications.

In Chapter 16, you learned about presenting BI and analytics data. Scorecards, dashboards, reports, and BI portals are the formats that have proven to be effective. The Balanced Scorecard (BSC) provides a strategic view of an organization's progress toward high-level goals.

BI and analytics have many practical applications. Analytics are used in such diverse areas as sports, science, government, marketing, finance, and risk management:

- **Sports** – selecting players, finding competitor weaknesses, calling plays
- **Science** – finding extraterrestrial planets, genomics
- **Healthcare** – diagnosing illness, detecting drug interactions, proposing treatments
- **Government** – detecting tax fraud, dispatching services effectively
- **Marketing** – segmenting customers, improving customer retention, allocating resources to marketing campaigns, cross-selling
- **Finance** – planning and budgeting, recommending financial trades
- **Risk Management** – hedging risk, evaluating credit risks, scoring risks
- **Fraud Detection** – finding suspicious credit card and other transactions.

Financial BI Applications

Use of financial analytics can greatly assist in the management of an organization's finances. Data is provided to financial analytics from data sources such as general ledger, budgeting, accounts payable, accounts receivable, payroll, and fixed asset management systems. Trend analysis and alerts can help organizations manage to their budgets and detect issues. Table 17-01 shows example financial analytics design elements.

Examples of financial BI applications include:

- Asset management
- Budget management
- Collections effectiveness
- Cost management
- Overhead reduction analysis.

Table 17-01: Financial Analytics Design Elements

Stars	Dimensions	Metrics
Asset Balance Fact	Calendar Date Dimension	Asset Balance Amount
Budget Line Fact	Currency Dimension	Budget Amount
GL Account Snapshot Fact	Facility Dimension	Budget Variance Amount
GL Transaction Fact	Fund Dimension	Equity Balance Amount
Payment Fact	Geographic Area Dimension	Liability Balance Amount
Revenue Transaction Fact	GL Account Dimension	Payment Amount
	Organization Unit Dimension	Stretch Goal Amount
	Product Dimension	Transaction Amount

Financial analytics make use of the BI operations of roll up, drill down, pivot, slice, and dice, as well as drill across. Hierarchies are supported in dimensions like the Organization Unit and Geographic Area Dimensions. This enables aggregated totals to be displayed for multiple levels of the organization. Storage of information at the financial transaction grain enables root cause analysis through drill down and drill across operations.

Financial performance is a key component of the Balanced Scorecard (BSC). Data managed in the financial data mart is a prime input to performance management scorecards and is critical to the management of successful organizations. Financial ratio KPIs can be calculated from the financial data.

Supply Chain and Manufacturing BI Applications

Supply chain and manufacturing analytics provide visibility to supply chain partners, including suppliers, manufacturers, transporters, wholesalers, and retailers. Data is provided to supply chain analytics from data sources such as procurement, manufacturing, inventory, and logistics systems. Table 17-02 shows example supply chain design elements.

Supply chain applications of BI include:

- Supplier performance analysis
- Plant and transportation hub location analysis
- Supply chain forecasting and planning
- Dynamic supply chain optimization
- Transportation efficiency analysis
- Inventory analysis
- Sales analysis.

Table 17-02: Supply Chain Analytics Design Elements

Stars	Dimensions	Metrics
Shipment Fact	Calendar Date Dimension	Inventory Balance Amount
Transport Fact	Currency Dimension	Inventory Turn Count
Requisition Fact	Facility Dimension	Procurement Lead Time
Supply Order Fact	Geographic Area Dimension	Manufacturing Lead Time
Billing Fact	Organization Unit Dimension	In Transit Unit Count
Procurement Fact	Product Dimension	Resource Capacity Unit Count
Fulfillment Fact	Supply Chain Partner Dimension	Per Product Scrap Cost
Inventory Snapshot Fact	Commodity Dimension	Maintenance Down Time
Demand Order Fact	Unit of Measure Dimension	Late Shipment Count
Inventory Transaction Fact	Work Order Dimension	Product Return Count
	Shipment Order Dimension	Unit Production Cost

Operations BI Applications

Operations management addresses the effective production of goods and services. Operations transform inputs (labor, material, facilities, machines) into outputs (goods and services) through a series of business processes and transformations. Table 17-03 depicts design elements that may be included in an operations data mart. Examples of operations application of BI include:

- Capacity planning
- Inventory analysis
- Operational performance and cost management
- Quality performance and safety analysis
- Scheduling of labor and facilities.

Table 17-03: Operations Analytics Design Elements

Stars	Dimensions	Metrics
Production Fact	Business Process Dimension	In Transit Unit Count
Activity Fact	Calendar Date Dimension	Inventory Balance Amount
Inspection Fact	Commodity Dimension	Inventory Turn Count
Inventory Fact	Currency Dimension	Late Shipment Count
Resource Fact	Facility Dimension	Maintenance Down Time
Labor Usage Fact	Geographic Area Dimension	Manufacturing Lead Time
Component Usage Fact	Organization Unit Dimension	Per Product Scrap Cost
Process Measure Fact	Product Dimension	Procurement Lead Time
	Resource Dimension	Product Return Count
	Unit of Measure Dimension	Resource Capacity Unit Count
	Work Order Dimension	Unit Production Cost

Performance Management BI Applications

Performance management applications of BI include:

- Balanced scorecard analysis
- Compensation analysis
- Resource and human capital management.

Risk Management BI Applications

Risk management includes numerous applications of analytics, such as hedging risk, evaluating credit risks, scoring risks, and detecting fraud. An example of flagging activity as potentially fraudulent is shown in Figure 17-01.

Figure 17-01: Fraud Detection Model

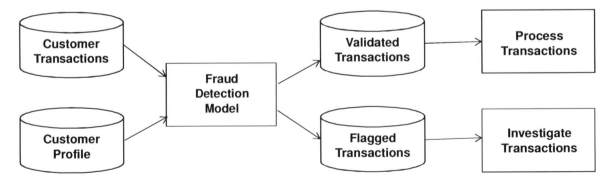

Risk management applications of BI include:

- Fraud detection

- Credit risk analysis
- Basel II and Solvency II analysis
- Hedging analysis.

Government BI Applications

Business intelligence and analytics have numerous applications in the government sector, where large volumes of data are gathered. Examples of government uses of BI include:

- Homeland security
- Crime prevention
- Tax fraud detection
- Military uniform sizing
- Education best practice analysis.

CASE STUDY: RICHMOND, VA POLICY DEPARTMENT

Business intelligence and analytics have helped the Richmond, Virginia Police Department (RPD) make dramatic steps in reducing crime. The city was able to drop its dangerous city ranking from 5th to 99th place through effective use of business intelligence.

To fight crime, the RPD decided to use analytics to find hidden patterns in its huge store of information obtained from 911 and other police systems. Analytics are used to predict the likelihood of crime and to effectively allocate police resources. Information is correlated from several data warehouses.

This was achieved by developing a statistical model using the IBM SPSS Modeler tool. Models are tied to color coded maps that are accessed by police officers in their patrol cars.

The use of analytics also enables proactive policing. Special units can be dispatched to where they can be most effectively utilized. In addition, certain property crimes are identified as having the potential to escalate to violent crimes. Proactive policing can head off more serious crime.

The results are impressive – from 2006 to 2007, crime rates fell; homicide declined 32%, rapes down 19%, robberies dropped 3%, and aggravated assaults fell 17%. These rates have continued to decline and the RPD continues to find new ways to use analytics to fight crime. (IBM SmartPlanet 2010)

Key Points

- BI and analytics can be used to produce results profitably in many areas.

- Financial analysis and KPIs are prime inputs to performance management and the Balanced Scorecard.

- Trend analysis and alerts support budget management and issue detection.

- Supply chain and manufacturing analytics can help to optimize procurement and delivery of goods.

- Manufacturing companies who use analytics can improve efficiency, inventory levels, and sales.

- Analytics for operations can contribute toward the effective production of goods and services.

- Performance management analytics such as the Balanced Scorecard (BSC) are great tools for improving the performance of the work force.

- Risk management can make use of analytic applications such as hedging risk, evaluating credit risks, scoring risks, and detecting fraud.

- Business intelligence can boost the effectiveness of law enforcement. Richmond Police Department used BI and analytics to improve law enforcement effectiveness and proactively reduce the crime rate.

- BI and analytics have additional applications in government, from homeland security to military uniform sizing to education.

Chapter 18
Customer Analytics

It's not who I am underneath, but what I do that defines me.

Batman Begins – 2005

When you have completed this chapter you will be able to:

- Understand the Single Customer View (SCV) conceptual data model
- Appreciate the benefits of the customer-centered orientation
- Specify the dimensions of customers
- Explain the benefits of customer-related analytics
- Segment customers using the RFM (Recency, Frequency, Monetary Gain) approach
- Categorize data into bands such as age band and education band
- Utilize the concepts of demographics, behavior, psychographics, interests, and transactions.

In Chapter 17, you learned about business intelligence applications and how those applications can help you to achieve benefits. The possibilities for using information to improve results are limitless. Examples of these applications include budgeting, logistics, manufacturing, and employee performance. One area of analytics stands out in the benefits that can be derived – customer analytics.

In this chapter, you will learn about the application of analytics to customers. Most organizations are heavily invested in creating and maintaining positive and profitable relationships with their customers. The importance of customers extends beyond for-profit businesses. The customers of governmental units are tax payers and specific recipients of services. The customers of non-profit organizations are the receivers of benefits.

If you are like most people, you have many questions about your customers. Use of customer analytics is a way to obtain answers to those questions. Table 18-01 shows questions that customer analytics can help you answer. Take time to review these questions and identify questions that are most important to you and your organization.

Table 18-01: Customer-Related Questions

Category	Question
Who	Who are our customers?
	• Identifiers –what identifiers set our customers apart?
	• Profiles – what kind of people are our customers?
	Who are our best customers?
	Who are our most profitable customers?
	Who is delinquent in paying their bills?
	Who is saying good things about us? (Promoters)
	Who is saying negative things about us? (Detractors)
	Who is harming our organization? (Committing fraud, etc.)
What / Which	What is a customer?
	What do our customers want?
	Which products or features are growing or declining in popularity?
	Which products should we offer a given customer?
	Which products are purchased together (market basket analysis)?
	Which offers will be responded to by which customers?
When / How Often	When is the best time to approach a customer?
	How often should we approach a customer?
Where	Where are our customers located geographically?
	Where do our customers go on our website?
	Where can we obtain customer data?
	Where should we open a new location?
	Where should we close a location?
How	How can we identify our customers?
	How do our customers learn about us?
	How can we sell more?
	How can we retain our customers?
	How can we better serve our customers?
	How can we detect when a customer is likely to leave?
	How are our customers related to each other?
	How do our customers want to be contacted?
How Much	How much money is spent by our customers?
	How much of a market share / wallet share / mind share?
	How much money was spent on each marketing campaign last month?
	How much should we charge for our products?
	How much credit should we extend to a given customer?
How Many	How many customers do we have and in what categories?
Why	Why is it a benefit to understand customers?
	Why do customers buy?
	Why do customers not buy?
	Why do customers leave? Reasons for attrition.

Customer Analytics is an approach to understanding customer behavior whose critical information is integrated in master data management, data warehousing, and other systems. This approach has some excellent benefits and uses:

- Improved customer service
- Cross sell and up sell opportunities
- Customer segmentation to enable targeted marketing and sales campaigns
- Improving customer loyalty
- Avoiding loss of profitable customers (retention).

For example, Larry Selden and Geoffrey Colvin found that the top 20% of a company's customers generate 150% of the company's profit, while the bottom 20% of customers drain 80% of the profits. (Selden 2003).

Successful organizations take action to understand their customers. ESPN, the sports network, has studied its customers and improved its offerings. Caesars Entertainment, the casino company, has built excellent relationships with its customers through analytics.

Single Customer View

The major obstacle that stands in the way of understanding and serving customers is that data about each customer is gathered in multiple places and cannot be integrated easily, as illustrated in Figure 18-01.

Figure 18-01: Customer Interactions

Single Customer View (SCV) is an approach that unifies information about customers so that all relevant activity and facts about each customer can be seen at a single point. One way to achieve this is Customer Data Integration (CDI), which is the process of integrating information about customers from multiple data sources into a single database.

Integrating customer data means associating all data about each customer to a common identifier or identifiers. This is a challenge, because customers may be associated with different identifiers in different systems. In addition, spellings of names and addresses may differ by system. Table 18-02 shows how data for a single customer can vary between and within systems.

Table 18-02: Customer Data Varies by System

System	Example Data
Help Desk	User Id = Bob29431 Email Address = RobertSmith312@bestmail.com Mobile Phone = 612-555-4567 Name = Robert Smith
Sales Order	Account Number = 89431 Name = Robert A Smith Telephone = 612-555-3579 Address = 100 East Main Street, Anoka, MN 55443 Email Address = RobertSmith312@bestmail.com
Warranty	Warranty Number = 100456 Name = Robert A Smith Telephone = 612-555-3579 Address = 100 East Main Street, Anoka, MN 55443 Warranty Number = 5431099 Name = Bob Smith Telephone = 612-555-3579 Address = 100 E Main St, Anoka, MN 55443
Syndicated Data	Name = Robert A Smith Address = 100 East Main Street, Anoka, MN 55443 Age Band = 5 (30-35 years) Income Band = 4 ($50,000 to $60,000) Lifestyle Segment = Upcoming Married Professional
Survey System	Email Address = RobertSmith312@bestmail.com

CDI software includes matching capabilities that enable matching data variations, such as spelling differences, format differences, address differences, nick names, and abbreviations. The integration point is the SCV Hub, illustrated in Figure 18-02.

Figure 18-02: SCV Integrates Customer Data from Multiple Sources

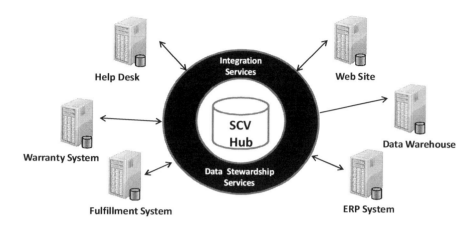

Common Customer Data Model

At the heart of SCV is a data model that supports the integration of customer data. Raw data is gathered for use in later analysis for profiling and segmenting customers. This includes detailed information that is accumulated in the SCV Hub and/or the data warehouse, such as identifiers, demographics, psychographics, location, products, measures, transactions, and interactions. See Figure 18-03 for examples of this.

Figure 18-03: SCV Data Model

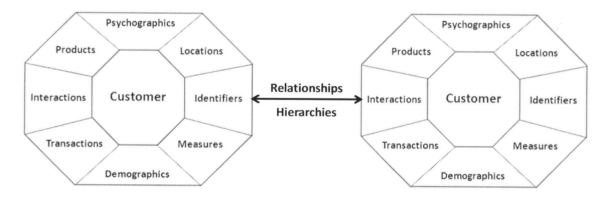

IDENTIFIERS

Identifiers are data elements that establish the unique identity of customers. They are the connecting points that enable the building of the single customer view using data from many sources. Frequently used identifiers include account number, DUNs number, and driver license number. Sometimes identifiers must be combined with other information such as birth date, name, and zip code to establish a unique identifier for an individual.

DEMOGRAPHICS

Demographics are descriptive information about a person that are the sorts of information gathered through the census to understand a population. Helpful demographic data elements include birth date, gender, marital status, number of dependents, occupation, and education level.

PSYCHOGRAPHICS

Psychographics are data inferred about the inner customer. This includes attitudes, beliefs, lifestyles, opinions, interests, motivations, preferences, and other psychological dimensions. This information is often discovered through surveys and social media research.

LOCATIONS (GEOGRAPHICS)

Location data is the answer to the "where" question. Postal address, work location, telephone numbers, and email addresses describe physical and virtual locations.

PRODUCTS

Product data describes the goods and services that the customer has purchased or has expressed an interest in. For a bank, this may be a listing of the types of accounts held by the customer. It can also include a list of products ordered. This information is useful for market basket analysis, as well as cross sell and up sell efforts.

INTERACTIONS

Interactions are customer touch points, where the organization and the customer are in contact. Interactions could be initiated by the customer or by the organization. Complaints, website visits, and warranty service requests are examples of customer initiated interactions. Outgoing sales calls and marketing campaigns are examples of organization initiated interactions. Building positive interactions is a key to building customer loyalty and retention.

TRANSACTIONS

A transaction is a unit of business exchange such as sales, shipments, deposits, withdrawals, and investments. Traditional data warehousing tended to focus on transactions, however, there is a marketing tendency to focus on interactions and relationships, rather than transactions.

MEASURES

Measures are quantitative metrics such as account balances, expenses, fees, and overdraft amounts. Some measures, such as Lifetime Customer Value (LCV), are calculated. For example, LCV may be calculated as the sum of projected revenues minus the sum of projected expenses discounted by a specified interest rate.

RELATIONSHIPS / HIERARCHIES

Relationships are associations between customers. For example, an individual may be a holder of a small account at a bank, while at the same time may be a CEO of a company with a large account. In this case, it would be an advantage to the bank to provide excellent service on the small account.

SINGLE CUSTOMER VIEW TIPS AND TRAPS

Following best practices in the area of Single Customer View increases the likelihood of success. Table 18-03 highlights tips and trips of SCV.

Table 18-03: Single Customer View Tips and Traps

Tips (Do This)	Traps (Don't Do this)
• "Start small, think big" • Get multiple perspectives on customers • Use Customer Data Integration (CDI) technologies • Create a common customer model • Include relationships between customers and their accounts • Consider external data sources	• Attempt to integrate all customer data at once • Fail to promote use by people who interact with customers • Fail to think from the customer perspective • Leave out the full picture when calculating customer value • Confuse CDI with DW and BI • Use duplicate and disparate data

Customer Segmentation

Customer Segmentation is the classification of customers for the purpose of improving profitability and/or achieving the organization's mission. Uses of customer segmentation can include:

- Determining the level of customer service
- Determining what to offer to the customer
- Determining whether to drop the customer.

There are a number of ways to segment customers. One of the most effective methods is through the use of segmentation factors that score or rank customers. The following steps are performed to segment customers using RFM (Recency, Frequency, and Monetary) analysis:

- Determine quintile ranking for each factor (quintiles are calculated by breaking data into five groups. These factors include:
  - o Recency – by date of most recent purchase
  - o Frequency – count of purchases over some time period
  - o Monetary – Dollar amount of purchases.
- This results in 3 sets of numbers with values 1 to 5.
- Each combination is a cell within a cube. This results in 125 cells for analysis.
- Each cell can be assigned a customer score and a treatment approach.
- Customers in cell 1-1-1 are the best customers. They buy the most goods, most often, and have bought most recently.
- Customers in cell 5-5-5 are the lowest ranked customers. They buy the fewest goods least often and have not purchased for a long time.

There are many characteristics which may be used to segment customers. Table 18-04 shows dimensions of demographics, behaviors, and interests that are supported by individual characteristics. The «xxx» entries are variables which apply to a particular customer group such as « plans to purchase a home » or « wants to retire early ».

Bands

A band is a grouping based on a range of values like those in Table 18-05. Bands support customer segmentation and simplify statistical analysis.

Figure 18-05: Customer Band Examples

Age Bands	Income Bands	Education Level Bands
Under 18	Less than $10,000	Not high school graduate
18 – 25	$10,000 – $35,000	
26 – 35	$35,001 – $50,000	High school graduate
36 – 45	$50,001 – $70,000	Some college
46 – 55	$70,001 – $100,000	Bachelor's
56 and above	More than $100,000	Master's
		Ph.D.

Table 18-04: Customer Dimensions and Attributes

Demographics	Behavior	Interests
Name	ATM Usage Count	Automobile Preference
Gender	Returns products	Hobbies
Birthdate	Requests service	Volunteer
Income Level	Mail Order Buyer	Products Purchased
Education Level	Files claim	Business Owner
IQ	Engagement Level	Favorite brands
Marital Status	Eats out	Plans to xxx
Number of Children	Loyalty Level	Wants to xxx
Household Size	Purchases by internet	Likes xxx
Living Parents	Purchases by direct mail	Dislikes xxx
Language	Answers email	Owns xxx
Ethnicity	Pays by credit card	Reads xxx
Race	Pays by debit card	Watches xxx
Occupation	Pays by check	Invests in xxx
Net Worth	Voting pattern	Fears xxx
Credit Score	Uses coupons	
Clothing Size	Pays in full	
Height	Pays minimum balance	
Weight	Uses Overdraft	
Accident Count	Risky behavior	
Felony Count	Visits to branch/store	
Relationships with other parties	Files complaint	
Telephone Number	Answers survey	
Address		
Length of Residence		
Zip Code		

Clusters

Clustering is a statistical technique for segmenting a population. This can include target market and customer service clusters. Acxiom PersonicX® provides segmentation on millions of United States consumers based on detailed information gathered about the American population. It has clustered people into 21 life stages divided into 70 segments/clusters. Examples of life stages include:

- **"Gen X Singles"** – Single households without children and low-middle income.
- **"Cash & Careers"** – Affluent people born in the mid-1960's and early 1970's who are childless and are aggressive money earners and investors.

- **"Boomer Barons"** – Wealthy baby boomers with high education levels who enjoy luxury homes.
- **"Mature Rustics"** – Near retirement blue-collar people with country values.

This information can be helpful in both understanding an overall market and in targeting offers to individual consumers. For example, a bank may target younger consumers who have the potential to become valuable customers.

Customer Analytics Terms

Customer analytics has its own terms, as defined in Table 18-06.

Table 18-06: Customer Analytics Terms

Term	Definition / Descriptions
Band	A band is a grouping based on a range of values such as age band and income band. Bands simplify statistical analysis.
Behavior	Actions taken by a party that are evaluated through analytics to gain insight into potential future behavior.
Campaign	A series of activities intended to market a brand, product, or service. Ideas for campaigns may be the result of customer analytics.
Communication Channel	A medium for communicating, such as telephone, email, mail, television, radio, or in person. Determining the effectiveness of communication channels enables more effective allocation of resources.
Clustering	Clustering is a statistical technique for grouping a population based on a shared characteristic. Factors commonly used in clustering include age, purchasing habits, income level, wealth level, education level, and preferences for luxury goods.
Cross-Sell	Cross-selling is the practice of selling multiple products and services to existing customers. Opportunities for cross-selling are the result of evaluating previous purchases and other customer characteristics.
Customer Data Integration	Customer Data Integration (CDI) is the process of bringing together information about customers from multiple data sources into a single database.
Customer Relationship Management	Customer Relationship Management (CRM) is an enterprise-wide strategy that seeks to make organizations customer-centric by finding, attracting, retaining, and serving customers. CRM mobilizes people, processes, and technologies to enhance customer relationships. It is a way of life and thinking, not just a software package.
Demographics	Information that describes characteristics of people such as gender, birth date, income level, and education level that may be used in analytics to segment the population to evaluate and predict future business opportunities.

Term	Definition / Descriptions
Detractor	A party who communicates negative information about an enterprise, brand, product, or service. Detractors feel negatively about an enterprise and are unlikely to recommend it to others. It is important to understand what they dislike to determine if there are factors within the business that need to be remediated.
Engagement	Activities involving a party interacting with an enterprise. A party is engaged when they interact by visiting a website or store, for example. Analytics evaluate the cause and results of a customer's engagement with an organization.
FICO	A credit score produced by the FICO corporation. The FICO score is frequently used to evaluate credit worthiness.
Hierarchy	A categorization that uses ranked order. For example, a geographic hierarchy could be organized with increasing rank by city, state, region, nation, and continent and used to determine similarities and differences in customers at the same or different levels of the hierarchy.
Interaction	An event during which a customer was in contact with the organization. There are a wide variety of interaction types, based on purpose and communication medium. Each interaction is an opportunity to gather more information about the customer and to provide an enhanced experience for them.
Interests	Something that holds the attention of somebody on an extended basis, such as a subject, hobby, or sport. Knowing a customer's interests provides some insight into how they may behave in relation to what the organization has to offer.
Lifetime Customer Value	Lifetime Customer Value (LCV) is a marketing metric that is calculated by summing the net present value of revenues and expenses projected for a customer relationship.
Customer Loyalty	Customer loyalty is a marketing metric that may be measured by: • Customer retention/defection rates • Referral count • Net Promoter Score • Tendency to purchase again or purchase different products
Marketing Channel	The path where products flow from producer to consumer. This path may be direct, where consumers buy directly from the producer, or complex, where many intermediaries are involved, such as wholesalers. Financial products might have a number of marketing channels such as: banks, wire houses, broker dealers and insurance agencies. Understanding the needs of marketing channels can lead to more effective product design, for example.
Personalization	The process of tailoring an interaction to the person involved and their preferences. Personalization could include showing information and products of interest.

Term	Definition / Descriptions
Preference	A choice made by a person, such as the type of preferred communication like email versus telephone or the frequency of communication like daily, weekly or monthly. The use of preferences requires capturing and storing those preferences.
Profile	A set of descriptors about a party that may have a specific subject such as demographics profile, interests profile, and behavior profile. Profiles are an aid to understanding customers and categorizing customers.
Promoter	A party who communicates positive information about an enterprise, brand, product, or service. Promoters feel positively about an enterprise and are likely to recommend it to others. The Net Promoter Score (NPS) is a method used to determine the promotion and detraction levels.
Psychographics	A customer segmentation method that uses criteria such as feelings, lifestyle, attitudes, personality, and motivation.
Relationship Marketing	A marketing approach that emphasizes a long term association with retention, rather than individual sales transactions.
Recency, Frequency and Monetary Analysis	Recency, Frequency, and Monetary (RFM) analysis results in a marketing metric that segments customers based on: • **Recency of purchase** – the more recent, the higher the score • **Frequency** – the more often, the higher the score • **Monetary** – the larger the purchase, the higher the score
Segment	A method of categorizing customers by divided them into groupings for analysis and marketing purposes.
Single Customer View	An approach that unifies information about customers so that all relevant activity can be seen at a single point. This often includes use of a database where customer data is integrated.
Syndicated Customer Data	Data about parties (individuals and/or organizations) provided by an external organization. For example, some organizations gather profiles of United States residents and make that data available to marketers.
Touch Point	A touch point is the same as an interaction.
Up Sell	Attempting to sell a higher end product or service to somebody who has purchased a lesser product or service. Customer analytics may be used to determine who to up sell to and which products to offer.

Analysis Types

There are many kinds of customer analysis. Table 18-07 provides an overview of several of these.

Table 18-07: Customer Analysis Types

Analysis Type	Description
Campaign Analysis	Campaign Analysis is an investigation into the effectiveness of marketing efforts. It tracks efforts to improve sales and the results of those efforts with a goal of making the best use of organization resources.
Call Center Management	Call Center Management is the direction and control of the call center, which is a group that provides service to customers over the telephone or internet.
Customer Churn Analysis	Customer Churn Analysis is an assessment of the degree that customers leave a company. Churn rate is another name for retention rate and is the inverse of customer loyalty.
Customer Satisfaction Analysis	Customer Satisfaction Analysis is an investigation about the feelings and perceptions of customers about a supplier. This analysis seeks to find the factors that cause satisfaction and dissatisfaction.
Market Basket Analysis	Market Basket Analysis is an investigation of the combinations of products that a customer purchases.
Market Share Analysis	Market Share Analysis is a procedure for determining the percentage of sales that a company, brand, or product has within a particular market area.
Market Analysis	An investigation of a market to understand its characteristics, including market size, growth rate, trends, and critical success factors.
Sales and Profitability Analysis	An assessment that compares the costs of sales with the sales revenue.
Sales, Marketing, & Channel Management	Analysis and management needs of marketing channels can lead to more effective allocation of marketing resources.
Store Operations Analysis	The use of analytic techniques to improve management of retail stores.
Subscriber Usage Pattern Discovery	The use of data analysis to understand how customers who subscribe to websites use those websites and the services within them. This includes navigation patterns, download usage, and timing.
Warranty Analysis	The analysis of repairs and services.

Learn More

Build your know-how in the areas of marketing and customer using these resources.

Visit a Website! Wikipedia provides a good introduction to customer analytics:

http://en.wikipedia.org/wiki/Customer_analytics

Get Research!

Search the web for research reports (filetype=pdf):

- Forrester Wave Marketing
- Gartner Magic Quadrant CRM

Read about it!

Try this book:

Blattberg, Robert C. *Database Marketing: Analyzing and Managing Customers.* Springer, 2009.

Key Points

- Understanding customers can result in improved customer service and loyalty.

- Customer analysis can help answer many questions about the customers, such as "What is the life-time value of this customer?"

- Single Customer View provides an integrated view of customer information. Customer identifiers such as account number and DUNs number support building an integrated customer view from multiple data sources.

- Demographic information such a birth date, gender and marital status are important to analyzing customers.

- Psychographic dimensions are also significant factors when analyzing customers.

- Customer segmentation is a method of classifying customers in order to improve profitability and achieve enterprise goals.

- RFM (Recency, Frequency, and Monetary) Analysis is a proven method for segmenting customers for many environments.

*The bitterness of poor quality remains long after the sweetness
of meeting the schedule has been forgotten.*

Urban Wisdom

In this chapter you will learn how to:

- Put together and execute a testing approach that ensures a trusted system
- Create and execute a plan for rolling out your data warehouse
- Organize a sustainable program to keep your BI and data warehousing efforts moving in the right direction.

In Chapters 1 through 18 of this book you gained knowledge about the data warehousing and BI software development lifecycle. You started with the business case and project management. Next you learned about business and technical architecture. You explored data topics and then BI tools and applications. Now is the time for a strong finish.

The chapter is organized in three sections that show how to successfully complete data warehousing / business intelligence projects.

- Section 19A – Testing the Data Warehouse
- Section 19B – Rolling Out the Data Warehouse
- Section 19C – Sustaining the Data Warehouse.

Section 19A – Testing the Data Warehouse

When you have completed this section you will be able to:

- Discuss elements of the data warehousing test plan
- Understand the roles needed for data warehouse testing
- Discuss data warehousing test responsibilities
- Link requirements with tests
- Specify the types of tests required
- Select test environments.

Testing the data warehouse and business intelligence system is critical to its success. Without testing, the data warehouse could produce incorrect answers and quickly

299

lose the faith of the business intelligence users. Effective testing requires putting together the right processes, people, and technology, and deploying them in productive ways.

DATA WAREHOUSE TESTING RESPONSIBILITIES

Who should be involved with testing? The right team is essential to success:

- **Business Analysts** elicit and document requirements
- **QA (Quality Assurance) Testers** develop and execute test plans and test scripts
- **Infrastructure People** set up test environments
- **Developers** perform unit tests of their deliverables
- **DBAs** test for performance and stress
- **Business Users** perform functional tests, including User Acceptance Tests (UAT).

BUSINESS REQUIREMENTS AND TESTING

When should your project begin to think about testing? The answer is simple – at the beginning of the project. Successful testing begins with the elicitation and documentation of requirements. Without requirements, it is difficult to measure system correctness.

Expect to produce a Requirements Traceability Matrix (RTM) that cross references data warehouse and business intelligence features to business requirements. The RTM is a primary input to the Test Plan.

DATA WAREHOUSING TEST PLAN

The Test Plan, typically prepared by the QA Testers, describes the tests that must be performed to validate the data warehousing and business intelligence system. It describes the types of tests to be performed and the required system features that will be covered.

Test Cases are the detailed components that enable implementation of the Test Plan. Each Test Case itemizes steps that must be taken to test the system, along with their expected results. A Test Execution Log tracks each test along with the results (pass or fail) of each iteration.

TESTING ENVIRONMENTS AND INFRASTRUCTURE

Typically, multiple environments and database versions are set up and maintained to support the system during its lifecycle:

- Development
- Quality Assurance (QA)
- Staging / Performance Testing
- Production
- Disaster Recovery (DR).

These database environments and versions improve productivity and system quality. Developers can be producing new system functionality at the same time as testers that are validating the system without interfering with the business who are using the production versions of the system. A Disaster Recovery (DR) version of the system is kept up to date so that service in not interrupted if the system stops functioning.

The following kinds of tools can facilitate testing and problem correction:

- **Automated test tool** – enables tests to be created, managed and run in a repeatable fashion through a user interface.
- **Test data generator** – produces data to test the data warehouse based on input parameters.
- **Test data masker** – hides or obscures confidential data such a social security number.
- **Defect manager** – tracks defects including description, correction and validation.
- **Automated test scripts** – tests to be run and validated in a repeatable fashion through files of text based commands.

UNIT TESTING FOR THE DATA WAREHOUSE

Developers should perform tests on their deliverables during and after their development process. The unit test is performed on individual components and is based on the developer's knowledge of the requirements and what their deliverable should produce. It should be performed before deliverables are turned over to QA. Tested components are likely to have fewer bugs.

QA TESTERS PERFORM MANY TYPES OF TESTS

QA Testers design and execute a number of tests including:

Integration Test

Tests the system operation from beginning to end, focusing on how data flows through the system. This is sometimes called "system testing" or "end-to-end testing".

Regression Test

Validates that the system continues to function correctly after being changed.

CAN THE DATA WAREHOUSE PERFORM?

Tests that determine how well the system performs with heavy loads of data should be designed and executed.

Extract Performance Test

Test the performance of the system when extracting a large amount of data.

Transform and Load Performance Test

Test the performance of the system when transforming and loading a large amount of data. High volume testing is sometimes called stress testing.

Analytics Performance Test

Test the performance of the system when manipulating the data through calculations.

BUSINESS USERS TEST BUSINESS INTELLIGENCE

Does the system produce the results desired by the business users? The main concern is functionality, so business users perform functional tests to make sure that the system meets their requirements. The testing is performed through the user interface (UI), which includes data exploration and reporting.

Correctness Test

The system must produce correct results. The measures and supporting context need to match numbers in other systems and must be calculated correctly.

Usability Test

The system should be as easy to use as possible. Usability testing involves business users exercising the business intelligence system to ensure it does what they wanted and expected.

Performance Test

The system must be able to return results quickly without bogging down other resources.

BUSINESS INTELLIGENCE MUST BE BELIEVED

Quality must be baked into the data warehouse or users will quickly lose faith in the business intelligence produced. It then becomes very difficult to get people back on board.

Putting the quality in requires both the testing described in this chapter and data quality at the source described in Chapter 10, Database Technology, to launch a successful data warehousing / business intelligence effort.

Testing Key Points

- Testing the data warehousing and business intelligence solution is critical to success. Without testing, the system may produce incorrect results and lose credibility with its users.

- Testing is a team effort that involves QA testers, business users, business analysts, and support personnel.

- Documented business requirements determine the criteria for system correctness and are essential for testing.

- Computer environments such as development, QA, and model office support testing.

- Multiple types of tests are needed, including unit tests, performance tests, business correctness tests, and usability tests.

Section 19B – Business Intelligence Rollout

Projects happen in two ways: a) Planned and then executed or

b) Executed, stopped, planned and then executed.

Urban Wisdom

After studying this section you will be able to:

- Prepare for rolling out your data warehouse
- Understand rollout critical success factors
- Avoid rollout traps and pitfalls.

In the prior section, you learned about the importance of testing for data warehouse and business intelligence success. Test plans were discussed, as well as testing by developers, QA people, and business people.

In this section, you will learn that rolling out a successful data warehousing project requires following a Data Warehousing and Business Intelligence Methodology to increase your probability of success. The following topics are explained:

- Pre-deployment and planning
- Deployment
- Training
- Follow up
- Assessment of results.

PRE-DEPLOYMENT FOR BUSINESS INTELLIGENCE ROLLOUT

Prepare an announcement that shows business users and others the benefits they can expect from the business intelligence and data warehousing system. When stakeholders understand how the new system can help them, they are more likely to be supporters instead of detractors. You need all of the supporters that you can get. Building and continuing to build support is a continuation of the effort to obtain support starting at the beginning of the project.

Documentation is also critical to successful data warehousing roll-out. Some important documentation items include:

- Preview of what is coming
- Schedule of activities and deliverables for the deployment
- Schedule of training
- Training manuals and other training materials
- Procedures and how to instructions
- Frequently Asked Questions (FAQ) or online help.

Capacity review and performance testing are also important parts of the pre-deployment step. Capacity review helps to confirm the computer resources that will be needed. Performance testing tests the load on the computer hardware and software to make sure that they can perform required activities in a timely manner as needed by the business. Finally, I recommend running a test in the production environment with a full database.

Sometimes a deployment does not work as expected. A rollback and fallback plan should be prepared to respond to this contingency. The fallback plan should describe what needs to be done to ensure that business can continue in case of problems.

A training plan is important to the success of the new system. It should emphasize benefits that trainees will derive from the system. For example, the trainees may spend more time doing the interesting work of analysis and less time doing the tedious work of data gathering In addition, the new system should enable the trainees to be more valuable to the business. Understanding of these benefits should raise their interest level and their focus, as well as help get them onboard with the new system.

The training plan should:

- Assess the need for training
- Develop the trainers and power users
- Plan a pilot deployment
- Plan training for a wider audience.

Training will also be needed for the follow-up phase. This will include training of users on a wider scale.

DEPLOYMENT OF DATA WAREHOUSES

I recommend a pilot deployment to a select group, probably power users or those in a particular department or division because you will be learning from the pilot deployment. Start small, using a pilot, then obtain feedback that can be added to the FAQ. This approach will head off future questions, enabling quick answers and smoother operation. Also, changes to the system may be required as the system is used in the real world. Be ready to make adjustments in response to results of the pilot deployment.

A phased deployment works well in many organizations. Start in one department and then extend to additional departments; or, as recommended above, begin with power users who will, in turn, train other users and expand use of the system.

TRAINING BUSINESS INTELLIGENCE AND DATA WAREHOUSE USERS

There are a number of ways training can be delivered. One way is through brownbag lunches. This leads to informal, friendly discussions with business people and other stakeholders. Brownbag lunches will enable them to ask questions and get immediate answers. These sessions are also a great source of feedback.

Webinars are another effective method of training for business intelligence and data warehousing. They are available through the Internet or you may create these training sessions yourself. Webinars are very helpful when people who are to be trained are spread out geographically. For example, you may have users in both Kansas and California. In that case, a webinar is a great way to obtain or provide training.

The data warehousing system's support people also need training and support documentation. Acquiring or developing training material should be part of the project plan. Support people should be included in system testing so they gain experience prior to deployment. They have distinct tasks that are different from business users. They need to be ready to carry out operations such as monitoring the system, backing out data and correcting problems. Monitoring tools and recovery jobs should be ready to assist the support team.

Administrative support people will require training, as well. The administrators will be configuring the system to make it more responsive. They will also be performing functions such as adding new users, executing reports and making reports available.

FOLLOW-UP SUPPORT FOR THE DATA WAREHOUSE

The business intelligence system does not run by itself. The business and other stakeholders will require ongoing support to have a successful system. A help desk that can be accessed by telephone or e-mail is a good way to provide follow-up support. The help desk can be equipped with trained people ready to answer questions in the FAQ and beyond.

A successful business intelligence system will gain in demand and users will want to do more advanced work. Follow-up training in advanced techniques will help with this process. In addition, new people may be joining the group of users, so earlier training sessions may need to be repeated for this audience.

BUSINESS INTELLIGENCE FOLLOW-UP ASSESSMENT

It is important to measure the success or failure of a program like the business intelligence / data warehouse program through follow-up with users of the system. Check with users to make sure business requirements have been met. Conduct surveys, face-to-face meetings, and focus groups to determine what went right and what went wrong. Ask what should be done differently.

A project audit report should be developed and shared with project stakeholders and management. Use the lessons learned from the project to add to the overall knowledge base for future projects. The project audit report answers questions:

- How well did the project meet goals and objectives?
- What went well?
- What did not go well?
- Was the schedule achieved?
- Was the budget met?

Deployment Key Points

- Communication is critical to the success of data warehousing and business intelligence rollout. Let business users and others know what to expect.

- Establish and define roles and responsibilities for deployment, training and system administration.

- Develop a training plan that is addressed to the appropriate audience, from power users to support personnel.

- Start with a pilot deployment and then gradually make the system available to a wider audience.

- Provide follow-up support including a help desk armed with needed information.

- A follow up assessment measures the degree of success or failure of programs. This leads to improvements in the system and better management of future projects.

Section 19C – Sustainable Business Intelligence

In our view, successful reform is not an event. It is a sustainable process that will build on its own successes – a virtuous cycle of change.

Abdallah II, King of Jordan

After studying this section you will be able to:

- Understand how DWBI can be sustained over longer periods of time
- Move data warehousing forward by following best practices
- Avoid data warehousing traps.

In the previous section, you gained an understanding of how to rollout a successful data warehouse. Topics covered included pre-deployment and planning, deployment, training, and follow-up and assessment of the results.

Are you concerned that your data warehousing and business intelligence effort could lose steam and grind to a halt? Remember that success is based on the 80/20 rule – 80% of success is based on people and process factors, while only 20% of success is based on technology.

BI / DATA WAREHOUSING PEOPLE AND PROCESS TIPS

The most critical factors in the success of business intelligence and data warehousing are people and process oriented. To maintain the "political will" to keep the DWBI initiative moving forward, be sure to:

- Communicate – stay "top of mind"
- Maintain executive support
- Support enterprise strategies and mission
- Focus on business needs and pain points
- Relate to business capabilities and process
- Add value beyond standard reporting
- Build in manageable-sized pieces
- Expand the user audience through training
- Obtain and keep funding
- Identify quantifiable measures
- Under promise and over deliver.

Successful DWBI initiatives are led through an ongoing governance process with buy-in from top executives. The Return On Investment (ROI) from a winning program can be high (100 to over 1000%) and thus earn executive support.

BI / DATA WAREHOUSING PEOPLE AND PROCESS TRAPS

Disregarding or minimizing the importance of people and process is often at the heart of failed DWBI efforts. Put people and process first to avoid these traps:

- Working in the background, keeping it quiet

- Focusing on technology rather than the business
- Talking in generalities and principles
- "Build it and they will come"
- Using "Big Bang" implementation
- Assuming that benefits are intuitively obvious
- Using informal organization instead of formal governance.

Failing DWBI initiatives often lose touch with the organization and people that they should be helping.

SUSTAINING BI / DATA WAREHOUSING TIPS

Technology is a necessary part of winning DWBI projects. While technology by itself cannot make a project successful, poorly chosen or utilized technology can be a killer. Use technology appropriately by:

- Monitoring data warehouse performance
- Enabling self-service
- Securing the data warehouse
- Adding processing capacity to support the user community
- Adding storage capacity to satisfy growing data needs
- Monitoring errors and correcting root causes
- Using proven architectural patterns
- Building a federated architecture to support varied environments and requirements.

The need for technical resources often skyrockets for the successful DWBI effort. More and more people access the system, increasing the need for processing power. Also, the amount of data storage needed increases as further detail is captured.

SUSTAINING BI / DATA WAREHOUSING TRAPS

Improper technology or an over-emphasis on technology can drag down the DWBI system. Avoid these traps:

- Ignoring increases in system use
- Ignoring system performance monitoring
- Neglecting upgrades
- Engaging in "Religious Technology Wars"
- Acquiring incompatible software or hardware.

The winning Business Intelligence / Data Warehousing effort focuses on the highest priority areas (people and process) while doing a good job with technology. Making the right moves while avoiding the bad plays should lead to victory.

Sustaining Key Points

- Keep up the momentum. Communicate direction and wins to a wide audience, including executive management.

- Quantify results – show that the business case is being realized.

- Avoid people and process traps such as keeping it quiet and using an informal organization rather than explicit governance.

- Provide good data warehouse and business intelligence performance by monitoring system performance and correcting any slowdown before it causes user problems.

- Avoid data warehousing technology traps such as neglecting to monitor the system or make upgrades.

Term	Definition
Abstraction	Abstraction captures the most important features shared by a group of similar entities. For example, a party is an abstraction of persons and organizations.
Additive Fact	An additive fact is a set of measurements in a dimensional data store where all numeric measurements can be correctly summed across all dimensions.
Aggregate	A process where data is added, producing summarized information. Calculating and storing aggregate results can greatly improve the speed and efficiency of data mart query results.
Analysis	The process of breaking a complex problem or situation into smaller parts to better understand and potentially change outcomes.
Architecture	The ANSI/IEEE Standard 1471-2000 defines the architecture of software-intensive systems as: "the fundamental organization of a system, embodied in its components, their relationships to each other and the environment, and the principles governing its design and evolution."
Atomic Stage	An area of a data warehouse system that is a simple integration point for data before it is placed in the atomic portion of the data warehouse.
Atomic Warehouse	An area of the data warehouse where data is broken down into its lowest level components in preparation for export to data marts. This area of the data warehouse tends to be normalized.
Attribute	An attribute is a sub-part of an entity that characterizes or describes the entity. Attributes are also referred to as characteristics and properties.

Term	Definition
Balanced Scorecard (BSC)	A management approach that evaluates and improves the overall performance of an organization. It combines multiple factors (financial performance, customer satisfaction, organizational learning, and production and innovation) to produce scores that can be included in scorecards. BSC was originated by Robert Kaplan and David Norton in 1992.
Best of Breed Vs. Total Product Line	The "Best of Breed" approach of software acquisition favors acquiring each piece of software based on its individual capabilities and performance. This can be a problem because each best of breed software component may be sourced from a different vendor and not integrate well with other tools. In contrast, the "Total Product Line" approach favors acquiring an integrated suite of products from a single vendor. This avoids productivity difficulties of integrating dissimilar software products.
Bridge Table	An associative table that implements a many to many relationship between a dimension table and fact table. It is used when there is an allocation of fact amounts to multiple dimension instances.
Business Activity Monitoring (BAM)	A technology that is used to monitor and measure business activities, including volumes, cycle times, errors, and exception conditions.
Business Architecture	A strategic blueprint of an enterprise or unit of an enterprise including analytic capabilities. The business architecture shows how multiple views of the future combine to support the organization's stated vision and mission. The multiple views include functional decomposition of the business value chain into business functions and capabilities.
Business Intelligence (BI)	The people, tools, and processes that support planning and decision-making, both strategic and operational, for an organization.
Business Intelligence Competency Center (BICC)	A team that focuses on the effective use of business intelligence in an organization. This cross-functional team is skilled in BI tools, processes, and people roles.

Term	Definition
Business Process	A series of on-going steps, implemented through a combination of people and technology, aimed toward achieving a business goal in support of a business capability.
Candidate Key	A set of one or more NOT NULL attributes that uniquely identify an entity instance or table row and could possibly be used as a primary key. The candidate key content must stay constant and include only the minimal number of attributes required for uniqueness.
Canonical Model	A model that is held in common. Data from multiple data sources, each with their individual models, can be integrated by storing in a database with a canonical model.
Cell	A data point within an OLAP cube that is a measure assigned to a specific combination of dimensions, such as dollar value of sales for product X in time period Y and territory Z.
Change Data Capture (CDC)	A process that captures only changed data, rather than all data. CDC typically works through analysis of database logs to increase efficiency.
Cluster	A grouping of data points with a large degree of affinity. The data points have much in common with data points in the cluster and differ from data points in other clusters.
Code	A substitute identifier and allowed value for an attribute that is limited to a specific set of values. For example, gender codes 'M' for male and 'F' for female.
Complex Event Processing (CEP)	A monitoring and processing system that accepts data describing many events throughout an organization, correlates the events, and then recommends action. For example, CEP may detect potential credit card fraud by monitoring a pattern of unusual credit card charges, then recommend follow-up with the account holder.
Conceptual Data Model	A graphic representation of high-level business or information subject areas. It may be represented as a domain model and/or a high-level class model.
Conformed Dimension	A consistently defined dimension that qualifies multiple facts. For example, a conformed product dimension could qualify both a sale_fact and a customer_feedback_fact.

Term	Definition
Cardinality	The number of entities that may participate in a given relationship, expressed as: one-to-one, one-to-many, or many-to-many.
Constraint	A limit or requirement that is placed on data. Constraints could be on integrity and/or specific values.
Control Group	A group of subjects who are not given an experimental treatment, but participate in all other aspects of an experiment in order to rule out other shared factors. For example, pharmaceutical control group participants are given a placebo.
Customer Data Integration (CDI)	The set of people, processes and tools that supports the management and unification of customer information from multiple sources.
Customer Equity	The total asset value that relationships with customers have to an organization.
Dashboard	A display of indicators that shows the current status of key metrics in a graphic format resembling aircraft control panels with gauges and charts.
Data	An isolated fact typically stored in the form of numbers, letters, or images. Data is the raw material making up information, which is data put into context.
Data Architect	A person who is responsible for laying out the data architecture for an organization, including databases, data integration, data models, and data definitions.
Data Cleansing	An automated process where errors in data are corrected.
Data Custodian	A person responsible for safe-guarding data content, as directed by a data owner or data steward.
Data Dictionary	An artifact that contains definitions of data, along with descriptions of characteristics such as data type.
Data Element	An element or piece of data. The same data element may be included in multiple entities.
Data Governance	The overall management of data and information, including people, processes, and technology that improve the value obtained from data and information by treating data as an asset.

Term	Definition
Data Integration	The technique of moving data or otherwise making data available across data stores. The data integration process can include extraction, movement, validation, cleansing, standardization, transformation, and loading of data.
Data Integration Competency Center (DICC)	A team that focuses on the effective use of data integration in an organization. This cross-functional team is skilled in tools and techniques such as data mapping, ETL, and SOA.
Data Lineage	Data lineage is a form of metadata that describes the flow of individual data elements from data source to intermediate storage to target.
Data Mapping	Data mapping is the process of documenting the movement of data from data source to data target at both the entity and attribute level.
Data Mart	A data mart is a database that is part of a data warehouse system where data is stored for presentation and user access. Early definitions of data marts specified that they were targeted to specific subjects and business processes. Later, in practice, the data mart has become a database that is organized into facts and dimensions which can cross subjects.
Data Model	A graphic representation of data and information used to understand and design data and databases.
Data Modeler	An individual who creates and maintains data models – graphic representations of data and information used to understand and design data and databases.
Data Mining	Data mining is the application of analytical methods to data. This can include finding patterns, clustering data, and predicting outcomes.
Data Owner	Individuals who have management accountability for specific domains of data at a tactical level. The data owner appoints one or more data stewards as guardians of the data.
Data Partition	A means of dividing data within a table. This can be done by placing specific rows at different locations or by separating the attributes of the table.
Data Profiling	A technique of understanding data through exploration and comparison. Patterns such as typical values, outlying values, ranges, and allowed values are identified.

Term	Definition
Data Quality Management	The discipline of ensuring that data is fit for use by the enterprise. It includes obtaining requirements and rules that specify the dimensions of quality that are required, such as accuracy, completeness, timeliness, and allowed values.
Data Source	Data sources are the origination points of data. They may include transactional systems, process-oriented systems, specification systems, and syndicated data.
Data Stakeholder	A party who is impacted by data and therefore has a voice in its governance.
Data Steward	An individual who is a guardian of specific data subjects at a tactical level, including determining data requirements, definitions, naming, security, quality, and compliance.
Data Warehouse	A database that contains data that will be copied to data marts for decision support. It serves as a data integration point for information gathered from source systems before it is placed in data marts.
Data Warehouse Appliance	A product that integrates a number of components together for an overall data warehouse solution. Components of a data warehouse appliance may include: Hardware (Servers, Disk) Operating System Database Management System Industry Data Model Data Integration Tools BI Tools and "Canned Reports".
Data Warehouse Architecture	A high-level blueprint for the design and implementation of a data warehousing system, including: Business architecture Application architecture Information architecture Technology architecture.
Data Warehouse Bus	A method of coordinating data marts by matching conformed dimensions to facts. This approach promotes drill across. This concept was pioneered by Ralph Kimball.
Data Warehouse System	An organized collection of people, data, processes, and technologies that manages data for decision support.

Term	Definition
Data Vault®	A concept originated by Dan Lindstedt which organizes data for decision support into hubs, links, and satellites. This method supports rapid and flexible loading of warehouse data.
Definition	A statement that communicates the meaning of a term. Definitions make it clear what a term includes and excludes. In addition, it may include classification as well as examples and uses of the term, to assist in clarifying the term.
Degenerate Dimension	A dimensional attribute that is directly added to a fact table without a supporting dimension table.
Denormalization	Restructuring data from a non-redundant (normalized) form that is optimized for transaction processing to a redundant form that is optimized for DSS.
Dice	An operation used to analyze dimensional data where the cube is rotated by looking at different dimensions to provide a different perspective. For example, analysis could be changed from a location perspective to a calendar perspective.
Dimension	A dimension is a database table that contains properties that identify and categorize. The attributes serve as labels for reports and as data points for summarization. In the dimensional model, dimensions surround and qualify facts.
Drill Down	An operation for navigating down a dimensional hierarchy to a lower, more detailed level.
DSS	Decision Support System
EIS	Executive Information System
Enterprise Application Integration (EAI)	A method of integrating software applications by using application program interfaces (APIs).
Enterprise Information Integration (EII)	A method of data integration that provides access to multiple data sources without the need to move the data to a common database such as a data warehouse. This method supports a federated schema, in which multiple data sources act like a single data source.
Entity	A person, place, thing, or idea of interest to the business. It is a primary unit of data modeling.

Term	Definition
Extract, Transform, And Load (ETL)	A batch process wherein data is obtained from a data source, modified, and placed in a data target.
Extracting	Obtaining information from a data source.
Fact	A set of measurements in a dimensional data store. It tends to contain quantitative data that are displayed in the body of reports. It often contains amounts of money and quantities of things. In the dimensional model, the fact is surrounded by dimensions that categorize the fact.
Factless Fact	A fact table, also called a junction table, that lacks specific measurements, but behaves like a fact in that it is related to dimensions.
Federated Data Warehouse	A federated data warehouse is an integrated set of data warehouses and/or data marts. It uses data virtualization or data movement to join data from multiple systems and/or locations.
Field Aggregation	Multiple columns in the same row/record are summed or otherwise manipulated.
Foreign Key	A set of one or more attributes that are also the primary key of a related entity, enabling navigation between the entities.
Functional Requirement	The features and functions of a system requested by the user(s) for whom the system is being developed. What the system is supposed to do for those who use it.
Grain / Granularity	The level of summarization of facts. A fine grained fact might contain information about a single transaction, while a course grained fact might contain information that summarizes multiple transactions over a period of time.
Grey Data	Data that varies in quality and completeness. It is often unstructured data such as web pages, free form text, emails, tweets, and other documents.
Hierarchy	An arrangement of member organized into levels where each member has one parent and may have multiple children. Some hierarchies have a fixed number of levels while others have an open ended number of levels.
Hierarchy Helper Dimension	A specialized type of dimension that enables navigation of a hierarchy. It relates parent and child entities while also showing the level within the hierarchy.

Term	Definition
Highly Summarized Data	An aggregation of a large amount of underlying data; typically over 20 rows of detail data summarized into 1 row of aggregated data.
Information	A meaningful arrangement or grouping of data.
Information Lifecycle Management (ILM)	Information Lifecycle Management is the discipline of specifying and managing information from its conception to its disposal. Information activities that make up ILM include classification, creation, distribution, use, maintenance, and disposal.
Instrumentation	An automated method of gathering information through measurement devices such as cameras, factory sensors, health monitors, smart phones, and gas meters. Instrumentation may provide an information stream at a faster rate than it can be stored and processed, therefore it may need to be processed immediately without storing details.
Junk Dimension	A dimension that contains unrelated attributes that have been placed in the same table for purposes of convenience or efficiency. This reduces the number of dimensions and the number of foreign keys needed in fact tables.
Key	One or more attributes that identify an instance or row of data.
Key Performance Indicator (KPI)	A metric that is linked to a specific target. Often, the KPI represents how far away the metric is from the target.
Knowledge	An understanding that is the result of interpreted information and that can lead to action.
Landing Stage	An area of a data warehouse system where data is first placed after extraction from a source system.
Logical Data Model	A graphic representation of data needed by a business area/system. It is often represented as an Entity Relationship Diagram (ERD). The logical data model is not aimed at a specific physical database solution.
Logical Key	A set of one or more attributes that are understood by users of a system and that identify an instance or row of an entity. This is the same as a natural key.
Loading	Placing data into a target database (data warehouse or data mart).

Term	Definition
Lightly Summarized Data	Data that aggregates a small amount of underlying data; typically under 20 rows of detail data summarized to 1 row of aggregated data.
Mapping	Documenting the assignment of specific source information to target information.
Master Data Management (MDM)	An activity focused on producing and making available a "golden record" of essential business entities such as customers, products, and financial accounts.
Materialized View	A SQL view of data containing predefined filters, joins, and aggregations designed to improve performance. This view is stored in a way that is rapidly retrievable and does not require a re-run of the underlying view.
Measure	A determination of quantitative characteristics of something such as count, amount, size, quality, weight, temperature, or timing.
Metadata	Information that describes and specifies data related objects. This description can include a definition of the data, its structure and storage, its business use, and processes that act on the data. Metadata is often called "data about data."
Metadata Repository	A system and data store that manages metadata, which is information that describes and specifies data related objects.
Metric	A direct quantitative measurement related to an organization.
Molap Cube	A structure within a multi-dimensional database that enables fast access of data from multiple perspectives, known as dimensions.
Multi-Dimensional Online Analytical Processing (MOLAP)	Multi-dimensional OnLine Analytical Processing – Where data is already stored in a multi-dimensional array, cube structure, which includes all possible combinations of data and enables each cell to be accessed directly.
Natural Key	A set of one or more attributes that are understood by users of a system and that identify an instance or row of an entity. This is the same as a logical key.
Next Best Action	An immediate action recommended by rules discovered through data mining or statistics that will produce optimal results.

Term	Definition
Normalization	A data modeling process that effectively minimizes data redundancy and dependency by adhering to these principles: "One fact in one place!" "The whole key and nothing but the key" "A place for everything and everything in its place"
OLAP	On-Line Analytical Processing
OLTP	On-Line Transaction Processing
Operational Data Store (ODS)	A database that can store data about business actions such as receipts, issues, purchase orders, etc. The ODS can also act as a data integration hub and data warehouse.
Optimization Analytics	The use of analytic methods such as data mining and statistics to make decisions with the best outcomes. For example, optimization analytics may recommend the most profitable price to offer to an auto insurance customer.
Outlier Dimension	A dimension that implements de-normalization by qualifying another dimension. This results in a snowflake schema.
Pattern	A reusable solution to a frequently occurring problem in software design. The star schema may be considered a pattern.
Performance Management	A set of management and analytic processes that is used to control and improve organizational performance, which is the accomplishment of goals through execution of tasks that are measured and compared to goals. Other names for this are Business Performance Management (BPM), Corporate Performance Management (CPM), and Enterprise Performance Management (EPM).
Performance Measurement	A quantification of work activities and results into financial, time, satisfaction level, or physical units. It is a kind of metric.
Physical Data Model	A graphic representation of data needed by a business area/system whose design takes into account specific physical database design and performance considerations. It is often represented as an Entity Relationship Diagram (ERD).
Pivot	An operation for navigating dimensional data where a dimension used in a query is changed to present data from a different perspective.

Term	Definition
Power User	A person who has a much higher degree of competence in the use of a system than typical users, and who is authorized to use advanced system features. The power user is called upon to solve difficult problems and to mentor others.
Predictive Analytics	The use of analytic methods such as data mining and statistics to anticipate future outcomes. For example, predictive analytics may provide insights into future demand for a product or the buying habits of a customer.
Project Plan	A document or set of documents that describes a project in terms of objectives, scope, schedule, budget, and resources.
Project Roadmap	A high-level plan that coordinates multiple project plans. The project roadmap is larger in scope than a single project plan.
Recommendation Engine	A software component that recommends a course of action based on an analysis of the facts. A recommendation engine may recommend the size of the credit limit to offer to a banking customer for example.
Reference Architecture	A proven template for a solution in an architectural domain. A reference architecture may specify a technical stack for data warehouse architectures, for example.
Regression Model	A statistical model that predicts the value of one variable based on the value(s) of one or more other variables. For example, the variable of credit worthiness might be predicted based on credit history, college grade point average, and driving record.
Report	A listing of information.
RFM	A method of customer segmentation based on Recency, Frequency and Monetary return: Recency – by date of most recent purchase Frequency – count of purchases over some time period Monetary – Dollar amount of purchases.
Relational On-Line Analytical Processing (ROLAP)	Where data is stored in a SQL database that is organized into tables and columns.
Roll-Up	An operation for navigating up a dimensional hierarchy to a higher, more summarized level and data is aggregated by removing one or more dimensions.

Term	Definition
Slowly Changing Dimension (SCD)	Slowly Changing Dimensions are dimensions where the logical key is constant and additional data rarely changes.
SCD Type 0	A dimension that does not change. Values are inserted and then never updated.
SCD Type 1	A kind of Slowly Changing Dimension where only the current version of data is stored. Updates are made to the data and history is not maintained.
SCD Type 2	A kind of Slowly Changing Dimension where a new row is inserted into the dimension table for each change. This preserves a history of all changes.
SCD Type 3	A kind of Slowly Changing Dimension where the dimension table contains one or more columns to store prior values.
Score	A number calculated from KPIs that expresses the accomplishments of a person or team and can be used for rankings.
Scorecard	A report or display that shows the performance of individuals or organizations for a specific time period. It typically contains multiple scores derived from KPIs, with weighted ranking between those scores.
Scrum	An iterative approach and framework that enables agile software development. The scrum master is the person who manages the scrum process. A scrum is organized into iterations called sprints.
Semi-Additive Fact	A set of measurements in a dimensional data store where there are limits to the measurements that can be summed. For example, summing may apply to some dimensions and not others.
Slice and Dice	An operation used to analyze dimensional data where the number of dimensions is reduced in order to focus on a specific area. For example, one could look at a slice for a specific product or group of products.
Slowly Changing Dimension	See SCD.
Snapshot Fact	A fact that captures measurements about an entity or process as of a point in time, such as customer account balance snapshot or insurance policy heading snapshot.

Term	Definition
Snowflake Schema	A form of dimensional model where each fact is connected to multiple dimensions which are, in turn, further categorized by outlier dimensions.
SOA	Service Oriented Architecture.
Source System	A system or application where data originates.
Star Schema	A form of dimensional model where each fact is connected to multiple denormalized dimensions that are not further categorized by outlier dimensions.
Statistics	The application of mathematics to understanding and predicting data. It tends to be directed and to use samples rather than full populations.
Storage Tier	Data storage categorized with a goal of balancing storage requirements with cost. Tier 1 might contain frequently used, high value data that requires more expensive storage media. Tiers 2 and 3 would be progressively less expensive.
Surrogate Key	A primary that substitutes for a natural key. It is typically a sequence number, assigned arbitrarily, and in a simple format such as an integer or string.
Target	A specification of a goal to be reached. It includes one or more measurements, a timeframe, and assignment of accountability. The target may be specified in terms of levels, with a minimum threshold and stretch targets.
Variance From Plan	The difference between actual performance and target performance. Variance from plan can be expressed in absolute units or as a percentage.
Wireframe Design	A visual blueprint for a user interface or report that depicts the main elements such as information content and navigation without specifying details like fonts or colors.
Wisdom	The ability to evaluate the best courses of action based on knowledge and experience.

Data Warehouse

Kimball, Ralph. *The Data Warehouse Toolkit: The Complete guide to Dimensional Modeling, Second Edition.* John Wiley & Sons, Inc., 2002.

Kimball, Ralph. *The Data Warehouse Lifecycle Toolkit, Second Edition.* John Wiley & Sons, Inc., 2008.

Adamson, Christopher, and Michael Venerable. *Data Warehouse Design Solutions.* John Wiley & Sons, Inc., 1998.

Imhoff, Claudia, Nicholas Galemmo, and Jonathan G. Geiger. *Mastering Data Warehouse Design: Relational and Dimensional Techniques.* John Wiley & Sons, Inc., 2003. Inmon, W.H. *Building the Data Warehouse, Third Edition.* John Wiley & Sons, Inc., 2002.

Todman, Chris. *Designing a Data Warehouse: Supporting Customer Relationship Management.* Prentice Hall PTR, 2001.

Hackney, Douglas. Understanding and Implementing Successful Data Marts. Addison-Wesley Developers Press, 1997.

Business Intelligence and Analytics

Ayres, Ian. *Super Crunchers: Why Thinking-By-Numbers is the New Way to be Smart.* New York NY: Bantam Books, 2007.

Malik, Shadan. *Enterprise Dashboards: Design and Best Practices.* John Wiley & Sons, Inc., 2005.

Kaplan, Robert S., and David P. Norton. *The Balanced Scorecard: Translating Strategy into Action.* Harvard Business Press, 1996.

Tufte, Edward. *The Visual Display of Quantitative Information.* Graphics Press, 2001.

Howson, Cindi. *Successful Business Intelligence: Secrets to Making BI a Killer App.* McGraw-Hill Companies, 2008.

Davenport, Thomas, and Jeanne G. Harris. *Analytics at Work: Smarter Decisions, Better Results*. Harvard Business School Publishing Corporation, 2010.

Brown, Mark Graham. *Keeping Score: Using the Right Metrics to Drive World-Class Performance*. Productivity, Inc., 1996.

Bale, Christian. *Batman Begins*. Directed by Christopher Nolan. Burbank: Warner Bros. Pictures, 2005.

Cass, Stephen. *IEEE Spectrum*, January 2004.

DAMA International. *DAMA Dictionary of Data Management*. Technics Publications, LLC., 2008.

Davenport, Thomas, and Jeanne G. Harris. *Competing on Analytics: The New Science of Winning*. Harvard Business School Publishing Corporation, 2007.

Davenport, Thomas, and Jeanne G. Harris. *Analytics at Work: Smarter Decisions, Better Results*. Harvard Business School Publishing Corporation, 2010.

Drucker, Peter F. *Management: Tasks, Responsibilities, Practices*. Harper & Row. 1974.

Friedlos, Dave. "RBS Consolidates Customer Details." *Computing*, May 31, 2007. http://www.computing.co.uk/ctg/news/1843456/rbs-consolidates-customer-details.

Gray, Glen L., Roger Debreceny, and Rick Hayes. *Cases In Strategic-Systems Auditing 3M Worldwide – Part B: 3M's Global Enterprise Data Warehouse*. KPGM/University of Illinois, 2005.

Hackathorn, Richard. *Current Practices in Active Data Warehousing*. Bolder Technology, Inc., 2002.

Imhoff, Claudia, Nicholas Galemmo, and Jonathan G. Geiger. *Mastering Data Warehouse Design: Relational and Dimensional Techniques*. John Wiley & Sons, Inc., 2003.

Kaplan, Robert S., and David P. Norton. *The Balanced Scorecard: Translating Strategy into Action*. Harvard Business Press, 1996.

Kimball, Ralph, and Joe Caserta. *The Data Warehouse ETL Toolkit*. John Wiley & Sons, Inc., 2004.

Kimball, Ralph. *The Data Warehouse Lifecycle Toolkit, Second Edition*. John Wiley & Sons, Inc., 2008.

Langseth, Justin. "Real-Time Data Warehousing: Challenges and Solutions." *DSSResources.com*, February 8, 2004. http://dssresources.com/papers/features/langseth/langseth02082004.html.

Linstedt, Dan, and Kent Graziano. *The Business of Data Vault Modeling*. Lulu, 2008.

Ortiz, Jorge L. "Astros pitching staff a full house of aces." *USA Today*, October 12, 2005.

Robertson, Suzanne, and James Robertson. *Requirements-Led Project Management*. Addison-Wesley Professional, 2004.

Reference	Details
ESPN 2011	Frankland, Dave with Suresh Vittal, Michael J. Grant, and Michelle Dickson. *Case Study: ESPN Drives Fan Value Through Customer Intelligence.* Forrester Research, Inc. 2011
IBM SmartPlanet 2010	*Curbing Crime with predictive analytics* IBM Corporation 2010
Linstedt 2004	Dan Linstedt. Data Vault article series www.tdan.com
McKinsey 2011	*Big data: The next frontier for innovation, competition and productivity* McKinsey Global Institute May 2011

Index

329

Made in the USA
Charleston, SC
28 June 2012